Films—
Too Good
for Words

Films—
Too Good
for Words

A Directory
of Nonnarrated
16mm Films

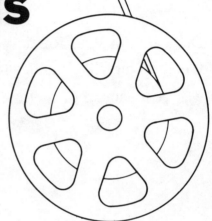

SALVATORE J. PARLATO, JR.
Media Coordinator
National Technical Institute for the Deaf
Rochester Institute of Technology

R. R. BOWKER COMPANY
New York & London, 1972
A Xerox Education Company

XEROX

0650179

4048

Dedicated to Paul Reed.
His thinking, like his death,
was years ahead of its time.

Published by R. R. Bowker Co. (A Xerox Education Company)

1180 Avenue of the Americas, New York, N.Y. 10036

Parlato, Salvatore J   1931-
   Films—too good for words.

   1. Moving pictures—Catalogs. 2. Moving pictures
in education. I. Title.
LB1044.Z9P34   016.37133'523   72-12831
ISBN 0-8352-0618-1

CONTENTS

4048

PREFACE

Just what is a nonnarrated film? A nonnarrated film is one that communicates pictorially. It does so on the strength of its visual unity, continuity, and coherence, without relying on a "voice-over" narrator, dialogue between on-screen actors, or face-to-face interviews. "Nonnarrated" does *not* imply the total absence of sound. In fact, most nonnarrated films do use sound, but not in the form of explanatory words. Instead, this medium uses sound *as* sound: music for the sake of mood, ambient noise for realism, and artificial sounds for special effects. Except for random exclamations or snatches of casual conversation, the spoken word rarely is used.

Most of the films listed in this directory are curriculum-oriented "educational" films. Semanticists may now refer to them as "films with a purpose" or (worse) "purposeful films," labels I consider inaccurate and unnecessary. If you think that instructional films need a new term, call them functional films. That will differentiate them from media-in-motion that are, or claim to be, an end in themselves—that is, art for art's sake.

While most of these films are designed with teaching and learning as their primary goal, many of them are indeed enjoyable experiences, to be used in or out of the classroom. Quite a few are pure entertainment, certainly a legitimate role for this vivid medium.

A few silent classics, like "Nanook of the North," are included here, along with more modern materials such as selected *Candid Camera* segments. Also found herein is another type of nonnarrated film: the one whose verbal message takes the form of musical lyrics—"song-track" films. These tend to be economical with their wordage, and usually avoid the monotony of canned patter. And, technically, they are nonnarrated in the literal sense of the term.

Whether nonverbal/sound or nonverbal/silent, all of the nearly 1,000 titles described herein have one characteristic in common: *visuality*. Many of the films also share the characteristic of "instructionality," but visuality is their basic feature.

This guide consists of three main parts, each serving a different but related function. Descriptions of individual films are found under thirteen numbered subject headings. These descriptions are factual, concept-oriented, and about a paragraph in length. Age-level suitability can be accurately inferred from the information given. Each description also includes information on the film's producer and/or distributor, its running time, whether it is in color, whether it has sound or is completely silent, and the date of copyright, if known.

The Films Indexed by Title section presents a complete list of titles in alphabetical order, with one-line outlines of contents and complete production data. This section is intended for quick reference and contains no formal data on topic or audience, but references are given to the section number in which the full descriptions appear. This section is useful not only for browsing but for isolating specific groups of films according to distributor, length, copyright date, or other factors.

The section entitled Films Indexed by Subject furnishes another way of grouping certain areas of interest. Here, finer and more detailed subject classifications make it easy to track down films that might otherwise be hard to find within the thirteen broad categories. For comparative viewing, too, this is the best place to look for a variety of films dealing with the same subject.

You will notice that there is very little overlap or duplication of titles among the thirteen subject categories. Of the 1,000 titles listed, only about 100 are described under more than one classification, and no film appears in more than two. For example, "Lost World" is fully described under both "Fantasy" and "Literature." Because of its landmark status in film history, it might also have been entered under "The Arts." Instead, it is found in the Films Indexed by Subject section under the heading Film Study: Techniques.

Once you've selected your film, consult either your local library or the film's distributor. An address list of over 100 companies and organizations from which films are available is located in the Producer/Distributor Directory section.

It should be noted that all films listed herein are available in 16mm form, for display on sound-speed projectors. Descriptions originate from producer/distributor catalogs, and have been edited only in the interests of brevity. As a matter of personal conviction, I have listed color films rather than black-and-white whenever a choice exists. Productions not devoid of narration carry only a minimum thereof, and are so identified.

The purpose of this directory is to provide a starting point in the search for nontheatrical films. With tens of thousands of titles on the market, film users need a preliminary "filtering out" process to help narrow down the bewildering and almost self-defeating array of choices. This guide, believed to be the only one of its kind, identifies the very films that are the most "filmish" of all—those that rely on visual impact alone to convey their message. Such narration-free films already number over a thousand, with more being released daily. It is important for users to know about these special resources, selected from the mass of conventional films that are already nearly unmanageable in quantity and unpredictable in quality.

While listing in this book is not to be construed as endorsement, the titles described are believed to be suitable for, though not limited to, the categories suggested. By the same token, omissions should not be interpreted as a reflection on the quality of a film or a company, but only as evidence of human oversight, despite the closest attention and kindest intentions.

INTRODUCTION

Films began as a purely visual medium that later acquired synchronized sound. Sound, once a supplement to pictorial motion, gradually grew overbearing, and before long became the major element in "sound-films." (Sound even got top billing!) What had started out promisingly as "audiovisual" soon degenerated into "verbal-visual." Instead of incorporating natural sounds into the screen action, most educational producers filled their new-found audio tracks with human (but humorless) voices that verbally paralleled the picture. It wasn't long before such verbalism, overemphasized by producers, threatened to greatly reduce—if not destroy—the films' visual impact.

With such a sad state of affairs prevailing, how did film companies survive, much less prosper and multiply? The fact is that they didn't—at least, not on their own. Two external factors came to the rescue and completely transformed their habits: the financial incentive provided by the Elementary and Secondary Education Act (ESEA) of 1965; and the artistic success of nonverbal films at Montreal's Expo '67.

ESEA, a valiant attempt at eliminating scholastic inequities in America, channeled millions of federal dollars into our inner-city schools. These were the very schools where conventional materials, print and nonprint, had failed most dismally. If the suburban world of "Dick and Jane" was foreign to our disadvantaged students, so was most of the vocabulary of educational films.

Almost simultaneously, North Americans were being dazzled by Expo's nonverbal films from all over the world, showing dramatically how films can bypass the barriers of language. Producers, to their credit, were quick to change. Recognizing that the answer to reaching students of limited literacy was not to be found in "canned" commentaries, they revived the truly visual approach to subject matter. Film-makers solved the problem of words by eliminating them. Once again, sound was used as a supplement, either to set a mood through music or, through ambient sound, to simulate an environment and a feeling of presence. Once again, voice became second to visual. That's when educators began to realize that middle-class students liked the same nondidactic media that disadvantaged children were enjoying, and the concept of visual literacy first loomed.

To keep these developments within historical perspective, remember that there were several forerunners in establishing the acceptance of nonverbal films. The National Film Board of Canada pioneered in the large-scale production of such materials. The bilingual nature of Canada's citizenry committed NFB to a word-free philosophy long before the idea became fashionable in the United States.

Another strong influence was Alexander Hammid's poetic "To Be Young," one of the hits of the 1964-1965 New York World's Fair. At about the same time Dan Gibson, an independent Canadian cinematographer, was winning international awards for his Birds of America series. And ten years earlier, Encyclopedia Britannica was successfully marketing Arne Sucksdorff's Stories Without Words series. Still, the watershed was Expo '67. Films changed then. They became pictures again.

The advantage of narrationless films centers on the difference between "visual" and "pictorial"—which are far from being the same thing. Media practitioners sometimes lose sight of the fact that something visual is not necessarily pictorial. For example, the page you're reading now is visual; it communicates through your sense of sight. But this page is not pictorial; it has no charts, drawings, or other images. Similarly, a motion picture that records a lecturer at his podium may be called visual, but not pictorial.

A pictorial film is one that documents an event—say, a trip to China. Metaphorically, a lecture about China equals a photocopy of scholarly notes; a documentary on China is a surrogate visit there. One treatment relies on words; the other builds on pictures. These pictures may be, and usually are, accompanied by narration on a sound track, which may or may not reinforce accompanying scenes. If a picture is self-explanatory, are words needed? If a picture is not self-explanatory, will adding words really improve it?

This is not to say that any film with built-in language is all wrong. In fact, many films, by the nature of their subject, need and figuratively give life to the spoken word. Good examples are productions of plays, interviews, speeches, and foreign language films. All such films are perfectly legitimate and highly useful applications of the motion picture medium. But granting that the prime use of film is to convey ideas, if words get in the way of expressing or understanding ideas, they should be eliminated. And that is what more and more producers are doing: trusting their talents to nonverbal modes of expression. The number and variety of films in this book will demonstrate the strength of this trend.

Sound-on-film is a great invention, but despite its permanent and worthwhile contributions to education, misuse has generated films that: (1) by arbitrary choice of vocabulary, underestimate or overestimate the audience's word power; (2) by vocally belaboring content, leave little opportunity for individual interpretation; and (3) by excessive reliance on vocal sound tracks, could be replaced as well, if not better, by print or another less dynamic medium.

By contrast, this directory provides a guide to films that, by the absence of narration: (1) presuppose no limits (upper or lower) to viewers' language skills; (2) encourage inductive reasoning and personal interpretation of ideas; and (3) present subjects peculiarly suited to the medium of movement, action, and change.

Owing to their wide range of applicability, nonnarrated films will be of special interest to two groups of teachers with opposite but equal frustrations: those who are trying to reach students with low language ability, and those who want to keep highly literate pupils from feeling "talked down to" by films with sugar-coated, condescending commentary. Indeed, because of the built-in flexibility of word-free films, practically every film programmer will find this compilation indispensable. Without narration, a film is freed from the limitations imposed by language levels. This versatility allows broad utilization potential across the whole spectrum of viewers: public schools, colleges, public libraries, programs for the deaf, industrial training, government programs, and (no less important) programs for entertainment.

Whatever the reasons for using these films, our first consideration should be neither words nor pictures, but the people who make up the audience. Keep *them* in mind when selecting from these films. That's what films are about. That's what films are for.

1. THE ARTS

Of all possible categories, this is the one you'd expect would include the most films, and it does. Almost 150 titles fall within this heading. This classification includes the "arts" (without the capitals), often referred to as crafts. The distinction between arts and crafts is a hazy and controversial one. Let's side-step that issue altogether—except to quote the Balinese chieftain who boasted of his tribe, "We have no art. We do everything as well as we can."

If it's a subterfuge to sneak crafts in under "The Arts," then it's a real coup to smuggle in photography and cinema. Attitudes in purist circles have recently softened enough, though, so that no justification is required for admitting camera studies into the company of the more traditional art forms.

Very few of these photo or cinema productions are of the "how-to" variety. Almost all of them are examples of technique and, as such, are more inductive than expository. Of course, such examples cross topical boundaries. The relatively few film-study recommendations described here are those whose techniques are particularly well highlighted or whose methods are, by the name and nature of their subject, most obvious. For example, "Red Balloon"—deservedly the most honored film of the 1960s—is not found in this group. Though a fine model of motion-picture art, it emphasizes story over technique. The style of a film like "Red Balloon" is so subtle and submerged that it really doesn't lend itself to analysis. ("Ars est artem celare": True art conceals itself). A contrasting example is the film "Sky," an excellent film that, by reason of its special emphasis on technique, is listed under "The Arts" instead of a more academic subject. Of course, another good (but not infallible) guide to technical mastery is the number, source, or type of awards a production has won. Awards are noted within the body of individual film descriptions.

Other visual arts covered here are painting, sculpture, and architecture. Also represented are the performing arts—music, dance, theatre, and pantomime. Are there any arts we've left out? That all depends on your definition of art. Mine is a liberal one, so if your favorite art isn't mentioned here by name, I hope you will find it where it can do the most good—on film!

ADAGIO
A protest film, reminiscent in part of the famous Picasso painting entitled "Guernica." Expressed in child-like Crayola drawings. Original music. (Produced by Fred Mogubgub)
PYRAMID. 4 min. Color. Sound. 1969

ARCHITECTURE, USA
Using original music and no narration, presents view of U.S. architecture that reflects America's cultural life. Includes educational and religious institutions, cultural centers, and the skyscraper.
NAT'L AV CTR. 13 min. Color. Sound. 1965

1

ART
A montage of over 2,000 works of art set to the tune of Beethoven's "Fifth Symphony." (Produced by Dan Mc-Laughlin)
PYRAMID. 4 min. Color. Sound. 1965

ART EXPERT
Three Candid Camera men are commenting on an abstract painting. They point out hypothetical boats, and onlookers always agree with these "experts." The Candid Camera men then notice that they have the wrong painting, or that it is upside down. The subjects change their opinions very readily, once the "experts" do. Demonstrates conformity and social influences on perception. Available only for purchase; no rentals.
CANDID CAMERA. 8 min. B&W. Sound

THE ART OF SEEING
An examination of everyday things, revealing hidden beauties and interesting facets in the world. A farmer takes strawberries to market, and the things he sees are explored. Encourages viewers to look at their surroundings for pleasure, and not to take them for granted or dismiss them as ugly or boring.
ACI FILMS. 10 min. Color. Sound. 1969

ART SCENE, USA
A lock at today's U.S. painters, sculptors and dancers, such as Wyeth, Warhol, Johns, Lichtenstein, Kienholz, Motherwell, Calder, Pollock, Shahn, Levine, Rivers, Marisol, the Martha Graham Dancers, the Once Group (A Happening), Hawkins, Cunningham, and the Alwin Nikolais Dancers. (U.S. Information Agency)
NAT'L AV CTR. 17 min. Color. Sound. 1966

AT YOUR FINGERTIPS—BOXES
Visiting a supermarket, we see boxes, cartons, and containers that are used in packaging everyday products. At home, these receptacles are transformed into playthings. Cereal boxes and milk cartons become cars, animals, and villages. Large boxes—like those used in crating refrigerators and filing cases—are made into playhouses and tunnels.
Awards: CINE and Venice.
ACI FILMS. 10 min. Color. Sound. 1969

AT YOUR FINGERTIPS—CYLINDERS
Designed to help children become aware of the creative possibilities of the cylindrical shape. Using materials found in the home—rollers from paper towels, toilet tissue, and containers such as salt boxes—children build totem poles, rockets, and other playthings. With cutout paper additions, they construct animals. By joining cylinders with brads, they create free-form sculpture. Tubes are also used to make hanging screens.
ACI FILMS. 10 min. Color. Sound. 1969

AT YOUR FINGERTIPS—FLOATS
Explains how air in a tightly corked bottle will keep it buoyant, and that in order for things to float they must be waterproof. After exploring what things float and why, the children in the film make their own floating playthings. A floating man is made out of cork and wire; balloons and milk cartons become boats, as do plastic meat-packing trays and styrofoam objects like water-paint trays.
ACI FILMS. 10 min. Color. Sound. 1969

AT YOUR FINGERTIPS—GRASSES
A ladybug on a blade of grass leads to an exploration of grasses and how they can be used. Different kinds of grass are compared to weeds. A fishing pole of bamboo is grass. A stalk of corn is grass. Fresh grass is held into the sun and forms artful patterns on paper. A print is made by placing paper on grass and rubbing with a crayon. Grass is used to

decorate boxes, to make collages, grass skirts, masks, and in weaving. ACI FILMS. 10 min. Color. Sound. 1969

AT YOUR FINGERTIPS—
PLAY CLAY
This film shows how to combine flour, salt, and water to make dough that can be modeled like clay. Illustrates how play clay can be dyed with vegetable coloring or painted with tempera. The modeling of forms is demonstrated, including animals, human figures, and elements for a necklace. The objects are finished with a lacquer spray. ACI FILMS. 10 min. Color. Sound. 1969

AT YOUR FINGERTIPS—
SUGAR AND SPICE
How festive objects can be made from ordinary sugar with water, to make a paste that is dried in molds. The molded form is decorated with icing. Children in the film demonstrate how to create party favors and decorations such as candlesticks, a centerpiece, and fortune balls. The making of Easter eggs, a snowman, and hangings for a Christmas tree is also demonstrated. ACI FILMS. 10 min. Color. Sound. 1969

AUTUMN FIRE
This "romance sentimentale" was made for its author's current inamorata. He was also enamored of the work of Eisenstein, Rutmann, and Kirsanoff, whose influences abound in the film. Not intended for commercial distribution, for a quarter of a century it was known only to a handful of people until it was added to the Cinematheque Francaise. Selected for showing at the Cinema Exposition in Paris. (By Herman G. Weinberg) McGRAW-HILL. 17 min. B&W. Silent. 1930

BALLET BY DEGAS
Camera studies of ballet paintings by Edgar Degas (1834-1917): "The Ballet Class," "Coryphee Resting,"

"Ballerina and Lady with Fan," "On Stage," "Dancers Practicing at the Bar," "Pink and Green." Piano accompaniment by Irma Jurist: Chopin's "Krakowiak" and an original piece. No commentary. (Produced by J. H. Lenauer) CCM FILMS. 10 min. Color. Sound. 1951

BEGONE DULL CARE
By painting directly on film, Norman McLaren and Evelyn Lambard have created this cinematic expression. Opening with a title page in eight languages, with hand-drawn sound track, the film moves into images interpreting jazz by the Oscar Peterson Trio. In three movements of "ragtime," "blues," and "boogie-woogie," colors, forms, figures, and lines move against a changing background in time with the music. Seven awards, including Venice and Berlin. (National Film Board of Canada) INT. FILM BUR. 8 min. Color. Sound. 1949

BLINKITY BLANK
An experiment by Norman McLaren in intermittent animation and spasmodic imagery. McLaren makes play with the law of persistence of vision by engraving directly on black emulsion-coated film, achieving a "now you see it—now you don't" effect. Music is in the form of improvisation, with percussive effects added by sounds scratched directly on film. Chosen Best Animated Film by the British Film Institute. (National Film Board of Canada) INT. FILM BUR. 6 min. Color. Sound. 1955

BOUQUET
Exploits the potential of film as medium and of flowers as subject. Editing incorporates split screen, kinestatic cutting, and other optical techniques to reveal a manifestation of nature. Original music. (Produced by David Adams) PYRAMID. 9 min. Color. Sound. 1971

BRONZE
Follows the work of sculptor Charles
Daudelin. Without dialogue or narration, director Pierre Moretti
traces the adventure of creation. We
see a gigantic sculpture as it begins
to take shape, and finally when it is
placed in the National Arts Centre in
Ottawa. Award: Silver Medal, Venice Film Festival. (National Film
Board of Canada)
LEARN. CORP. 14 min. Color.
Sound. 1969

CANDLEFLAME
A study, in extreme close-up, of a
candle as it burns. The flame and
the constantly changing patterns of
melting wax achieve an almost surrealist quality. The viewer may
become conscious of hidden images
in everyday objects, and enjoy new
visual impressions for their own
sake or for inspiration for other art
forms. No narration; musical score.
(Made by Hungarofilm)
ACI FILMS. 7 min. Color. Sound.
1971

CANON
A visual definition of the musical
form, the canon, with colors and
shapes representing the voice parts,
and designs illustrating movement
patterns and intervals. Shows how
the parts work together and depend
on each other for the sense of the
theme. The film suggests how the
sound "looks." Awards: New Delhi,
Argentina, Melbourne, Canada.
(Produced by Norman McLaren)
INT. FILM BUR. 9 min. Color.
Sound. 1963

CHILD OF DANCE
About children and dance; the chil-
dren, aged 4 to 6, are members of
Virginia Tanner's Creative Dance
Studio at the University of Utah.
They are engaged in exercises, ex-
pression, and simply having fun.
This film includes two Bach flute so-
natas. No narration. (A film by Ju-
dith and Stanley Hallet)
FILM IMAGES. 9 min. Color.
Sound. 1970

CHILDREN'S DREAMS
Paintings by children, aged 6 to 15,
from Austria, France, Germany,
Great Britain, Holland, India, Italy,
Japan, Sweden, Turkey, and the
U.S.A., selected, arranged, super-
imposed, and animated so that a
child's dream of a fantasy journey
may be interpreted by the audience.
No narration. Music. (Produced by
Ervin Alberti for Centropa Film,
with the cooperation of the Austrian
Ministry of Education)
CCM FILMS. 14 min. Color. Sound.
1960

CHRISTMAS CRACKER
A seasonal pleasantry of three seg-
ments by National Film Board of
Canada artists and animators, with
music. The film contains three parts:
Jingle Bells, in which paper cut-outs
dance; a dime-store rodeo of tin
toys; and a new Christmas story.
Seven awards, including: Nomination,
Hollywood; Rome; Naarden, Holland.
(National Film Board of Canada)
McGRAW-HILL. 9 min. Color.
Sound. 1964

CHRISTMAS LIGHTS
The colorful lights of Christmas—
decorations, trees, ornaments, store
windows—are photographed to a
background of choral music. The
film combines the sights of the season with the singing of some favorite
carols: "We Wish You a Merry
Christmas"; "The Holly and the
Ivy"; "Hark, the Herald Angels
Sing"; and "Silent Night."
STERLING. 11 min. Color. Sound.
1965

CIRCUS
This film was created and drawn by
children. Its scenes illustrate the
various activities of a circus from a
child's-eye point of view. Designed
to stimulate and motivate viewers in
their own creative activities. No
narration. (A Willis E. Simms
Film)
BFA ED. MEDIA. 8 min. Color.
Sound. 1961

CONCERT FOR CLOUDS
Cloud formations and movements ascend, swell, and recede under the influence of air currents, change from
cumulus puffs to towering thunderheads, then disappear in the upper
blue sky. Sun rays bathe the varying
formations in myriad colors. No
narration. (Portafilms)
PERENNIAL ED. 9 min. Color.
Sound

CRASH, BANG, BOOM
What is music? What feelings does
music evoke? "Crash, Bang, Boom"
gives some of the answers by in-
troducing 11 percussion instruments,
showing how each is played and what
kind of sound each makes. There is
no spoken narration, the story being
told in song by a chorus of voices.
(Produced by Eric Productions, Inc.)
XEROX FILMS. $9\frac{1}{2}$ min. Color.
Sound. 1970

A CREATION:
THE ARTIST AT WORK
Prize-winning Hungarian glass designer Erzsebet Szabo creates a
large glass vase from its conception
on paper through the many trials to
the final form that pleases her. She
guides and encourages her two
skilled assistants who blow and press
the glass into shape. No narration.
(Hungarofilm)
BFA ED. MEDIA. 12 min. Color.
Sound. 1969

CRYSTALS
Crystals radiating brilliant prismatic colors grow and merge as if
they were dancing to the accompanying soundtrack of electronic tingles
and taps.
PYRAMID. 6 min. Color. Sound.
1969

CURRIER AND IVES
Nathaniel Currier (1813-1888) and
James Merritt Ives (1824-1895).
Their hand-colored lithographs are
now memorable Americana: quaint,
sentimental, and moralistic repre-
sentations of American life in the

last half of the nineteenth century.
The nostalgic scenes in the film are
accompanied by American folk
songs—"Shenandoah," "America,
the Beautiful," "Hop Up, My Ladies," "The Wabash Cannonball,"
"There's No Place Like Home,"
and others. (Produced by Lewis
Jacobs)
FILM IMAGES. 13 min. Color.
Sound

CUT-UPS
A pair of scissors dances onto the
screen, hovers over colored paper,
and proceeds to cut out circles.
Cutout children appear and play with
the circles. Diamonds are cut out
and become kites, rectangles become
stairs, a curve becomes a slide, and
new shapes are transformed into
birds, animals, trees, clouds, a sun,
a camel caravan. Concept: Complex
things are composed of basic shapes.
Minimum narration. Teacher's guide
available.
MOD. MEDIA. 5 min. Color. Sound

DANCE SQUARED
This film is an encounter with geo-
metrical shapes. "Dance Squared"
employs movement, color, and music
to explore the symmetries of the
square. Every movement of the
square and its components presents
an opportunity to observe its properties. Awards: Chicago, Argentina,
Portugal, Iran.
INT. FILM BUR. $3\frac{1}{2}$ min. Color.
Sound. 1962

DANZE CROMATICHE
In this film Ugo Torricelli approaches the idea of dance on the
most fundamental level. He takes
pure colors and gives them movement. He harmonizes the life and
movement of these colors with 12
pieces of music, creating many different dances and moods. Award:
Golden Eagle from the Council on International Nontheatrical Events
(CINE).
XEROX FILMS. $8\frac{1}{2}$ min. Color.
Sound. 1969

DAY OF THE PAINTER
The "biography" of a work of modern art. A painter who knows how to
make good in the contemporary market spends the day hurling, dripping,
splashing, and spray-gunning paint
onto a board. An art dealer chooses
one segment that the painter has
sawed off. The other parts of the
masterpiece float down the stream
with some puzzled gulls and swans.
No narration. Awards: Academy
Award, Best Live Action Short Subject; Best Fiction Short Subject, San
Francisco. (Little Movies, Inc.)
CCM FILMS. 14 min. Color. Sound.
1959

DEGAS DANCERS
Degas was an innovator in structural
composition that gave his subject a
motion never before attained by an
artist. No narration. Music. (From
Les Films de Saturne, Anthony Roland Collection)
TIME-LIFE. 13 min. B&W. Sound

DELACROIX (1798-1863)
Born into an age marked by revolution and extremes, Eugene Delacroix
was an arch-romanticist whose su-
perb draftsmanship vitalized the
most simple of his preparatory
drawings. No narration. Awards:
Salerno; Cannes; Vancouver; Wiesbaden; Centre National de la Cinematographie, Paris; Columbus;
Yorktown. (From Les Films de Saturne)
TIME-LIFE. 13 min. B&W. Sound

DINA IN THE KING'S GARDEN
(Maillot Sculpture)
Robust and with a compelling earth-
mother quality, Dina was the perfect
model for Aristide Maillot to use for
the adaptation of classical elegance
in his sculpture. No narration; music by Richard Strauss is used
throughout. Award: Centre National
de la Cinematographie, Paris.
(From Les Films du Prieure)
TIME-LIFE. 10 min. Color. Sound

THE DIRECTOR
Shot in cinema verite style at a major studio, this film documents the
many problems of a feature film director, following a production from
the first script conference, through
casting sessions, rehearsals, and
shooting, on to the editing room and
completion.
UNIVERSAL ED. 31 min. Color.
Sound. 1969

DISCOVERING THE FOREST
This film is designed to raise questions, and to encourage viewers to
observe, then interpret their observations. Without narration, the film
takes a field trip to the forest, where
the mood is established through
sounds and the varied forms of life
found there. Original music.
ENCYC. BRIT. 11 min. Color.
Sound. 1966

DURER: THE GREAT PASSION
Albrecht Durer (1471-1528) grasped
the importance of printmaking, the
artistic equivalent of printing in his
time. His work reflected the faith of
the Middle Ages, the restlessness of
the Renaissance, and his own striving
for knowledge. This film depicts his
series of scenes in the life of Christ,
from original woodcuts in Vienna.
No narration; music by the Vienna
Symphony Orchestra. (Produced in
Austria)
FILM IMAGES. 14 min. B&W.
Sound

ECCE HOMO
(Czechoslovakian Art 1400-1600)
The richly painted and gilded wood
sculpture of the birth, life, death, and
resurrection of Christ were late
manifestations of the Gothic influence
in Czechoslovakia in the fifteenth and
sixteenth centuries. No narration.
Award: Bergamo. (From Kratky
Films Praka)
TIME-LIFE. 9 min. Color. Sound.
1969

ENCRE
A look at three artists in Paris
working at lithography. Each one

creates his design in a different way.
They then work together preparing
the stone plates, inking the presses,
and making the lithographs. No nar-
ration; music. (Produced by
SOFIDOC with the artists Alechinsky,
Appel, and Ting)
INT. FILM BUR. 20 min. Color.
Sound. 1971

ERNST BARLACH: THE FIGHTER
Barlach (1870 - 1938), identified with
the German Expressionist school, led
a lonely, creative life as sculptor,
poet, draftsman, and playwright.
His works—sometimes harsh, sometimes pure and poetic—reveal the
truth, glory, and misery of contemporary man. Best known for his wood
sculptures, he also worked in bronze
and stone. Examples are shown,
without commentary, in this film.
Music by Tchaikovsky. (Produced in
Germany)
FILM IMAGES. 14 min. B&W.
Sound

ERNST BARLACH: THE VICTOR
In the second half of Barlach's life,
his humanity overcame the forces
that had tormented him and found
expression in his work. No longer
was Man portrayed as driven towards
a tragic destiny, but rather as a reflection of God. That interpretation
emerges in Barlach's mature works.
Sculpture from this period and examples of woodcuts, including those
made to illustrate Schiller's "Ode to
Joy," are shown without commentary. Music by Anton Bruckner.
(Produced in Germany)
FILM IMAGES. 15 min. B&W.
Sound

EXERCISES # 4
An early attempt to create "visual
music" by handmade (as opposed to
computer-generated) means. This is
the most complex of the five exercises. Original synthetic sound is
synchronized to the moving images.
Award: First Prize at the First International Experimental Film Fes-

tival. (Produced by James and John
Whitney)
PYRAMID. 6 min. Color. Sound.
1944

EXPOSITION
The surreal rotating, vibrating, sus-
pended, and static displays of Montreal's Expo '67 have been transformed into a futuristic montage of
lights and shapes. Reveals the curious interplay between spectator and
exhibit. The documentary footage
becomes a statement, not just on the
fair and its exhibits, but on modern
art, architecture, and design. Original music from the Czech Pavilion.
PYRAMID. 10 min. Color. Sound.
1968

EYES ARE FOR SEEING
Designed to develop an awareness
and perception of the common and
uncommon. It is a purely visual experience. Familiar and extraordi-
nary visuals are integrated throughout the film to make statements
about color, mass, and form. The
film can lead to language art activities, painting, model construction,
mobile construction, experiments
with light, and cutouts of geometric
shapes.
STERLING. 9 min. Color. Sound.
1967

FANTASY FOR FOUR STRINGS
The essence of Robert Cambier's
score in Albert Pierru's animated
screen patterns, painted directly on
film.
CCM FILMS. 5 min. Color. Sound.

FIDDLE-DE-DEE
A film of dancing music and dancing
color. To "Listen to the Mocking
Bird" by an oldtime fiddler, patterns
ripple, flow, flicker, and blend. The
artist, painting on film, translates
sound into sight. Five awards, including Brussels and Rome. (National Film Board of Canada)
INT. FILM BUR. $3\frac{1}{2}$ min. Color.
Sound. 1948

FILM IMPRESSIONS
Through impressionistic visuals and
music, demonstrates the capabilities
of a film company. Awards: CINE
Golden Eagle; Locarno.
MINI-FILMS. 5 min. Color. Sound.
1969

THE FIREMAN IS SAD AND CRIES
A child's real and fantasized world,
done with montages of children's
paintings. Photographic images of
the world, and children in the act of
expressing, through art, their emotional reactions to the world. No
dialogue or commentary; the electri-
cal musical score evokes the environment of today's child. (Produced in Argentina)
McGRAW-HILL. 10 min. Color.
Sound. 1965

THE FOUR SEASONS
Vivaldi's string concerto, "The
Four Seasons," provides the theme
and sets the musical pace for a montage of scenes in which man and nature share in the cycle of change.
Camera techniques accentuate the
movement of clouds, the rhythm of
skiers and skaters, the flight of
birds, and unite the visual action
with that of the concerto. (Produced
by Condor-Films, Ltd.)
THORNE FILMS. 14 min. Color.
Sound. 1968

FRANCIS BACON:
PAINTINGS 1944-1962
Bacon's paintings realize a vision of
the human predicament rare, in modern art, in its violence and grandeur.
This film attempts not so much to interpret that vision as to approach its
meaning, without using words. No
chronological sequence is followed.
Instead, certain images are juxtaposed to suggest what Bacon is saying about the nature of modern man
and how, in brushstroke and pigment,
he is saying it. (Arts Council of
Great Britain)
FILMS INC. 11 min. Color. Sound.
1963

FRESCOES IN DANISH CHURCHES
The world of the old frescoes in Danish village churches is presented
with music in this evocation of Biblical history and art produced by
Luciano Emmer. No narration.
(Produced for Danish Culture Films)
CCM FILMS. 10 min. B&W. Sound.
1954

FROM THE INSIDE OUT
Six 15-year-old girls express their
thoughts and feelings through movement in creative dance, defined as
"the exercise of body and imagination in order to bring the whole being
into play." All dances were choreo-
graphed by the girls themselves,
each having been encouraged to express herself in her own way, working "from the inside out." The
dances and improvisations cover a
wide range of mood and form. No
narration. (Produced by Carolyn
Bilderback)
FILM IMAGES. 13 min. Color.
Sound. 1967

FROM TREE TRUNK TO HEAD
This film reveals Chaim Gross'
technique of sculpturing in wood. It
follows the step-by-step development from a block of raw wood to
an heroic portrait head. The artist's technique is presented to the
viewer without recourse to commentary or captions. The work
shown won a prize when exhibited at
The Carnegie Institute of Art.
FILM IMAGES. 28 min. B&W.
Silent

THE FUGUE
Here we join a group of people in a
church as they listen to an organ concert of music by Bach. As the music
creates a sense of unity and peace,
we find a brief escape from the restlessness and noise outside in the
streets. (Produced by Czechoslovak
Television)
McGRAW-HILL. 19 min. B&W.
Sound. 1966

GALLERY
Using variable-duration scenes, split

screen, tilts, pans, zooms, and other techniques, Ken Rucolph has taken the highlights of Western art—over 2,000 paintings, drawings, and etchings—and fashioned them into a chronological approach to art history. Unlike Dan McLaughlin's "Art," which allows 1/12 second per image, "Gallery" employs individually paced superimposed images. (Produced by David Adams)
PYRAMID. 6 min. Color. Sound. 1971

GALLERY: A VIEW OF TIME
A visit to the Albright-Knox Gallery in Buffalo. Many great works of art are employed—along with the architecture of the building itself—to give a sense of time and place, timelessness and placelessness. (Produced, directed, and filmed by Don Owen)
CCM FILMS. 14 min. Color. Sound. 1969

GRAND CANYON
The grandeur of this natural spectacle—including its many moods and its inhabitants (bobcat, jackrabbit, owl, tarantula, Gila monster, and others)—is portrayed to the musical background of Ferde Grofe's "Grand Canyon Suite." No narration.
WALT DISNEY. 29 min. Color. Sound

THE GREAT TRAIN ROBBERY
One of the first American films to carry a story-line—a Western, naturally. Lots of action, gun-play, and a chase. Combines on-location scenes with studio settings. Directed by Edwin S. Porter.
BLACKHAWK. 8 min. B&W. Silent. 1903

GROWING
(A Computer-Animated Film)
A computer-animated approach to the concept of growing. Viewers should see it twice—to become acquainted with computer animation, and then to consider the concepts of seasonal changes and growth.
ENCYC. BRIT. 7 min. Color. Sound. 1970

HANDS AND THREADS
Rugs being made in a village in Mesopotamia. The film relates the young girls' sensitive fingers drawing the wool through the warp to those of string musicians in an orchestra. No narration. (Zagreb Films)
FILMS INC. 10 min. Color. Sound. 1971

HARLEM WEDNESDAY
Paintings and sketches by Gregorio Prestopino are arranged to suggest activities of an ordinary day in Harlem. (A Contemporary Films release, directed by John Hubley)
McGRAW-HILL. 10 min. Color. Sound. 1959

HARRY BERTOIA'S SCULPTURE
Designer-sculptor Harry Bertoia and his works of metal sculpture. Imagination and skill combine with metal to produce these forms—matter catalyzed into spirit. No narration. Music by Bertoia. (Produced by Clifford B. West)
FILM IMAGES. 23 min. Color. Sound

HENRY MOORE
AT THE TATE GALLERY
The 1968 Henry Moore exhibition at the Tate Gallery was spoiled by success. Over 100,000 visitors made it impossible to see the exhibits in relationship to one another. This film offers the illusion of being alone with the sculptures and contemplating them in silence. The film is a rarity in its absence of words, music, and other familiar props. (Arts Council of Great Britain)
FILMS INC. 14 min. Color. Silent. 1970

ILLUSIONS
Tony Montanaro, performer and teacher, in eight pantomime vignettes: Warm Up, Rope Climb, Chicken, Lion Tamer, Wheels, Tug-of-War, Monkey, and Eagle.
CMC/COLUMBIA. 15 min. Color. Sound. 1969

IMAGES FROM DEBUSSY
This film derives from Claude Debussy. Three of his compositions
are performed and for each the
film director finds a visual equivalent. "Arabesque en mi" is seen
as sunlight on the water moving
through reeds and water lilies.
"Reflets dans l'eau" is now placid,
now shimmering reflections of landscape and sky; and "Arabesque en
sol" is a lively, almost abstract
dance of light and water. No narration. (Directed by Jean Mitry)
FILM IMAGES. 13½ min. B&W.
Sound

IMAGES 67
Live-action menage of architecture,
furniture, and the female form.
Brief introductory sentence and final
"Auf Wiedersehen" are the only
words. (Produced in Germany)
ASSN./STERL. 9 min. B&W. Sound.
1967

INTERPRETATIONS
Three painters interpret one subject—a woman in a boat as the sun
rises over the lake. By observing
the widely differing styles of each
artist, viewers will better understand how different processes can be
valid statements of the same subject.
The film contains no narration, allows viewers to respond to what they
see—just as the artists interpret
reality in their individual styles.
(Produced by Educational Film Studio for Film Polski, Warsaw)
ENCYC. BRIT. 13 min. Color.
Sound. 1970

JAPAN'S ART—FROM THE LAND
The Japanese mirror the beauty of
their land in their music, painting,
architecture, and other forms of art.
The camera follows the artist, Shu-
son Kono, painting a mountain landscape, and records the serenity of
nature. There is no commentary;
soundtrack of bamboo flutes and a
vocal chorus.
STERLING. 10 min. Color. Sound.
1962

JOSEF HERMAN:
20TH CENTURY ARTIST
The simple laborer, with his quiet
dignity and essential pride-of-being,
has been personified by Herman with
a realism that shows him to be a universal man. No narration. Music.
Awards: Centre de la Cinamatog-
raphie, Paris; Columbus. (From Les
Films de Saturne, directed by Anthony Roland)
TIME-LIFE. 13 min. B&W. Sound

KINDNESS WEEK or
THE SEVEN CAPITAL ELEMENTS
Master of the collage and the sa-
tirical twist, Max Ernst uses Vic-
torian engravings to animate a
Gothic-type tale of a world where
only the inconceivable represents the
norm. Very little narration. Music.
Award: Centre National de la Cine-
matographie, Paris. (From Les
Productions Tanit)
TIME-LIFE. 19 min. B&W. Sound

KOREAN ALPHABET
An animated film by a young Korean
filmmaker in the National Film
Board of Canada's animation division, with synthetic sound by Norman McLaren. The film was made to
teach the alphabet to Korean children, but its style of animation, and
tunes produced without instruments,
give it a wider appeal. Award: Teheran. (National Film Board of
Canada)
UNIVERSAL ED. 7¼ min. Color.
Sound. 1968

LA CATHEDRALE DES MORTS
The interior sculpture of the historic
cathedral of Mainz, Germany, a Ro-
manesque structure with Gothic additions and details. No spoken commentary. Music. (Produced by
Compagnie Nouvelle Commerciale)
MUS./MOD. ART. 12 min. B&W.
Sound. 1935

LA POULETTE GRISE
One of Norman McLaren's films,
this illustrates the imagery of a
simple lullaby traditional in France

and Canada. Photographed from pastel drawings as the artist changed each, and varied the lighting. Illustrates how a single drawing can "animate" a scene. Sung by Anna Malenfant. (National Film Board of Canada)
INT. FILM BUR. $5\frac{1}{2}$ min. Color. Sound. 1947.

LINES—VERTICAL AND HORIZONTAL
Nonobjective art joining design and music. The design consists of lines cut on film so that they are constantly in motion against colored backgrounds. Lines gyrate, group, and regroup in accord with music. For "Lines Vertical," the accompaniment was composed and played on the electronic piano by Maurice Blackburn; for "Lines Horizontal," by Pete Seeger on wind and string instruments. May be shown separately or together; when together, "Lines Vertical" should be first. Six awards including Venice, Edinburgh, and London. Also available as two films, "Lines Vertical" and "Lines Horizontal," each $6\frac{1}{2}$ min. (By Norman McLaren and Evelyn Lambart)
INT. FILM BUR. 13 min. Color. Sound

LITHO
Beginning with early types of lithography—with the stone and the press—using examples of Lautrec's posters, the film then brings us to the actual steps in present-day mass color reproduction. The processes are depicted entirely in imagery and a jazz score. (Produced by Elektra Films for the Amalgamated Lithographers of America)
McGRAW-HILL. 14 min. Color. Sound. 1961

LOPSIDELAND
Children love to stand on their heads to see the world upside down. This film shows them this world—and the people and animals in it—upside down, right side up, sideways, and diagonally. Provides a lesson in looking at things from different perspectives.
ENCYC. BRIT. 5 min. Color. Sound. 1969

LOREN MacIVER
An American contemporary painter, her paintings, and her environment. All three emerge as interwoven, and constitute this two-part film, each part self-contained. MacIver is seen during the four seasons, roaming and absorbing objects, color, and movement in city and country. The film reveals their transposition to canvas. (Produced by Maryette Charlton)
FILM IMAGES. 46 min. Color. Silent

MAITRE
A satire on the problems faced by the artist in contemporary society. Our protagonist is rejected by art galleries, is chased by dogs and by gunshot. Concludes with applause, photographs, and cash-register sounds as our artist is finally recognized. Original music instead of narration. Animated.
SIM PROD. 12 min. Color. Sound. 1970

MAKING FELT (Pushtu)
Throughout Central Asia, women of the Pushtu tribe make felt mats for their families' comfort and for decorating the hard floor of their black camel-hair tents. Pushtu men shear the tribal sheep. Their Moslem wives, with unveiled and weathered faces, pound and separate the wool fibers, deftly flicking their hands over the flattened, outstretched wool, and pressing in the vivid colors. Mountain People of Central Asia series.
IFF (BRYAN). 9 min. Color. Sound. 1968

MAN AND COLOR
An adaptation of the films for the Expo '67 Kaleidoscope Pavilion. A single-faceted collage of color and motion. Beginning with the natural

world of ocean, sun, and stream, it
moves gradually to examine the motion and color of rockets, computers,
autos, and lights, and finally into the
realm of the totally fantastic. (Produced by Morley Markson)
PYRAMID. 12 min. Color. Sound.
1968

MARCHING THE COLOURS
An experiment in film animation
without a camera by Guy Glover,
visualizing a military march in color
abstractions. Bold hues move,
march, blend, and separate in a series of mobile forms, transforming
into color and shape the sound of the
accompanying music. (National
Film Board of Canada)
INT. FILM BUR. 3 min. Color.
Sound. 1942

MEN'S DANCE (Pushtu)
The Pushtu are dependent upon traditional dances to provide entertainment and pleasure. The rugged
tribesmen are shown against a backdrop of snow-capped peaks in an unusual national dance that portrays
man's endless combat with evil.
Mountain People of Central Asia series.
IFF (BRYAN). 11 min. Color.
Sound. 1968

THE METAMORPHOSIS
OF THE CELLO
A study in technique; the art of con-
struction and the skill of interpreta-
tion on the violoncello, as per-
formed by the French virtuoso,
Maurice Gendron. Music by Hayden,
Bach, Chopin, and Boccherini. No
narration. Orchestra directed by
Pablo Casals. (Directed by Domi-
nique Delouche)
FILM IMAGES. 14 min. B&W.
Sound

MIME OVER MATTER
A humorous treatment of man's relationship to the material objects that
make his life more comfortable. It

stars Ladislav Fialka, Czechoslovakia's leading mime artist. (Produced by Kratky Films)
SIM PROD. 12 min. Color. Sound.
1970

MOSAIC
The idea for this display of movement, color, and sound was suggested
by superimposing the two films
"Lines Vertical" and "Lines Horizontal." The intersection of the
moving lines results in a series of
designs. Because it is largely a play
on the retina of the eye, "Mosaic"
might be called an example of cinema
"op" art. Awards: New York, Melbourne, Buenos Aires, Vancouver.
Rental only. (National Film Board
of Canada)
INT. FILM BUR. $5\frac{1}{2}$ min. Color.
Sound. 1965

MOTHLIGHT
A fluttering light collage that the
filmmaker describes as "what a
moth might see from birth to death,
if black were white." Made without
a camera. (Produced by Stan Brakhage)
PYRAMID. 4 min. Color. Silent.
1963

MOTION PICTURE
From the Midwest to New York in
four minutes! A "tour de force" of
time compression, capturing the variety, confusion, and beauty of aspects of all the land between start
and finish.
CINEMA 16. 4 min. Color. Sound

MOZART AND BARRIOS
ON SIX STRINGS
Abel Carlevaro, a pupil of Segovia,
gives a recital on the guitar, playing
Fernando Sor's "Variations on a
Theme by Mozart," and "The Bees"
by the Paraguayan composer Bar-
rios. Reveals the range of the guitar
and its ability to interpret classical
music. No narration. (Directed by
Ramon Biodiu)
FILM IMAGES. 9 min. B&W.
Sound

MUSIC
This is a picture-and-sound story of
music, told without narration and
with only scattered, incidental dialogue. The range of music presented
runs from a school band to the
Beatles recording "Hey Jude" to the
Bath Festival Orchestra. Exempli-
fies the many and varied roles of
music in the modern world.
NBC-TV. 54 min. Color. Sound.
1969

NANOOK OF THE NORTH
A classic epic of Eskimo life—the
world's first, and by many standards, the finest documentary ever
made. (Produced by Robert Flaherty)
McGRAW-HILL. 55 min. B&W.
Silent. 1922

THE NAVAJO SILVERSMITH
Similar to "A Navajo Weaver" in
structure, this film traces the creation in silver of some small Yei-
bachai figures—from the mining of
the silver to the finished figure. Navajos Film Themselves series.
CMC/COLUMBIA. 20 min. B&W.
Silent

A NAVAJO WEAVER
Susie Benally, a young Navajo, depicts her mother weaving at the
loom and includes all of the necessary steps prior to the actual weaving. Navajos Film Themselves series.
CMC/COLUMBIA. 22 min. B&W.
Silent

NIGHT ON BALD MOUNTAIN
Produced in shadow pin-board animation by Alexander Alexeieff and
his wife, Claire Parker. To the
music of Moussorgsky's "Night On
Bald Mountain," the film creates
an eerie mood as it interprets the
composition. (A Contemporary
Films release)
McGRAW-HILL. 8 min. B&W.
Sound. 1933

NOTES ON A TRIANGLE
Animation of a single geometric
form. A white triangle divides into
three parts colored red, yellow, and
blue. Further divisions and movements produce many complex designs, all accompanied by appropriate music. Finally, the forms return to the basic triangle, and the
colors disappear. Music. Awards:
London, Teheran, Buenos Aires,
Melbourne. (National Film Board
of Canada)
INT. FILM BUR. 5 min. Color.
Sound. 1968

N.Y., N.Y.
A highly personal, visual interpreta-
tion of the temper and personality of
New York City. Awards: Cannes,
London, Edinburgh, and New York.
(Produced by Francis Thompson)
PYRAMID. 16 min. Color. Sound.
1959

ONCE UPON A TIME
THERE WAS A DOT
Images and a uniform style follow the
antics of a dot that "magically"
transforms itself into a circle, a
wheel, an airplane, musical instruments, people, cars, clothing, and
other things. The "dot" creates a
colorful world for children, showing
how imagination can form complex
concepts from basic origins. (Produced by Zagreb Film)
McGRAW-HILL. 8 min. Color.
Sound. 1964

OPUS: IMPRESSIONS OF
BRITISH ART AND CULTURE
Survey of the contemporary arts in
Britain, highlighting modernist
trends in sculpture, painting, archi-
tecture, drama, and ballet. Awards:
International Festival of Color
Films; Hemis-film Festival; First
United Nations Festival of Short
Films; Argentina Festival of the
Arts.
PYRAMID. 29 min. Color. Sound.
1967

OPUS 3
Sound and images were created with minimum of photographic or electronic equipment. The film is composed of images of a few simple geometric forms—squares, circles, lines, ellipses, etc.—arranged to generate an increasing number of images. Award: Melbourne.
NAT. FILM BD. 7 min. B&W. Sound. 1968

OVERTURE/NYITANY
To the score of Beethoven's "Egmont Overture," time-lapse photography with a microscopic camera unfolds the development of a chick embryo. (A Mafilm production, Hungary)
McGRAW-HILL. 9 min. Color. Sound. 1965

PACIFIC 231
A visualization of the journey of a locomotive across the French countryside. Based on the symphonic composition of the same title by French composer Arthur Honegger. Rental only. (Produced in France by Andre Tadie)
AUDIO/BRANDON. 10 min. B&W. Sound. 1952

PAS DE DEUX
The creation of Norman McLaren. Through optical printing and stroboscopic effects, McLaren takes a simple pas de deux and enlarges it into a cinematic and dance experience. Multiple images of movement capture the mystery of a man and woman reaching out to one another. Awards: Academy Award Nominee; Landers Award; Blue Ribbon and Emily Awards; American Film Festival; Columbus Film Festival. (National Film Board of Canada)
LEARN. CORP. $13\frac{1}{2}$ min. B&W. Sound. 1969

PEOPLE MIGHT LAUGH AT US
On a reserve in the Baie des Chaleurs region of Quebec, Micmac Indian children make birds and dolls of brightly colored paper that they hang in trees. But they are reluctant that visitors should see them, claiming, "People might laugh at us." No narration; background music. (Canadian Film Award)
NAT. FILM BD. 9 min. Color. Sound

PERMUTATIONS
Culmination of John Whitney's five-year study of computer graphics, a "vocabulary of shapes and rhythms." Dots become analogous to letters; circles of dots, to words; and formations of circles, to "sentence structures." A South Indian rhythm duet is synchronized to the imagery. Award: CINE Golden Eagle.
PYRAMID. 7 min. Color. Sound. 1968

A PHANTASY
A surrealist abstract art interpretation with pastel drawings and cut-out animation by Norman McLaren. In a dream-like landscape, inanimate objects come to life and disport themselves in grave dances and playful rituals. Music for saxophone and synthetic sound. Awards: Venice, Canada, Boston. Rental only. (National Film Board of Canada)
INT. FILM BUR. 8 min. Color. Sound. 1948

PHYSICS IN F-MAJOR
Film artists at the Popular Science Film Studios in Hungary pose many questions in this film: How does sound look? How does light sound? Starting with the sine curve on an oscilloscope, the film progresses through simple lab experiments designed to exhibit the artistic potentials of physics. Colors and sounds are synchronized with the music of Scarlatti. (Released in co-operation with Faroun Films of Canada)
XEROX FILMS. 9 min. Color. Sound.

A PLACE TO STAND
An Expo '67 multi-image film showing the variety, beauty, and achieve-

ments of the province of Ontario, Canada. Winner: eight cinema awards. (Produced by Christopher Chapman) McGRAW-HILL. 18 min. Color. Sound. 1967

POSADA
Jose Guadalupe Posada (1851-1913) produced over 20,000 lithographs, woodcuts, and etchings. They commented on history, politics, and events of the times. Illustrations for ballads, caricatures, news stories of the Mexican Revolution, superstitions, the Day of the Dead, and even Halley's Comet are depicted. Mexican folk tunes on the guitar accompany the images. No narration. (Produced by Jose Pavon) FILM IMAGES. 10 min. B&W. Sound. 1964

POSTERS: MAY-JUNE 1968
(Revolutionary Art of the French Students)
Documents the anti-DeGaulle posters made by students during the confrontations. It begins with a tour of the schools, from the Sorbonne to the National School of Decorative Arts, where the posters were produced. The very first poster, "Vive la Revolution Creatrice," is shown being printed, and then a steady stream of revolutionary art. Soon they cover every available space on buildings. No narration; music. FILM IMAGES. 23 min. Color. Sound. 1968

POTEMKIN
Considered one of the most important films in the history of silent cinema. It brought to world attention Eisenstein's theories of cinema art: montage, intellectual contact, and employment of the masses (instead of the individual) as protagonist. Story is based on an incident that occurred on the ship Prince Potemkin during the 1905 Russian uprising. The sailors themselves and the people of Odessa were used as actors. Musical score. English titles; no dialogue. CCM. 67 min. B&W. Sound. 1926

POTTERY MAKING (Tajik)
From a series on the mountain people of Central Asia, specifically the Tajik tribe on the 10,000-foot plateaus of northeastern Afghanistan. No imposed narration; natural sound and native music. Printed supplements available on request. Mountain People of Central Asia series. (Made by German photographer Hermann Schlenker) IFF (BRYAN). 15 min. B&W. Sound. 1969

RAIN (Regen)
Joris Ivens, active in the first film club in Holland, filmed in the streets of Amsterdam for three months to produce this impression of a rain shower in the city. Released in 1929 as a silent film; 1931 sound version with music. No narration. FILM IMAGES. 12 min. B&W. Sound. 1931

RED STONE DANCER
A study of one of Gaudier-Brzeska's most important sculptures, Red Stone Dancer. The film shows the sculpture in changing patterns of movement and light. The film is introduced by a statement by Gaudier-Brzeska: "Sculptural feeling is the appreciation of masses in relation. Sculptural ability is the defining of these masses by planes." (Produced in England by Arthur Cantrill) FILM IMAGES. 5 min. Color. Sound

RE-DISCOVERY
Gift-wrapping paper is used to represent almost anything—from an idea to a musical composition. Nothing material is permanent; people with imagination will find new ways of expressing an idea. If applied to people, it raises the question as to whether they change with each contact with another person. Minimal narration, natural sound effects, and music. (Produced by Graphicom) AIMS. 6 min. Color. Sound. 1971

THE REED
This film uses serious music for counterpoint and mood, as men go to harvest reeds in the Danube Valley. In winter fishermen from surrounding villages skate across the ice to the reed forests; their battle for the reeds for the cellulose industry is about to begin. No narration; excerpts from Carl Orff's "Carmina Burana."
CCM FILMS. 9 min. B&W. Sound. 1967

REMBRANDT'S CHRIST
This film examines drawings in which members of Rembrandt's family and the townspeople of Amsterdam are compassionately represented as biblical characters encountering Christ as He fulfilled His mission on earth. No narration; music. Awards: Art Documentary of the year, Assisi; Columbus. (From Les Films de Saturne)
TIME-LIFE. $40\frac{1}{2}$ min. B&W. Sound

ROYAL ROCOCO (1725-1750)
Versatile and elegant, eighteenth century Rococo was the last of the grand styles to be universally embraced. The Castle of Augustusberg and its nearby lodge, with an interior glorifying falconry on blue and white tiles, are examples of German adaptation of imaginative decor. No narration. Award: German Government. (From Euphono Film)
TIME-LIFE. 12 min. Color. Sound

SAME SUBJECT, DIFFERENT TREATMENT
Designed to alert the viewer to the many ways artists have portrayed familiar objects. The motion picture is divided into five parts. In each a brief introduction presents the subject—the eye, the head, the human figure, the chair, the sun—and then a variety of images shows how it has been presented. These include photographs, paintings, posters, and sculpture.
ACI FILMS. 10 min. Color. Sound. 1969

SECOND WEAVER
This film is the result of Susie Benally teaching her mother to use a camera. It depicts the daughter weaving a belt. Navajos Film Themselves series.
CMC/COLUMBIA. 9 min. B&W. Silent

THE SHAPE AND COLOR GAME
Abstract toys and materials translate, through play situations, concepts of color, form, texture, and structure. There is no story line; the film follows some structured activities, but mainly relies on spotlighting free play. Child viewers, as players, may select a few of the ideas presented as ways to bring into focus the aesthetic definitions of the physical world. (A John Korty film)
STERLING. 8 min. Color. Sound. 1967

SHEEP IN WOOD
The process of making a woodcut of two sheep, by a contemporary master of the medium, Jacque Hnizdovsky. Based on the pastoral views of his native Ukraine. Composer Marian Kouzan provides the score for chamber ensemble.
ARTSCOPE. 10 min. Color. Sound. 1970

SHORT AND SUITE
Abstract imagery interprets lively jazz in this film by McLaren and Lambart. Effects are drawn directly onto the film, resulting in a kind of "visual music." Different themes, instruments, and movements are interpreted by line and color variations and motion. An example of art inspired by music. Awards: Bergamo, Venice. (National Film Board of Canada)
INT. FILM BUR. 5 min. Color. Sound. 1960

SKETCHES
As performer and teacher, Tony Montanaro has been seen across the country with his mime in theaters

and on television. In this film, he reveals the intricacies of his art in four vignettes: Athlete, Games, Sculptor, and Nightmare.
CMC/COLUMBIA. 16 min. B&W. Sound

SKY
From the Rockies of the western plains, this film catches and condenses the spectacle of a day in the life of the sky. Photographed with many lenses and different camera speeds; every changing mood of the sky is registered. Awards: Columbus, Ohio; Swift Current, Saskatchewan. (National Film Board of Canada)
McGRAW-HILL. 10 min. Color. Sound. 1958

SPANISH GYPSIES
A Gypsy festival offers an opportunity to witness authentic flamenco songs and dances as performed by Juan Salido and other artists in a grotto at Sacro-Monte, near Granada. No narration. (Produced by Pierre Braunberger)
FILM IMAGES. 11 min. B&W. Sound

SPHERES
Norman McLaren's film is a ballet of white spheres cavorting to the music of Bach, multiplying and dividing, advancing and receding against colorful backgrounds. The visuals for the film were completed by McLaren and Rene Jodoin over 20 years ago, but the music was chosen and the film released by the National Film Board of Canada in 1970.
INT. FILM BUR. 8 min. Color. Sound. 1970

THE SPIRIT OF THE DANCE
Classical dance and the many facets of the professional activity of a ballerina of the Paris Opera Ballet. Highlighted are the exacting disciplines this art demands. In the finale, the dancer performs a solo in which her technique and lyrical style are shown. No narration; music by

Adolphe Adam, Bach, and Gluck. (Directed by Dominique Delouche)
FILM IMAGES. 21 min. B&W. Sound

STAINED GLASS:
A PHOTOGRAPHIC ESSAY
A young craftsman expresses his love for beauty as he makes a stained glass work of art—simple enough in its conception and execution to teach, beautiful enough to inspire. No narration. (A Greg Smalley Film)
BFA ED. MEDIA. $8\frac{1}{2}$ min. Color. Sound. 1970

STAR OF BETHLEHEM (1700-1750)
Neapolitan craftsmen reflected the refinement of the late Baroque period in retelling the story of the Nativity with minute wood-carved religious figures, dressed in fabrics and styles of the seventeenth century. No narration; music. (From Film-Studio Walter Leckebusch)
TIME-LIFE. 12 min. Color. Sound

STARLIGHT
A "personal" film presenting an eclectic and fast-moving stream of clouds, boats, rivers, animals, and people. An example of the personal cinema that originated in San Francisco with avant-gardists like Stan Brakhage and Bruce Baillie. (Produced by Bob Fulton of Summit Films)
PYRAMID. 5 min. Color. Sound. 1970

A STUDY IN PAPER
Puppet-like figures tear themselves from newspapers and move by animation. The film demonstrates that even a simple design can develop a theme without the use of words. By means of tear-outs, the artist expresses the struggle between Peace and War. All the actors and "props" are handmade, and all the action is achieved by single-frame exposures. (Produced by L. Bruce Holman at Syracuse University)
INT. FILM BUR. $4\frac{1}{2}$ min. B&W. Sound

SUR LE PONT D'AVIGNON
Puppets, dressed in medieval cos-
tumes and set against painted back-
grounds reminiscent of the Palace of
the Popes and the ancient bridge at
Avignon, dance to the tune of this old
folk song. (National Film Board of
Canada)
INT. FILM BUR. 5¾ min. Color.
Sound

SURPRISE BOOGIE
Albert Pierru's impressions of
Robert Cambier's original jazz
score was one of the surprises of
the Experimental Film Competition
held at the 1958 Brussels World's
Fair. Animated. Awards: French
Government Prize; First Prize,
Mannheim; selected for exhibition at
Berlin, Oberhausen, Brussels, and
E.F.L.A. (Educational Film Li-
brary Association)
CCM FILMS. 6 min. Color. Sound.
1958

SYMMETRY
The figures in this animated film
obey strict mathematical principles—the embodiment of science in
art. The music gives the basic
rhythm to the movement of the figures. Tone and timing characterize
the different symmetries. Designed
and directed by Philip Stapp. No
narration. (Produced by Sturgis-
Grant)
McGRAW-HILL. 10 min. Color.
Sound. 1966

T'AI CHI CH'UAN
The Chinese art of T'ai Chi Ch'uan
is a series of orderly, balanced
exercises in a definite and traditional sequence. Philosophically
comparable to the Yoga system of
seeking inner peace with the universe; physically analogous to boxing
or the dance. Performed by Professor Nan Huau-Chin. Filmed in Taiwan (Formosa). Nonverbal, with
electronic sound effects and music.
Approved by the American Federation of Art.
DAVENPORT. 9 min. Color. Sound.
1970

THE TENDER GAME
An exercise in free association of
popular music and popular images to
the tune of "Tenderly" sung by Ella
Fitzgerald, accompanied by Oscar
Peterson. Animated by John Hubley
and Faith Elliot.
McGRAW-HILL. 7 min. Color.
Sound. 1958

TEXTILES
How the artist/designer interprets
and transforms the textures and
colors of nature into woven and
printed textiles. Shown by the juxta-
position of trees, flowers, rippling
water, and the finished product—
fabric, weaving, or rug. Included are
sequences showing the designer at
work, as well as weaving and silk
screening. No dialogue.
MOD. MEDIA. 15½ min. Color.
Sound

TEXTURES
Explores the factors that determine
a person's impression of a surface
or texture. Foremost among these
factors is the point of view. A given
surface is quite a different thing to
an insect than it is to a human being.
Also influencing impression of texture are the direction and quality of
light, and function. Shows that textures are directly related to aesthet-
ics. Almost no narration. (A
Wheaton Galentine film)
ACI FILMS. 10 min. Color. Sound.
1970

THROUGH THE LOOKING GLASS
Instead of inventing new abstract
forms, Jim Davis here simply dis-
torts the familiar forms and principles of nature. Heads, eyes, hands,
and arms form, dissolve, and reform
again in a constant, rippling metamorphosis in an irrational and surreal world.
FILM IMAGES. 10 min. Color.
Sound. 1953

THE TORCH AND THE TORSO:
THE WORK OF MIGUEL BERROCAL
The work of this contemporary Span-

ish sculptor is based on the dissociative principle: his works may be dissembled and reassembled. Berrocal is of the generation of sculptors liberated and stimulated by the mastery of welding. He is shown at work in his studio, with his helpers, creating metal figures. They are surrounded by a panoply of materials and tools of all sizes. No narration; music. (Produced and directed by Jules Engel)
FILM IMAGES. 11 min. B&W. Sound

TUKTU AND
HIS NICE NEW CLOTHES
Tuktu and other children are shown being dressed and fitted for warm winter clothes, beautifully made by the Eskimo women. We see the cutting, stitching, and use of Arctic clothing, and we learn how important it is for an Eskimo wife to be clever with her needle. Stories of Tuktu series. (National Film Board of Canada)
FILMS INC. 14 min. Color. Sound. 1968

TUKTU AND THE CLEVER HANDS
A look at some of the things made by Eskimos and a commentary on the clever use that Eskimos make of the few materials available in their harsh environment. We come to the conclusion that the Eskimo is highly skilled and intelligent, and has overcome problems that seem almost unsolvable. Stories of Tuktu series. (National Film Board of Canada)
FILMS INC. 14 min. Color. Sound. 1968

TUKTU AND
THE TRIALS OF STRENGTH
Strong and hardy Eskimo hunters demonstrate and test their strength in Eskimo boxing, tug-of-war, and other strenuous activities. We see and hear the Eskimo drum dance, a demonstration of Eskimo poetry and rhythm. Stories of Tuktu series. (National Film Board of Canada)
FILMS INC. 14 min. Color. Sound. 1968

TURNER (1775-1851)
Credited with liberating color from its role of describing the subject, William Turner evoked an intensity of feeling in his landscapes that future impressionists and abstract artists were to try to capture in their work. No narration; music. Awards: Salerno, Vancouver, Wiesbaden, Columbus, Paris. (Les Films de Saturne)
TIME-LIFE. 12 min. Color. Sound

UN CHIEN ANDALOU
(An Andalusian Dog)
An attempt at pure surrealism (a work of art created entirely from the subconscious). Dream imagery is used in a free-association technique that discards conventional standards of esthetics, in order to shock the viewer. Audiences should be forewarned of content and style. (Produced by Salvador Dali and Luis Bunuel)
PYRAMID. 16 min. B&W. Silent. 1929

UNTITLED 2
In this film, an artist achieves success, not by talent or hard work but by finding a piece of junk. He describes it as art, calls it "Untitled 2," puts it in a gallery, and has an elaborately formal opening. Several serious questions are posed: If you find something and show it off, are you an artist? Is art communication or manufacturing? Just what is art and what is communication? (Produced by Murray Duitz)
XEROX FILMS. 9 min. Color. Sound

VERGETTE MAKING A POT
A master potter at work. The film is a close-up portrayal of the process of ceramics—wedging, throwing, trimming, glazing, and firing. Represents a respect for craftsmanship and for the man who can create a work of art from a lump of clay. No narration; original music by Teiji Ito. Award: CINE Golden Eagle.
ACI FILMS. 9 min. Color. Sound. 1966

THE VIOLIN LESSON
Accompanied by a violin solo, the camera peruses old photographs, paintings, and statues of great musicians. As the great men and fine music set a scene, the violin solo gets stuck. An old man removes the record. The old man opens the door to an anxious mother. Her young son is carrying a violin and looking quite stubborn. The lesson ends with an unusual twist—a spoof on this classic situation, accomplished with no dialogue. (Produced by Julia Newman and VPI)
McGRAW-HILL. 10 min. Color. Sound. 1970

VIVALDI'S VENICE
Venice, queen of Italian cities, is photographed by Life photographer Carlo Bavagnoli. Six eighteenth-century concerti of Vivaldi sustain the camera as it reflects Venice's glories and variety of moods through four seasons. No narration. Award: Venice Film Festival Silver Medal.
TIME-LIFE. 27 min. Color. Sound. 1968

WEAVES
This film, set to music with no commentary, is an impression of a textile designer-weaver. Shows how she creates and weaves, how her handiwork is made ready and is hung in an exhibition. Shows various weaving processes, the weaver at her handloom, and the reaction of visitors to the display. (Produced by Homi D. Sethna)
INT. FILM BUR. 12 min. Color. Sound

WEAVING CLOTH (Pushtu)
The ageless art of weaving. This process is not simply an art to the Pushtu wives traditionally assigned the role of weavers—it is a craft vital to their tribe's survival. They are seen working the crude portable wooden looms that date back to the days of Ghengis Khan, and even today are used throughout most of the mountains of Central Asia. Mountain People of Central Asia series.
IFF (BRYAN). 9 min. Color. Sound. 1968

WHERE TIME IS A RIVER
Without narration or dialogue, the film uses camera techniques to animate the imagery of Henri Rousseau, Paul Gauguin, Marc Chagall, and Fernand Leger. Details from over 100 paintings, concentrating on mood and feeling rather than content. Includes an orientation for use of the film, a biography of each artist, questions for discussion, supplementary activities, book, slide, and print bibliographies.
CMC/COLUMBIA. 18 min. Color. Sound

WHITE MANE (Crin Blanc)
Written and directed by Albert Lamorisse, director of "Red Balloon." This is a tragic and mythic story of a boy's love for a wild horse, photographed against the watery wilderness of the Camargue region of southern France. Rental only.
MUS./MOD. ART. 39 min. B&W. Sound. 1953

WILLOW
An aesthetic experience with nature. Visuals and music were selected to evoke the qualities of dignity, mass, intricate structure, strength, solemnity, and cheer—as related to a particular tree. Further dissection of the film reveals principles of good cinema composition, which is the film's primary purpose.
SYRACUSE UNIV. 7 min. Color. Sound. 1971

WINDOWS
The steps in the creation of a modern stained glass window. Without narration, this film follows the artist through the design, laying out the cartoon, selection of glass, cutting, assembling, to the installation. A CINE Golden Eagle award winner and official U.S. entry at the Venice Film Festival (A Yehuda Yaniv film)
ACI FILMS. 11 min. Color. Sound. 1969

2. OTHER PLACES, OTHER CUSTOMS

For some reason, I was surprised to find so many films whose topics fall under this heading. I shouldn't have been. After all, producers like Julien Bryan are usually overseas more often than home. And—continuing with Mr. Bryan as my example—maybe it was his international outlook that led him to the pioneering of nonnarrative interpretations of far-flung cultures.

Another rich source of similar materials comes to us, via Films, Inc., from Germany's Institut fur Film und Bild. FI's Man and His World series, while not completely free of words, holds narration to a minimum, averaging only three minutes of commentary for every 16 minutes of screen time.

The materials under "Other Places, Other Customs," in another time or context, might have been called travel films or travelogs. But these are not tourist films. Travelogs show only the surfaces of places, rarely the people themselves unless in costume or unreal pageantry. By contrast, the films you'll find here are "people" films, with people in the forefront, living the geopolitical relationship between man and land, land and man. Marshall McLuhan has said: "Man shapes his environment, then his environment shapes man." These films help us to understand that paradox.

AI-YE
An interpretation of the story of mankind's voyage, filmed along the Pacific coast of South America. Chants, songs, and drumming are integrated with the images. No narration. Awards: Venice and Edinburgh Film Festivals.
FILM IMAGES. 24 min. Color. Sound

AMAZON FAMILY
Filmed in Bolivia, 2,500 miles up the Amazon River. Here at Cabaceras Mati a crew of three Americans lived two months, studying and filming the life of these simple village people. Pedro, the father, is a serengueiro, whose daily task is gathering latex from wild rubber trees. His work, his food, his recreation, his family life are all portrayed. No narration.

How We Live series. (Photography by Francis Thompson)
IFF (BRYAN). 19 min. Color. Sound. 1963

ANNUAL FESTIVAL OF THE DEAD (Dogon People)
The Dogon tribe devotes its most important festival to those who died in the past year. The villagers perform war games in the village square. With dance movements, the warriors enact the accomplishments of their departed. Women bring offerings for relatives of the departed. The men parade to the houses of those who died within the past year. The festival concludes with the men drinking millet beer and the women dancing. African Village Life series.
IFF (BRYAN). 14 min. Color. Sound. 1967

ARCTIC PEOPLE

The Eskimos are native to a setting that is barren and cold. Because agriculture is impossible, hunting is the usual means of livelihood. In the Canadian northland, the Eskimo integrates custom with a modern life style. In contrast, the Lapps of the low Arctic face a less hostile environment, permitting the more varied activities of husbandry and fishing. Places People Live series.
STERLING. 14 min. Color. Sound. 1970

AT THE CARIBOU
CROSSING PLACE, Part I

Early autumn. The woman wakes and dresses the boy. He practices with his sling while she spreads a caribou skin to dry. The boy picks berries, and then the men come in their kayaks with another caribou. This is skinned. Soon night falls. In the morning, a weasel runs through the camp. One man leaves with his bow while the other makes a fishing mannick and bait of caribou meat. The woman works at the skins, this time cleaning sinews and hanging them to dry. The man repairs his arrows and then sets a snare for a gull. Netsilik Eskimo series.
MOD. MEDIA. 30 min. Color. Sound. 1969

AT THE CARIBOU
CROSSING PLACE, Part II

Two men arrive at the camp and help build from stones a long row of manlike figures, "inukshuit," down toward the water. They wait for caribou, then chase them toward the stone figures and into the water where other men in kayaks spear them. The dead animals are floated ashore and skinned. The boy plays with the visitors, the woman cooks meat, the men crack the bones and eat the marrow and then feast on the plentiful meat. Netsilik Eskimo series.
MOD. MEDIA. 30 min. Color. Sound. 1969

BAKING BREAD (Pushtu)

The simple but physically demanding domestic life of the nomadic Pushtu—no cleansers, no appliances, and no concern for "rough, red hands." The unveiled and weathered face of the Pushtu wife—cloaked in her traditional garment as she prepares and kneads the precious flour into dough—reflects the relentlessness of her environment. She skillfully fashions large flat discs of dough, then bakes each separately by pressing it to the convex side of a great copper pan. Mountain People of Central Asia series.
IFF (BRYAN). 10 min. Color. Sound. 1968

BARGEMEN ON THE RHINE

For 2,000 years the Rhine has been the great waterway of western Europe. The barge is the main workhorse, carrying goods and produce down the 700 miles of its length to the North Sea. Cameras follow the tug Braunkolle as it moves a unit of two coal barges from Cologne, Germany, to Karlsruhe, about 150 miles and 48 hours away. Minimal narration. Man and His World series. (Institut fur Film und Bild)
FILMS INC. 13 min. Color. Sound. 1970

THE BEDOUINS OF ARABIA
(Edited Version)

The desert is the setting for a look at the Bedouin, picturing their relationship with land, family, and tribesmen. Chanting and music form the background. The Bedouin emerge as figures of strength and affection, of courtesy and loyalty, men who learned to live with hardship and with nature. Today, as oil derricks dot the desert, the Bedouin can look forward only to an existence as an unskilled laborer, grist for the mill of civilization. Man and His World series. (I.I.T. Production)
FILMS INC. 20 min. Color. Sound. 1969

BOAT FAMILIES

Living and working on their barge, a French family makes the Rhone

River their home. The barge is loaded with seeds, and travels down the river and through canals with many locks. In Thailand, waterways are the principal carriers of freight, and home to many Thai families living in their sampans. Even shopping is done at the floating market place. Places People Live series. STERLING. 14 min. Color. Sound 1970

BOYS' GAMES (Pushtu)
An ancient game known throughout Asia is played by Pushtu boys. The toughness of these rugged young men, as well as the value these tribal people place on physical superiority, is demonstrated. Mountain People of Central Asia series.
IFF (BRYAN). 5 min. Color. Sound. 1968

BOZO DAILY LIFE (Mali)
The Bozo tribe meets the demands of environment through a division of labor determined in part by the fluctuations of the Niger River. The Bozo emerge from their thatched huts while dawn breaks over the Niger. The men man the boats and the women begin their day at the water's edge. These black Africans are shown as they fish, weave, cook, and mill rice—the activities that form the backbone of their daily lives. No narration. African Village Life series.
IFF (BRYAN). 16 min. Color. Sound. 1967

BUILDING A BOAT (Bozo People)
Boat-building, fundamental to the existence of all river peoples, is the work of a group of specially skilled Bozo men. The timber, from the coastal rain forests many miles away, is skillfully converted into the long, narrow boats in which the Bozos fish, trade, and even move their families, as the seasons change. Glue, nails, strips of cloth, and even mud are used to make the boat watertight. No narration. African Village Life series.
IFF (BRYAN). 8 min. Color. Sound. 1967

BUILDING A BRIDGE (Tajik)
At 10,000 feet in northeastern Afghanistan, 100 Tajik men and boys from one village work together to rebuild their hand-constructed bridge—their lifeline to market and their only means of contact with the outside world. These 100 Tajiks, in just three days of actual construction, bridge the river with a remarkable cantilever span of 120 feet. Mountain People of Central Asia series.
IFF (BRYAN). 10 min. B&W. Sound. 1968

BUILDING A HOUSE (Bozo People)
The construction of a storage house suggests many aspects of the Bozo culture—the division of labor between men and boys; the artistry of the simple construction, using materials yielded by the river; the joy of working to fulfill a common need. Reeds are soaked and twisted into rope; poles form the framework; woven reed matting forms the floor and walls; thatch, the roof. No narration; music, sound effects. African Village Life series.
IFF (BRYAN). 7 min. Color. Sound. 1967

BUILDING A KAYAK, Part I
Now it is July—summer. The runoff is in full spate, and open water shows offshore. Ice cakes melt on the shingle. On the bay are ducks. It is time to build a kayak, a task shared by two men. They gather materials: valuable scraps of wood, bone, seal skins and sinews. Now there is much cutting, fitting, joining and binding. The woman helps by cutting additional thongs, scraping skins, providing food. She must also amuse the child who seems left out by the single-minded work of the men. Then the work breaks, and a man harpoons a fish in a tide pool, and all share the pleasure of fresh food. Netsilik Eskimos series.
MOD. MEDIA. 32 min. Color. Sound. 1969

BUILDING A KAYAK, Part II
As the kayak takes shape, there are
more ribs to be split and shaped to
fit, more soaking, bending and binding, more skins to soak and scrape
and soak again before stretching
them tightly on the frame and sew-
ing them in place. Now the outer
rim is put in position and, while the
ice floats in the bay, the men launch
and test their new kayak with evident
pleasure in its able performance.
Netsilik Eskimos series.
MOD. MEDIA. 33 min. Color.
Sound. 1969

BUZKASHI (Afghan Tribes)
This once-forbidden sport is performed on horseback by the tribes of
Afghanistan. Fierce tribesmen honor
the King by competing at the week-
long annual festival. Buzkashi is one
of the toughest sports in the world,
requiring incredible riding ability.
The intense pride and rivalry of a
tribal society, as well as the role of
physical superiority and competition,
are implicit. No narration; natural
soundtrack. Festivals Around the
World series.
IFF (BRYAN). 8 min. Color.
Sound. 1968

CASTING IRON PLOW-SHARES
(Tajik)
From a series on the mountain peo-
ple of Central Asia, specifically the
Tajik tribe on the 10,000-foot pla-
teaus of northeast Afghanistan. No
narration; natural sound and native
music. Mountain People of Central
Asia series. Printed supplements
are available on request. (Made by
German photographer Hermann
Schlenker)
IFF (BRYAN). 11 min. B&W.
Sound. 1969

CHANGING GREENLAND
Along the rugged coastline of Greenland a hardy people are carving a
modern country. Once one out of
three people died of tuberculosis,
the long winters sealed off most of
the country from the outside world,
and many children were illiterate.

Now hospitals are found in the
larger towns, helicopters operate
between settlements year-round,
and schooling is provided for
everyone. Minimum narration.
FILMS INC. 14 min. Color. Sound.
1971

CHILDREN OF ISRAEL
We see young Israelis of different
ages and backgrounds in school, in
an arts and crafts class, on a kib-
butz, in synagogue, on the beach, at
home, and like teenagers all over the
world, spending endless hours on the
telephone. No narration; includes
authentic Israeli music. How We
Live series.
IFF (BRYAN). 13 min. Color.
Sound. 1969

CHILDREN OF PARIS
Kids—shining faces—Paris in summer! In this little-narration film, the
camera catches the excitement of
vacation-time in a fascinating city.
Faces young and old, rich and poor—
in the parks or the Flea Market, the
Louvre or Montmartre, the Sacre
Coeur or the back alleys. (Produced
by Films/West)
AIMS. 12 min. Color. Sound. 1971

COFFEE PLANTERS
NEAR KILIMANJARO
Naftali is a member of the Tschaga
tribe. He and his two wives live in
Tanzania. Naftali raises coffee
plants and the ripe beans are sold
through a cooperative. His son goes
to a modern school that owes its
existence to the Native Cooperative
Union. Blacks and whites sit together on the coffee "Board." The
races have learned to work together
to ensure improved living conditions
and educational opportunities. Man
and His World series. (Institut fur
Film und Bild)
FILMS INC. 14 min. Color. Sound.
1969

COOPERATIVE FARMING
IN EAST GERMANY
This is the story of a cooperative

farm in the village of Mestlin. The
cooperative owns the land and machinery, and each member is assigned a job. Everyone works for
the benefit of the whole—but how
different is this concept from the
communal relationship of primitive
tribes? Man and His World series.
(Institut fur Film und Bild)
FILMS INC. 15 min. Color. Sound.
1969

CORK FROM PORTUGAL
What are the people like who harvest
and process the cork we have on our
bulletin boards? This film gives us
insights into the workers who peel
the bark from the extensive cork oak
forests. Cork is Portugal's most
important export. Lisbon is Portugal's shipping center for cork products. We watch ships from many
countries load the cork. Man and
His World series. (Institut fur Film
und Bild)
FILMS INC. 12 min. Color. Sound.
1970

COTTON GROWING AND SPINNING
(Dogon People)
In small fields bounded by protective
thorn fences, the Dogon tribe grows
its cotton. A tribesman harvests
the cotton and brings it back to his
village hut, and a weathered Dogon
woman prepares the cotton fiber before spinning the thread. No narration; music and sound effects. African Village Life series.
IFF (BRYAN). 6 min. Color.
Sound. 1967

DAIRY FARMING IN THE ALPS
The village of Feeshin is located on
the Austrian-German border. The
viewer is given a picture of trans-
humance as practiced in Alpine Europe. Milk is brought to a cheese
factory where it is processed into
the famous Emmentaler cheese. In
early fall, the annual roundup is
held, festival time for the local people and tourists. Cultural characteristics of the region are expressed
in the dress of inhabitants and in the
ceremony of bedecking cattle with

flowers. Man and His World series.
FILMS INC. 16 min. Color. Sound.
1970

DEAD BIRDS
A study of the tribal life of the Dani,
a people of western New Guinea.
Shows how these people have based
their values on an elaborate system
of intertribal warfare and revenge.
(A Contemporary Films release by
Robert Gardner)
McGRAW-HILL. 83 min. Color.
Sound. 1963

DEEP SEA TRAWLER
A trawler steams from its port on
the North Sea to the Grand Banks off
Newfoundland. The ship is a "factory at sea," with electronic fishing
aids, mechanized cleaning and pack-
ing facilities. Through an animated
sequence, we see how huge nets are
dragged on the ocean bed and then
brought on board with tons of fish.
Once the hold is filled, the trawler
heads for home, and the men wait to
see their families, from whom
they've been separated for months.
Man and His World series. (Institut
fur Film und Bild)
FILMS INC. 18 min. Color. Sound.
1969

DESERT PEOPLE
Water means life to those who live
in the desert. In the Sahara, the
Tuaregs, a nomadic people, search
incessantly for water and grazing
lands. In contrast to the Tuaregs,
the Rajputs of the Great Indian Desert are cultivators. Moving water
through an ancient irrigation system by camel power and natural
flow, they toil to reclaim the desert.
Places People Live series.
STERLING. 14 min. Color. Sound.
1970

DIAMOND MINING IN EAST AFRICA
South of Lake Victoria is "diamond
country." The mine looks like a
well-protected industrial plant.
Trucks deliver the stones to a plant
where they are split. Inside, there
is constant surveillance of every

process. Policemen watch the workers to forestall any attempt at steal-
ing. In the more responsible jobs,
young Africans work on tasks for-
merly assigned to white employees.
Although the workers are the best
paid in East Africa, one wonders how
the pressure of being watched affects
these people. Man and His World
series. (Institut fur Film und Bild)
FILMS INC. 9 min. Color. Sound.
1970

EGYPTIAN VILLAGERS
Mustafa and his family live in an
agricultural village near the Nile.
The fields are irrigated by large,
hand-operated waterwheels. Three
crops are grown. Agricultural ad-
visors help the farmers use modern
methods. Life in the village is a
curious mixture of old and new cultures. The women who don't work in
the fields perform the household
tasks; children attend a modern
school and benefit from a government health program. Man and His
World series.
FILMS INC. 14 min. Color. Sound.
1969

THE ESKIMO: FIGHT FOR LIFE
Eskimos on the edge of the Arctic
Ocean struggle for existence as their
ancestors have done for centuries.
Compared by many to the classic
documentary on the Eskimo, ''Nanook
of the North.'' The sound-track
consists of the natural sounds of the
region, with a brief commentary by
Prof. Asen Balikci of the University
of Montreal. Awards: Emmy (TV),
American Film Festival, Atlanta,
San Francisco.
ED. DEV. CENTER. 51 min. Color.
Sound. 1970

ETHIOPIAN MOSAIC
A glimpse of Ethiopa. Editing of both
picture and sound have provided an
intimate look at Ethiopia's people
without any need for narration. Especially interesting is the use of
silence and a dark screen to coun-

terpoint the many scenes. (National
Film Board of Canada)
INT. FILM BUR. 10 min. Color.
Sound. 1970

THE FAMILY FARM
A contrast in modernity and tradition. On a highly mechanized farm
in Denmark, efficient land management embraces many skills, including machine shop work, use of machinery, and bookkeeping. The
family farm in Yugoslavia is worked
with few modern implements. The
manual labors of the Yugoslavian
family exemplify the endurance of
custom.
STERLING. 14 min. Color. Sound.
1970

FAMILY OF THE MOUNTAINS:
A PERUVIAN VILLAGE
The life of a family in the mountains
of Peru is depicted from sunrise to
sundown. The camera follows the
children going to school, the men,
women, and children working in the
fields, and caring for the llama and
sheep herd. No narration; the visuals are accompanied only by original
Peruvian music.
McGRAW-HILL. 22 min. Color.
Sound. 1971

FISHING AT THE STONE WEIR,
Part I
Full summer, and the tundra is bare.
The skin tents are up, and it is time
to attend to the fishing as the fish
move upstream. The men are in the
river, lifting stones and putting
them in place to form enclosures to
trap the fish. A woman skins a duck
and then braids her hair in the old
way, stiffly around sticks. From a
bladder she makes a balloon for the
child. The men are fishing with the
three-pronged leisters, spearing the
fish and stringing them on a thong,
one after the other, until it is as
much as a man can do the drag his
catch from the water. The woman
works quickly, cleaning the fish, and
then all enjoy bits of the raw fish.
Netsilik Eskimos series.
MOD. MEDIA. 29 min. Color.
Sound. 1969

FISHING AT THE STONE WEIR,
Part II
There are many men fishing now,
and even the children on shore imi-
tate the motions of the men. Rain
sweeps over the tundra but the work
goes on, with the men splashing
through the weir, furs hitched high,
seemingly little affected by the cold
water. The haul is large. A man
makes fire with a bow-drill, and
soon there is a blaze under the stone
cooking pot. Fish are stewed and
eaten, the men staying in their own
group. There is a little play at cat's
cradle while stories are told, and
then the women return to cleaning
fish, and the men to building stone
caches to store and protect this
plentiful harvest for the leaner days
to come. Netsilik Eskimos series.
MOD. MEDIA. 27 min. Color.
Sound. 1969

FISHING IN ROMANIA
An unnarrated film that details a day
in the life of a Romanian fisherman.
IFF (BRYAN). 10 min. Color.
Sound. 1971

FISHING ON THE COAST OF JAPAN
The contrast of scenic beauty with
the ancient, creaking wooden boats
and the drudgery of the fishermen's
work. No narration; authentic Japanese music. How We Live series.
(Photography by Kenneth Snelson)
IFF (BRYAN). 13 min. Color.
Sound. 1965

FISHING ON THE DANUBE DELTA
(Rumania)
The famed Danube River pours into
the Black Sea as the ageless Ruma-
nian fisherman works the swamps
and lagoons of its three-forked delta.
Clinging to methods sanctified by
centuries, he pulls his catch from
the swollen river waters. Among the
fish he draws from the reeds and
flooded marshes are carp, crayfish,
and sturgeon, source of black caviar.
IFF (BRYAN). 15 min. Color.
Sound

FISHING ON THE NIGER RIVER
(Bozo People)
For the Bozo tribe, fishing is particularly important, since the fish in
the Niger provide the only abundance
in an otherwise parched and hostile
environment. This film studies each
of the Bozo's methods of catching
fish—some requiring the skill of a
single person; some requiring the
combined efforts of groups; and
others, the cooperation of the entire
village. No narration. African Village Life series.
IFF (BRYAN). 18 min. Color.
Sound. 1967

FOREST PEOPLE
The forest regions of the world provide many jobs and different life-
styles. Highlighted in this film are
lumber operations in Nova Scotia and
in Finland, where natural waterways
are integral to the transportation of
logs from forest to sawmill. In
contrast to the logging is sap gathering in France. Forests yield not
only lumber but other products, including resin, which is processed
into turpentine and cellulose products. Places People Live series.
STERLING. 13 min. Color. Sound.
1970

GRANTON TRAWLER
A study of the fishermen engaged in
dragnet fishing off the east coast of
Scotland. The only commentary is
the men's conversation at their work,
with the sound of the sea and the
boat's engine in the background.
(Photography by John Grierson)
McGRAW-HILL. 10 min. B&W.
Sound. 1934

GRINDING WHEAT (Tajik)
A Tajik man lifts a stone, and a
mountain brook is diverted to turn a
mill wheel that grinds wheat into
flour. From the first turn of the
grinding stone to the Tajik woman's
traditional tithe to the miller, the
camera gives the viewer a look at
the age-old process that provides
bread for these remote mountain
people. An evocation of the ingenuity

of early man in utilizing natural resources. Mountain People of Central Asia series.
IFF (BRYAN). 7 min. B&W. Sound. 1968

GROUP HUNTING
ON THE SPRING ICE, Part I
Late June, and much of the land is bare. There are sounds of running water, and melt ponds shine everywhere. The woman carries heather and moss to camp; the man makes a whirling bullroarer for the boy. Another child pretends to drive a dog sled. A woman is working sinews into bowstrings, while another is busy with a seal skin. A woman prepares a meal, and a man makes a bow from bone and sinews. It is a demanding task to combine such materials into a strong supple weapon; the result is pleasing to the man. The next day the men move out on the sea ice with a dog to look for seal pups. Netsilik Eskimos series.
MOD. MEDIA. 34 min. Color. Sound. 1969

GROUP HUNTING
ON THE SPRING ICE, Part II
The men are out on the sea ice, and the women work at the tasks of camp. Seal skins are pegged to dry in the sun. A woman, baby on her back, picks over a pile of gulls. The birds are skinned and then go into the pot with water from a melt pond. A baby sucks on a bone. The people eat, and then the women visit an old man in his tent. Now the women are out gathering moss for the fires, and we see the birds and flowers common to the area. A woman skins a seal pup while another sews skins for a tent. The children play at making camp, and some of the older girls pretend to nurse the fat pups. Then the adults join the fun, playing at juggling. Netsilik Eskimos series.
MOD. MEDIA. 28 min. Color. Sound. 1969

GROUP HUNTING
ON THE SPRING ICE, Part III
The men are moving about on the sea ice, probing for unsafe ice and watching for seals. The snow cover is nearly gone now, and the breathing holes have widened. The men sit and wait. One makes a strike with his harpoon, and others come to watch. They are ready to eat and relish the good warm blood and liver. Another hunter succeeds, and then another, but this one loses his catch when his thong breaks and the seal slides back into the water. But the party has three seals in tow when they return to camp, and soon the women have the meat exposed, and all eat. Then the blubber is packed into sealskin bags, and the men haul it away to the cache. Netsilik Eskimos series.
MOD. MEDIA. 35 min. Color. Sound. 1969

HARVEST IN JAPAN
A Japanese family at harvest time. Opens with rice fields and the cutting and drying of the grain. Then the tiny streets of the little village, the washing of vegetables, the making of rope from rice straw, the village cow, and housecleaning in honor of the harvest festival. Next preparations for the meal, patching the paper windows, and finally the feast— relatives in western dress for the occasion, drinking sake, eating with chopsticks, looking at the family album. The singing of Japanese folk songs ends the film. How We Live series.
IFF (BRYAN). 10 min. Color. Sound. 1964

HARVESTING
Here the reality is the horizon-wide fields of grain that must be cut and threshed by the combines before frost lays the crop to waste. What is seen suggests a military maneuver as a phalanx of the giant machines lumbers across the golden acres. Music. (National Film Board of Canada)
PYRAMID. 10 min. Color. Sound. 1968

HERDING CATTLE (Peul People)
A glimpse of the Peul (or Fulani)
tribe. These black nomads wander
with their cattle from one grazing
ground to another. The viewer joins
the Peul as they drive their cattle
across the Niger. He hears the
grunts and snorts of the struggling
swimming beasts, the shouts of the
graceful drovers, and the lapping of
water about the boats of hired river-
men, who carry calves and pick up
stragglers. No narration. African
Village Life series.
IFF (BRYAN). 7 min. Color.
Sound. 1967

HIGHLAND INDIANS OF PERU
"Is the highland Indian better off in
the highlands, or moving to Lima,
where he probably will not be able to
find a job and will live in a slum?"
From views of modern Lima, the
film moves to the highlands, where
the Indians labor as farmers and
herdsmen on land owned by absentee
landlords. There are no schools except in the villages, and 50 percent
of the highland Indians are illiterate.
Man and His World series. (Institut
fur Film und Bild)
FILMS INC. 18 min. Color. Sound.
1969

HIGHLAND PEOPLE
In an isolated environment, invention
and necessity work closely together.
The Aruaco Indians of Colombia live
in mountain foothills. An isolated
tribe, they depend entirely on their
agriculture and sheep for food and
clothing. Highland counterparts, the
Dogons of Mali live in rocky hills.
The uninviting cliffs have been transformed into a multistoried community. The Dogons are also an agrar-
ian people.
STERLING. 12½ min. Color. Sound.
1970

HIROKO IKOKO
Played without words against a background of Japanese life, "Hiroko
Ikoko" is about two young Japanese
girls whose fascination with fish
takes them through parks, markets,

and city streets until they find
themselves lost. American children
can identify with the girls' experience, leading to discussion on cultural differences and similarities.
(National Film Board of Canada)
XEROX FILMS. 20 min. Color.
Sound. 1970

HOLLAND: TERRA FERTILIS
For geography and social studies on
agriculture, it provides a lesson in
the accomplishments of the small but
highly developed country. It is also
a travel film. No narration. (A
Carillon Film)
ACI FILMS. 11 min. Color. Sound.
1969

THE HUNTERS
The slow pace of the action, and the
silent photography broken only infrequently by narration, slow plucking
of native instruments, and song,
evoke the peace of the lives of these
hunters of the Kalahari Desert. Detailed as to the thought processes,
personalities, and techniques of survival of these people. A visual demonstration of the close interrelationship of earth, animal, and primitive
man. Also available in B&W. Preview recommended.
McGRAW-HILL. 72 min. Color.
Sound. 1958

HUNTING WILD DOVES
(Dogon People)
The daring, skill, and bravery of the
young men of the Dogon tribe. The
agile young men of this black African culture scale the steep cliffs in
search of doves that nest in the
craggy pockets. Their lives are sus-
pended high above their onlooking
elders by the strength of the rope
handwoven from the bark of the bao-
bab tree by a fellow tribesman. No
narration. African Village Life series.
IFF (BRYAN). 8 min. Color.
Sound. 1967

IMPRESSIONS OF
A GUATEMALA MARKET DAY
To the beat of marimba music, young

girls carry water from a well.
Women, with babies on their backs,
stroll among fruits and vegetables.
Bells indicate that Sunday is more
than a day for shopping, as men burn
incense on the church steps, while
others engage in processions or
dances as old as their Mayan heritage. (Produced by Garry Young)
PYRAMID. 10 min. Color. Sound.
1969

IN INDIA THE SUN
RISES IN THE EAST
Includes farmers and city dwellers,
craftsmen and professionals, tem-
ples and houses, cities and villages,
bazaar and beggars, sunrise and sunset. No narration, no dialogue—only
the natural effects surrounding people and places, and the music native
to the country. Award: Chris Award,
Columbus Film Festival. (Produced
by Richard Kaplan, Inc.)
McGRAW-HILL. 14 min. Color.
Sound. 1970

INDIAN VILLAGERS IN MEXICO
On a market day, we visit the province's capital, Oaxaca. We see the
old Spanish houses that line the
streets, and the many churches that
dot the city not far from the large
central square of the market. Despite the changes in the world around
them, the villagers continue to lead
their lives as their ancestors did.
Man and His World series. (Institut
fur Film und Bild)
FILMS INC. 12 min. Color. Sound.
1970

INDUSTRIAL REGION IN SWEDEN
Can a country become industrialized
and still maintain beautiful forests,
clear rivers, and lakes? This film
shows how it is done in the resource-
rich central region of Sweden, which
was producing iron long before paper was made from wood, and electricity generated by water. Industrial centers like this are scattered
throughout the region, instead of
being concentrated in major centers.
Man and His World series.
FILMS INC. 18 min. Color. Sound.
1969

INDUSTRY COMES TO PAKISTAN
In Pakistan large-scale industry is
slowly replacing the inefficient time-
worn methods employed in small-
scale domestic manufacture. Technical training programs have been
introduced and there is already evidence of technological improvements
in transportation, building, and manufacture. Industrialization is part of
Pakistan's transition to modern na-
tionhood. Minimal narration.
FILMS INC. 17 min. Color. Sound.
1972

INTREPID SHADOW
Called by Margaret Mead "one of the
finest examples of animism shown on
film." This film deals with subjec-
tive rather than objective aspects of
Navajo life. In the film, Al Clah at-
tempts to reconcile the Western
notion of God with his traditional
Navajo notion of gods. Navajos Film
Themselves series.
CMC/COLUMBIA. 18 min. B&W.
Silent

ISLAND PEOPLE
Size and resources are important
factors in determining the character of any community. Isolated
from others of their kind, a family
of the Njemps tribe sustains itself
on an almost barren island in Lake
Baringo, East Africa. By contrast,
the island of Marguerita, near Venezuela, allows for a more complex
society. The work of the people is
diversified, and the marketplace
offers a variety of goods and services. Places Pleople Live series.
STERLING. $13\frac{3}{4}$ min. Color. Sound.
1970

JAPANESE FARMERS
Despite the harshness of the moun-
tainous terrain, the Japanese farmer
has used his ingenuity to develop
cultivation techniques that make use
of every inch of arable land. Men
and women work year-round, to
squeeze productivity from the earth.
Many farmers are moving to the
city. What will happen to this high
level of agricultural productivity?

Man and His World series. (Institut
fur Film und Bild)
FILMS INC. 17 min. Color. Sound.
1969

JERUSALEM
Using the highly compressed form of
the "time capsule," this film is both
a kinestatic history and an impressionistic overview of the Holy City.
Beginning with David, over 800
photos and film clips bring the
viewer through time to the 1967 Six
Day War. Special emphasis is
placed on the blending of Arabic and
Israeli cultures, and on the artistic
flavor of the city's past and present.
(Produced by David Adams)
PYRAMID. 5 min. Color. Sound.
1971

JIGGING FOR LAKE TROUT
More signs of winter's end as more
wildlife returns. The family makes
an excursion for fresh fish from a
lake. They build a karmak and move
in their furs, cooking troughs, etc.
The woman sets up her lamp, spreads
the furs, and attends to the children.
There are signs of returning wildlife. The man moves out on the lake
ice and chips a hole for fishing. He
baits his hook and lowers it, jigging
the line to attract the fish. Crouched
by the hole, he persists with his purpose and takes some fish, as does
his wife who has joined him. Both
remain at the hole through a severe
blizzard. Netsilik Eskimos series.
MOD. MEDIA. 32 min. Color.
Sound. 1969

JUGGERNAUT: A FILM OF INDIA
India is revealed through the eyes of
her people as they watch the incon-
gruous journey of a modern-day
"juggernaut" (a nuclear reactor) on
its 600-mile route through their
land. The camera comments on the
irony of this symbol of the modern
world in scenes that reveal almost
every aspect of Indian life: the arid
countryside, the landmarks, the ancient customs, the nation's deeply
Eastern philosophy. Minimal nar-

ration. Award: American Film
Festival. (National Film Board of
Canada)
LEARN. CORP. 28 min. Color.
Sound. 1968

LAKE PEOPLE OF SCOTLAND
The lake is the famous Loch Lomond.
The people are the shepherds, farmers, and foresters. The time is fall,
winter, and early spring—when the
tourists are not there, and life is
quiet and personal. The lake people
are skilled conservationists. They
also protect game, though a deer
that destroys trees is shot. And
they nurture their livestock, bottle-
feeding orphan lambs. Man and His
World series. (Films of Scotland)
FILMS INC. 16 min. Color. Sound.
1970

LAND FROM THE NORTH SEA
How land is reclaimed from the sea,
how land is built up through sedi-
mentation, how dikes are constructed, and why certain plants are
sown. Farmers on the reclaimed
land grow grain. Some raise pigs or
cattle. At times, the rising water
becomes a problem but the people
install pipes to lead the water to the
sea. Shows the drainage system
that protects the land. Man, in this
film, has used his ingenuity to re-
shape his environment. Man and His
World series. (Institut fur Film und
Bild)
FILMS INC. 18 min. Color. Sound.
1969

LIFE IN NORTH CHINA
Workers from the country join with
the city workers of North China,
once known as Manchuria, to celebrate National Liberation Day.
Scenes of the Chinese in festive
mood thronging through the streets
and squares of the city to watch the
parade. Minimal narration.
FILMS INC. 18 min. Color. Sound.
1971

THE LINE
The first crossing of Australia by the

standard gauge railway line between
Sydney and Perth. Natural sound and
folk music replace conventional
narration.
AUSTRALIA. 13 min. Color. Sound.
1969

MAGIC RITES: DIVINATION BY ANIMAL TRACKS (Dogon People)

Shows a common method of divining.
The soothsayer, an elder of the village, enters the sacred ground. Re-
sponding to questions by members
of his village, he uses symbolic
language to draw a representation
of the village in the sand. He then
drops peanuts at strategic places to
lure the night jackals into the field.
The following morning he returns to
prophesy from the tracks left by the
jackal. No narration. African Village Life series.
IFF (BRYAN). 7 min. Color.
Sound. 1967

MAGIC RITES: DIVINATION BY CHICKEN SACRIFICE (Dogon People)

The Dogon religion requires a steady
practice of living animal sacrifice to
insure a good relationship with the
divine forces. This film details the
most common sacrifice—the ritual
execution and devouring of the
chicken. When the dying fowl is
thrown to the ground, it is considered a good omen if it lands with
its feet in the air. No narration.
African Village Life series.
IFF (BRYAN). 7 min. Color.
Sound. 1967

MAKING BREAD (Tajik)

The Tajiks prepare their flat bread,
using a somewhat different method
from their Pushtu neighbors. In the
grim Hindu Kush mountains, a
Moslem woman of the Tajik tribe
kneads her dough into a flattened,
rounded form, slapping it to the
walls of her clay oven. The crisp,
flat, unleavened bread is like that
of biblical times. Compare this
film with "Baking Bread." Mountain
People of Central Asia series.
IFF (BRYAN). 11 min. B&W.
Sound. 1968

MAKING GUN POWDER (Tajik)

A Tajik tribesman makes gunpowder
by an ancient technique similar to
that used during the time of the
American Revolution. The tribesman is shown as he grinds a careful balance of charcoal, potassium
nitrate, and sulphur in a stone
mortar, and stores the finished product in a moisture-proof powder
horn. Mountain People of Central
Asia series.
IFF (BRYAN). 10 min. B&W.
Sound. 1968

MAN CHANGES THE NILE

The Nile is the key to life as it
courses through this land. But man's
ingenuity is already effecting
changes. Dams have made Egypt's
agricultural economy independent
of seasonal flooding. Power plants
and a nitrogen factory provide elec-
trical energy and fertilizer. In parts
of Egypt, men or animals are used
to draw water. However, pumps are
gradually replacing old methods. A
new way of life is opening up in this
old land. Man and His World series.
(Institut fur Film und Bild)
FILMS INC. 13 min. Color. Sound.
1969

MAN OF ARAN

Robert Flaherty's classic film of the
fishermen of the Aran Islands and
their difficult struggle for existence.
The film is dominated by the sea,
while the sound track is an or-
chestration of natural sounds, folk
songs, and snatches of conversation.
McGRAW-HILL. 77 min. B&W.
Sound. 1934

MASAI IN TANZANIA

A look at the African warrior tribe,
the Masai, noted for height and lack
of negroid features. Cattle are
prized possessions. Young herdsmen
take the stance peculiar to the
Masai—standing on one leg with the
other foot against the knee. Close-
up shots show them drinking blood
from cattle—their chief nourish-
ment. The Masai now trade peacefully with neighboring tribes, but be-

fore the prohibition of weapons in the marketplace, the Masai provoked bloody battles at trading sites. Even now, they seem uncomfortable with the new ways of barter. Man and His World series. (Institut fur Film und Bild)
FILMS INC. 13 min. Color. Sound. 1970

MEN'S DANCE (Pushtu)
The Pushtu are dependent upon traditional dances to provide entertainment and pleasure. The rugged tribesmen are shown against a backdrop of snow-capped peaks in an unusual national dance that portrays man's endless combat with evil. Mountain People of Central Asia series.
IFF (BRYAN). 11 min. Color. Sound. 1968

MINERS OF BOLIVIA
Focuses on Indians living in the highlands. They eke out an existence in the mine and along the creeks and rivers. Almost everyone chews cocoa leaf, to relieve the hardships of their lives. The beauty of the locale is a sharp contrast to the squalor of their lives. Man and His World series. (Institut fur Film und Bild)
FILMS INC. 15 min. Color. Sound. 1969

MOON'S MEN
Wordless study of the early morning world of the shrimp fishers of the northwestern English coast. We see the men harness their mares, ride in a wooden wagon to the water, and gather nets filled with fish. We watch a crab, tossed back, disappear into the wet sand. Horses trudge through deep water so that the fishermen may place their nets.
CMC/COLUMBIA. 13 min. B&W. Sound. 1964

MOSLEM FAMILY IN YUGOSLAVIA
Yugoslavia's little-known but substantial minority of European Moslems maintain their religion and customs in the middle of a modern state. Authentic folk music underscores this narrationless film.
IFF (BRYAN). 9 min. Color. Sound. 1965

MOUNTAIN FAMILY IN EUROPE
Contrasts are shown between farming in the U.S. and the traditional style of farming of an Alpine family as they milk, make butter and cheese, bake bread, and reap and dry the hay. See 'n Tell series. (Institut fur Film und Bild)
FILMS INC. 9 min. Color. Sound. 1970

MOUNTAIN PEOPLE
In the Swiss village of Guardia, tradition is strong. Surrounded by mountains, a hard-working people have shaped and retained their harmonious way of life. Thousands of miles away, on the slopes of the Himalayas, live the Gurungs of Nepal. Despite the scarcity of land and the climatic extremes, the Gurung culture has endured with little change for centuries. Places People Live series.
STERLING. 13½ min. Color. Sound. 1970

NANOOK OF THE NORTH
A classic epic of Eskimo life—the world's first, and by many standards, the finest documentary ever made. (Produced by Robert Flaherty)
McGRAW-HILL. 55 min. B&W. Silent. 1922

NAWI
During the dry season, the Jie of Uganda leave their homesteads and take their cattle to temporary camps, or nawi, where fresh grass is abundant. The film is about this drive and the life of the Jie at the cattle camp. Without commentary but with subtitles translating the conversation of the people. (By David MacDougall)
CHURCHILL. 22 min. Color. Sound. 1970

NEW LIFE
FOR A SPANISH FARMER
Ramon Cortes makes a decision to
move his family from the arid land
of his ancestors to an agricultural
project. By donkey cart, they travel
to their new home. The land changes
as they approach. Irrigation has
brought flourishing crops. Cortes'
family moves into their new home,
part of a housing unit. He goes to
classes where farming techniques
are taught. Officials bring him a new
cart and implements. His big day ar-
arrives when he goes to the farmland
allocated to him. Cortes and his son
begin preparing for the life ahead.
Man and His World series. (Institut
fur Film und Bild)
FILMS INC. 18 min. Color. Sound.
1969

NIOK
About a jungle boy's devotion to a
baby elephant deserted in the forest
by its parents. Niok's greatest sac-
rifice comes when he sets it free
rather than see it sold into captivity.
This film also depicts living condi-
tions in a small Cambodian village.
Very little narration. (Directed by
Albert Lamorisse)
WALT DISNEY. 29 min. Color.
Sound. 1960

NORTH SEA ISLANDERS
The islanders have learned through
the years to respect the sea. The
stone breakwaters protect the shore-
line, and the homes are constructed
to withstand gales. Old houses are
torn down to make way for new,
stronger homes. Children play
along the streams that interlace the
island. During school, a storm approaches and the children are sent
to the safety of their homes. Living
on an island as contrasted to living
on a land mass is portrayed. Man
and His World series. (Institut fur
Film und Bild)
FILMS INC. 19 min. Color. Sound.
1970

A NORWEGIAN FJORD
Eric, a teen-age Norwegian boy,
lives at Hardanger-Fjord, one of
Norway's largest. We join Eric on
a fishing trip and see the fjord from
his rowboat. What does the future
hold for a boy in a small community?
Eric can go into farming, work in the
plant, or go to college and make his
way elsewhere. The decision will
not be parochial, for his counterparts around the world face the same
problem. Man and His World series.
(Institut fur Film und Bild)
FILMS INC. 13 min. Color. Sound.
1969

THE NUER
The sounds, gestures, and events that
portray the harmony and rhythm of
the life of the Nuer, the tall and
graceful Nilotes of Ethiopia and the
Sudan, who call themselves Nath or
"the real people." Award: Ameri-
can Film Festival. (A Contemporary
Films release by Hilary Harris and
George Breidenbach)
McGRAW-HILL. 75 min. Color.
Sound. 1970

NZURI: EAST AFRICA
The moods, life styles and harmonies
of the East African nations of Kenya,
Uganda, and Tanzania. Gold Medal
Award: Atlantic Film Festival.
(Produced by Summit Films)
PYRAMID. 30 min. Color. Sound.
1970

O CANADA
A nonnarrated film that gives a
brief picture of Canada from the ar-
rival of the French to the modern
times. (Produced by Murray Sweig-
man)
PYRAMID. 4 min. Color. Sound.
1970

OASIS IN THE SAHARA
The natural forces that play upon the
Sahara add up to a journey dominated
by the unpredictable. The route
leads through the Tanesruft, a desert
within a desert. It is divided by the
Tropic of Cancer, separated by rains
from the northern desert during the
winter, buffeted by winds, and faced
with floods during the summer.

Viewers are shown a land of contrasts and the "power" of the desert. Man and His World series. (Institut fur Film und Bild) FILMS INC. 16 min. Color. Sound. 1970

OIL IN LIBYA

The film takes the viewer into the desert that comprises the country of Libya. We move through the rocky hills along a road that passes oil-drilling sites, a source of the country's most important export. Marsa el Brega is the termination point of the pipelines. Tankers take on oil from a loading island. We visit Tripoli, its market, business district, and offices. Man and His World series.
FILMS INC. 16 min. Color. Sound. 1969

ONION FARMING (Dogon People)

Documentation of the division of labor, of the unity of the tribal group at work, and the order, grace, and dignity of a black African people. Each step is shown as the Dogons process their onion crop. Women harvest the onions, and men pound them and squeeze out the fluid to preserve them in the torrid heat. The compressed balls are then dried and stored for use in flavoring or for trade with nearby tribes. African Village Life series.
IFF (BRYAN). 7 min. Color. Sound. 1967

OVER THE ANDES IN ECUADOR

A journey across Ecuador with a crate of machine parts, from Guayaquil to the city of Quito, then to a village near the headwaters of the Amazon. The first part of the trip is made by train. We get glimpses of the people, the customs, and the native dress. At Quito's modern airport, the crate is transferred to a light plane. The plane delivers the crate to a missionary station, and returns a woman to the hospital at Quito. Man and His World series. (Institut fur Film und Bild) FILMS INC. 18 min. Color. Sound. 1969

PAPUA AND NEW GUINEA

Tribalism, remote villages, and illiteracy have kept Papua and New Guinea primitive, but they are determined to create a modern society. Stepping-stones to the future are new roads, better use of natural resources, and a growing economy to train workers, establish towns, and afford educational opportunities. Development is aided by Australia, trustee for the territory. Man and His World series.
FILMS INC. 17 min. Color. Sound. 1970

A PLACE TO STAND

An Expo '67 multi-image film showing the variety, beauty, and achievements of the province of Ontario, Canada. Winner: eight cinema awards. (Produced by Christopher Chapman)
McGRAW-HILL. 18 min. Color. Sound. 1967

PLAINS PEOPLE

Along the Great Rift Valley of Kenya and Tanganyika live the Masai, a tribe of seminomadic herdsmen. They neither hunt nor grow crops, but subsist on the milk, meat, and blood of livestock. Ranching is the way of life for many Cheyenne and Crow Indians on the reservation in Montana. The ranch is a family enterprise, and everyone works for it. Places People Live series.
STERLING. 14 min. Color. Sound. 1970

PLATEAU FARMERS IN FRANCE

Roger Merle, a government agricultural agent, describes his work with farmers in southeast France. We travel around the area with the agent as he talks to farmers. We see some of the prosperous farms and the reasons for their success, and we see the abandoned farms and villages. Film demonstrates that even dry, rocky land can be productive if people are willing to accept change. Man and His World series. (Institut fur Film und Bild) FILMS INC. 15 min. Color. Sound. 1969

POTTERY MAKING (Tajik)
From a series on the mountain people of Central Asia, specifically the Tajik tribe on the 10,000-foot plateaus of northeastern Afghanistan. Natural sound and native music; no imposed narration. Printed supplements available on request. Mountain People of Central Asia series. (Made by German photographer Hermann Schlenker)
IFF (BRYAN). 15 min. B&W. Sound. 1969

RAINFOREST PEOPLE
Isolated from the outside world, the pygmies of the Congo are nomadic hunters and gatherers. The tropical rainforest provides them with all basic needs. The Waika Indians live along the Orinoco River in the rainforests of southern Venezuela. Primarily an agricultural people, bananas and plantains are their main crops. The river is the sole means of transportation to the outside world. Places People Live series. STERLING. 13½ min. Color. Sound. 1970

RAINY SEASON IN WEST AFRICA
A boy watches a rainmaker sacrifice a chicken. As though in answer, a storm deluges the village. The villagers huddle in huts. Within a few days, the ground has softened and they plant corn and millet. Parched earth is now a green paradise. But the cycle will repeat when the sun and lack of rain again parch the land. There is a long way to go in this country. The elements and old beliefs have to be conquered before a modern economy can be established. Man and His World series. (Institut fur Film und Bild)
FILMS INC. 14 min. Color. Sound. 1970

RANCHERO AND GAUCHOS IN ARGENTINA
We see the celebrated gauchos with the herd, and observe the scientific farming methods used by the owner. Although the rancher is a progressive businessman, the gauchos are not far from poverty. The questions arise—should management concern itself only with profit and loss? Which is more important—rebuilding the deteriorated ranch or providing better living conditions for employees? Man and His World series. (Institut fur Film und Bild)
FILMS INC. 17 min. Color. Sound. 1969

RICE FARMERS IN THAILAND
Payong, a rice farmer, is a step ahead of his neighbors. He has built a water pump to flood his land so that he can plant two successive crops, while other villagers wait for rain. The villagers listen to a government expert who encourages them to irrigate. When Payong's harvest is in, he invites the Buddhist priests to bless his crop. The old ways of life contrast with new ideas. Man and His World series. (Institut fur Film und Bild)
FILMS INC. 19 min. Color. Sound. 1969

RIVER JOURNEY ON THE UPPER NILE
This trip to Juba unfolds a panorama of flora and fauna. The White Nile drains what appears to be a continually moving swamp and the riverboats have difficulty navigating the shifting channel. As the boats near Juba, elephants and hippos can be seen on the banks. The south Sudan, where Juba is located, is poor, but the government is developing the area. Man and His World series.
FILMS INC. 18 min. Color. Sound. 1969

RIVER PEOPLE
Along the Magdelena in Colombia live a people whose lives are determined by the river. Their houses are on stilts, they travel by boat, and the river is their principal source of food. On the Niger in Mali, the Mopti vary their habitats with the season. During the wet season they live in boats, and during the dry season

they build huts on shore. Places People Live series.
STERLING. 12 min. Color. Sound. 1970

RIVER PEOPLE OF CHAD
In the African country of Chad, people in villages live as they have for generations. You perceive family and group relationships that depict culture traits dating back to earlier centuries. Their existence depends upon everyone—men, women, and children—working together. The film shows life as it is in this part of Africa. Can this way of life continue? Should it? Man and His World series. (Institut fur Film und Bild)
FILMS INC. 20 min. Color. Sound

ROMANIA
The plains region of Romania is traversed by the Danube as it winds its way to the Black Sea. Along the Black Sea are resort towns and seaports. Collective farms form the basis of the agricultural economy. Grain is a major export and useful for supporting cattle. The change from a rural to an urban society is seen in the modernized cities around the oil fields and around the new factories producing fertilizer, synthetic fibers, cellophane, and paper. Man and His World series. (Institut fur Film und Bild)
FILMS INC. 18 min. Color. Sound. 1970

SAHARA FANTASIA:
A DESERT FESTIVAL
As nomadic desert tribes converge in Southern Morocco to celebrate their "moussem," the viewer is immersed in this unique Saharan festival—its tribal dancing and frenzied music, colorful tents of trade, and the celebration of the "fantasia," a traditional event combining the precision of ancient musketry with skilled horsemanship.
IFF (BRYAN). 9 min. Color. Sound. 1970

SCHOOL DAY IN JAPAN
A typical day of a Japanese boy and his sister. They set out for school, obeying the traffic signals and the crossing guard. The girl and other children in class act out a story about a little pig. Her brother uses an abacus in arithmetic class, and learns the art of calligraphy. Although there is little difference between Japanese and American schools, the childrens' attitudes and way of life present a contrast. See 'n Tell series. (Institut fur Film und Bild)
FILMS INC. 10 min. Color. Sound. 1970

SEACOAST PEOPLE
York Harbor, Maine. A long day lies ahead for the lobster fisherman. Picking up the bait in the morning, he checks and baits his traps, gathers his catch, and returns at the end of the day to sell it to a wholesaler. The Maine lobster fisherman and the Norwegian crab fisherman have developed similar methods of harvesting the coastal waters. In Norway, the fisherman sells his catch directly to the people at the dock. Places People Live series.
STERLING. $14\frac{1}{4}$ min. Color. Sound. 1970

THE SEEING EYE
Mark Fine's film about a lonely boy on an island in the South China Sea. The eye that sees is the eye of the boy, observing particularly the grand procession through the island of Cheung Chau, firecrackers exploding. Sound effects and music of harpsichord, recorders, and Chinese violins.
McGRAW-HILL. 28 min. B&W. Sound. 1966

SHEARING YAKS (Tajik)
From a series on the mountain people of Central Asia, specifically the Tajik tribe on the 10,000-foot plateaus of northeast Afghanistan. Natural sound and native music; no narration. Printed supplements available on request. Mountain

People of Central Asia series.
(Made by German photographer Hermann Schlenker)
IFF (BRYAN). 9 min. B&W. Sound. 1969

SING OF THE BORDER
A series of folk songs explores the Scottish border country and its history, beginning with the Battle of Flodden. Examines historic ruins and the home of Sir Walter Scott. The people celebrate past battles for freedom by riding over the countryside "lest baron or landlord ever forget" that the land belongs to the people. (Produced by British Transport Films)
INT. FILM BUR. 19½ min. Color. Sound

THE SINGING STREET
This film, which is without commentary, consists entirely of songs and games sung and played by Edinburgh children in their native city. Phrases of ancient ritual, myth, and lost language are mingled with symbols of present-day life—taxis, telephones and powder-puffs—the favorite themes being of love and death.
BRITISH. 20 min. B&W. Sound

SOUTH AMERICA: MARKET DAY
With a minimum of narration, this film allows viewers to draw conclusions about economic and social life in South American villages. They will observe the variety of foods and spices, modes of transportation, clothes, utensils, child-parent relationships, entertainment, reading materials, machine-made and handcrafted goods, and means of exchange. (An Art Evans Production)
BFA ED. MEDIA. 10¼ min. Color. Sound. 1971

STALKING SEAL
ON THE SPRING ICE, Part I
The family is on the shore of Pelly Bay in May and June. A seal basks beside its hole under a warming sun. The hunter stalks the seal, kills it,

and drags it to the family camp on shore. Man and wife skin the seal, cutting the hide into rings that girdle the body. Stripped of blubber, the rings are then cut spirally into long thongs. The boy plays on the shingle, imitating the circling gulls, while the man stretches his thongs between rocks and scrapes away the fur. The woman dresses the seal, wasting nothing, braiding the intestines. Netsilik Eskimos series.
MOD. MEDIA. 27 min. Color. Sound. 1969

STALKING SEAL
ON THE SPRING ICE, Part II
A seal is seen nosing from a snow-melt pool. The hunter sits at the door of his tent, shaping a new bone tip for his harpoon. When he finishes his harpoon, he sets out after seal. After a long imitative stalk, the hunter moves too soon, alerting the seal, and his harpoon misses. He prepares for a night vigil at the breathing hole. Next morning the hunter still waits for the seal. When again he fails, he turns to egg collecting on the cliff where the gulls nest. Finally the family packs its belongings on a bear skin, and shifts along the coast to another area. Netsilik Eskimos series.
MOD. MEDIA. 35 min. Color. Sound. 1969

STEPPE IN WINTER
In the chilling cold of the steppe land of southeastern Europe, men, women, horses, dogs, cattle, and sheep endure the long winter. In documentary style and without narration, this film shows a way of life influenced but not dominated by wind, cold, and snow.
STERLING. 13 min. B&W. Sound. 1966

STROMBOLI: A LIVING VOLCANO
The unpredictable and precarious existence of a volcanic island. The Stromboli volcano has been active since recorded history. On September 2, 1930, without warning, it erupted. Before that day, 5,000 peo-

ple lived on Stromboli; today, only 300 remain. These lead an existence touched by severe memory and daily apprehension.
ACI FILMS. 10 min. Color. Sound. 1969

SUGAR IN EGYPT
In the days of the Pharaohs, plows drawn by water buffalo or oxen were used to cultivate the fields. The farmers in Egypt's Upper Nile region still use this method, contrasting with the modern machinery on the government-supervised plantations in the same area. Progress comes slowly in this part of the world, and only in recent years have leaders introduced modern techniques to boost the economy. Man and His World series.
FILMS INC. 13 min. Color. Sound. 1969

SUNDAY BY THE SEA
A view of the English enjoying the pleasures of the seaside, showing people in a realistic, yet kindly light, even with their inhibitions down. Instead of the usual commentary, the activities are accompanied by ballads made famous in English music halls. Music hall ballads sung by Joan Sterndate-Bennett and John Hewes. Award: Grand Prize at the Venice Film Festival. Rental only. (Produced by Leon Clore)
McGRAW-HILL. 15 min. B&W. Sound. 1955

THREE BROTHERS IN HAITI
A government official visits the village with Mr. Mouton of the U.N. The farmers listen to explanations of better methods with suspicion. Mouton realizes he must proceed differently. He begins by clearing the land of stone. Despite initial scorn he is soon joined by several farmers. Mouton shows the farmers the elements of efficient farming. Soon, the farmers bring in a good harvest that is successfully sold. Change is universally opposed, but often benefits all—including the op-

position. Man and His World series. (Institut fur Film und Bild)
FILMS INC. 16 min. Color. Sound. 1970

THRESHING WHEAT (Tajik)
From a series on the mountain people of Central Asia, specifically the Tajik tribe on the 10,000-foot plateaus of northeast Afghanistan. Natural sound and native music; no narration. Printed supplements available on request. (Made by German photographer Hermann Schlenker)
IFF (BRYAN). 9 min. B&W. Sound. 1969

TIMBER IN FINLAND
Aerial photography shows the lakes and rivers that give Finland the natural highways that carry her major economic asset to the pulp and paper mills. Most Finnish farmers depend upon their forests for a part of their income, and receive help from foresters who arrange for each year's wood supply. The Finns are making excellent use of natural resources and, with governmental supervision and aid, have built in safeguards against exhausting these resources. Man and His World series. (Institut fur Film und Bild)
FILMS INC. 15 min. Color. Sound. 1969

TUKTU AND THE INDOOR GAMES
A look at the Eskimos and the games they play in the big igloo. The wind and blizzard howl, but Tuktu's family and friends ignore the weather. They juggle stones, skip, and play with a delightful Eskimo child. Finally Tuktu falls asleep and dreams about the good time he has had. Stories of Tuktu series. (National Film Board of Canada)
FILMS INC. 14 min. Color. Sound. 1968

TUKTU AND THE SNOW PALACE
After a trek to new hunting ground, Tuktu's family and friends build igloos, including a giant igloo where feasting, dancing, and games are

held. Stories of Tuktu series. (National Film Board of Canada)
FILMS INC. 14 min. Color. Sound. 1968

TURKEY: NATION IN TRANSITION
Traces the historic background of this country through animated sequences. Includes evidence of democracy slowly beginning to function in elections following the students' revolt of 1961. The picture is allowed to speak for itself, using only authentic Turkish music.
IFF (BRYAN). 27 min. Color. Sound. 1971

TWO BROTHERS IN GREECE
Two brothers live in a village in the Peloponnesus. The younger has decided to become a farmer like his father. The older hopes to become an engineer. To help with expenses, the older brother decides to work on a tourist boat. He takes visitors to Delos, an island renowned in mythology, famous for its ruins. At home, the younger brother helps with the harvesting. The two brothers have decided which road each will travel to reach his goal. Man and His World series. (Institut fur Film und Bild)
FILMS INC. 17 min. Color. Sound. 1969

UIRAPURU
A reenactment of a primitive Brazilian legend. Brief narration and the music tell the story of the hunt for a legendary Uirapuru, the bird of love. Music by the Philharmonic Orchestra of New York under the direction of Efrem Kurtz. Awards: Edinburgh and Venice Film Festivals. Includes some scenes of nudity. Rental only. (Produced by Sam Zebba and filmed among the Urubu Indians of Maranhoa)
AUDIO/BRANDON. 17 min. Color. Sound

UNDALA
Village life in the Thar desert in northwest India during the months before the monsoon. For the farmers a time of leisure and repair; for women, water-bearing; and for craftsmen, little change in routine. Among the views of Rajasthani life are pottery-making, spinning, leather work, ropemaking, and the important task of drawing water. No narration; original musical score in Hindustani classical and folk styles. Awards: Winner, CINE Golden Eagle; Brussels; Cracow; Florence. (Directed by Marek Jablonko)
CMC/COLUMBIA. 28 min. Color. Sound. 1967

VENEZUELA
Venezuela as it is—a contrast between the wealthy and the poor; the city of Caracas and the jungles. The argument for nationalization of oil is countered by the claim that outside capital was essential in developing the industry. Venezuela is beginning to develop a broader industrial structure, hoping this will create jobs and better living standards. Man and His World series. (Institut fur Film und Bild)
FILMS INC. 14 min. Color. Sound. 1970

VILLAGE LIFE IN TONGA
The Tonga islands in the South Pacific are known as "The Friendly Isles." Visitors have been charmed by the attractive, friendly islanders and their relaxed life that seems to be able to accept the benefits of civilization without losing the integrity of Polynesian culture. Filmed in the village of Hoi, with natural sound and music but no narration. (A Harvard University film)
ACI FILMS. 20 min. Color. Sound. 1971

WEAVING CLOTH (Pushtu)
The ageless art of weaving. This process is not simply an art to the Pushtu wives traditionally assigned the role of weavers—it is a craft vital to their tribe's survival. They are seen working the crude portable wooden looms that date back to the days of Ghengis Khan, and even today are used throughout most of

the mountains of Central Asia.
Mountain People of Central Asia series.
IFF (BRYAN). 9 min. Color. Sound.
1968

WINEMAKERS IN FRANCE

The camera visits a small village in
Burgundy, where the ancient winery
is the focal point. From the crushing of the grapes to the hand bottling
of the wine, the film gives the viewer
a picture of a traditional French industry. Here, in this village, tradition and quality have not been super-
seded by modern mass production
methods. Man and His World series.
(Institut fur Film und Bild)
FILMS INC. 15 min. Color. Sound.
1969

WOMEN OF RUSSIA

Here are ballerinas and bricklayers,
fashion models and airdrill operators, pretty university students and
90-year-old ladies in an old people's
home, husky bathing beauties and
rugged crane operators. Teachers,
peasants, doctors, scientists. All
women; all working hard for their
families and for their country. No
narration; original musical score.
IFF (BRYAN). 12 min. Color.
Sound. 1968

WOOL IN AUSTRALIA

First, a great sheep fair at Sydney.
Then to a sheep ranch in the out-
back. Here we see a rancher and
his family in this isolated area,
where water is scarce, and mail is
delivered once a week. School for
the children is by correspondence.
Separated from the conveniences of
the populated coastal areas, they
have achieved a self-sufficient plane
of living by adapting to their environment. Man and His World series.
(Institut fur Film und Bild)
FILMS INC. 19 min. Color. Sound.
1969

YUGOSLAV FARM FAMILY

A hardy, independent farm family on
the Dalmatian coast struggles with
the harsh land and a government that
wants to collectivize all farming.
They live in a stone house over 600
years old. They are shown growing
food on the rocky ground and grinding oil from precious olives. No
narration; original score based on
Yugoslav folk melodies. (Photographed by Kenneth Richter)
IFF (BRYAN). 14 min. Color.
Sound. 1965

YUGOSLAVIAN COASTLINE

Shows us a cultural interface. Hvar
is a city unspoiled by tourists. In
the marketplace, produce and fish
are displayed. The face of the coastline is seen in a canning factory and
a bauxite mine. In another area,
limestone is converted to cement.
Shipyards abound. The camera helps
reveal the new and the old. Man and
His World series. (Institut fur Film
und Bild)
FILMS INC. 15 min. Color. Sound.
1970

3. SCIENCE

Science has historically been a rich source of film fare, so it's only predictable that so many science films have turned up in nonnarrated form. Here are over one hundred titles on science, which has been construed to include mathematics and technology. Excluded from this category are the numerous nature films commonly associated with biology. Inclusion of nature films under "Science" would have created too large a classification for easy reference. As a result, "Nature" is treated separately, in the section following this one.

This "Science" section includes films of fairly narrow scope, conceptually more specific than most other films, and therefore more closely—and unfairly—associated with "straight" instructional films. Yet, consider the dilemma facing producers and users: If there have been failures in certain science series, it has been because producers were willing to experiment with format; if science films stuck to too predictable a pattern, they were criticized for dullness.

Still, because of the needs of teachers and the convictions of businessmen, science films proliferated and producers profited. Even now there are probably more educational films on science than on any other classification. And it's only right that science films occupy such a prominent place in our collections. The early history of the media movement would have been dismal indeed without the leadership, commitment, and imagination of science teachers. It's no coincidence that so many science teachers climaxed their careers as media coordinators. What they had practiced as teachers, they preached as administrators.

While scientists enjoy an embarrassment of riches in this medium, mathematicians are practically destitute. Despite much attention and experimentation, mathematics has never yielded up nearly enough worthwhile teaching films. Of the rare successes, very few are nonnarrated. Those few are described within. But math specialists might well find related films in other areas. See especially "The Arts" category for motivational materials such as "Notes on a Triangle" and "Dance Squared." There are no words during such films, but there should be plenty after.

ACID BASE REACTION IN
ELECTROLYSIS OF WATER
The 60 films in the series, many of them produced under a grant from the National Science Foundation, are examples of the style of teaching where the films may be utilized as part of a series or treated as a single unit. The method is left entirely in the hands of the instructor. Detailed information on film content will be sent upon request. Contact CCM. Yale Chemistry Films series. CCM Films. 2 min. Color. Silent

AETNA
Mt. Aetna on the island of Sicily ... Europe's highest volcano ... a crater

and cone that constantly fluctuate. This film has no narration, but through close-up photography, extreme slow motion and a musical score, audiences will learn more about our Earth and the forces that shape it.
AMERICAN ED. 11 min. Color. Sound. 1971

AFRICAN ANIMALS
A day on the African savanna. The approach of elephants to the waterhole disturbs the water buffalo and a rhinoceros. Gnus, antelopes, impalas, and zebras congregate around the waterhole, but are watchful since life depends upon alertness. Vultures and hyenas await the scraps. A sated lion walks through a herd of gnus, but the animals instinctively know he is not dangerous since he has eaten. See 'n Tell series. (Institut fur Film und Bild)
FILMS INC. 9 min. Color. Sound. 1970

AMMONIA FOUNTAIN
The 60 films in the series, many of them produced under a grant from the National Science Foundation, are examples of the style of teaching where the films may be utilized as part of a series or treated as a single unit. The method is left entirely in the hands of the instructor. Detailed information on film content will be sent upon request. Contact CCM Films. Yale Chemistry Films series.
CCM FILMS. 2 min. Color. Silent

ANIMALS IN AMBOSELI
Using a typical region of East Africa, the Masai Amboseli Game Reserve, this film shows particularly the faunal association of the open grassland, woodland, and waterhole areas. The relationship of one species with another, and how baboons coexist with ungulates, carnivores, elephants, etc., is explored. Introductory narration only.
MOD. MEDIA. 20 min. Color. Sound. 1969

ANIMALS IN AUTUMN
Typical autumn activities of a variety of animals show them searching for food, building warm homes, preparing to migrate or hibernate. Includes deer, fox, weasel, cold-blooded birds, and insects.
ENCYC. BRIT. 11 min. Color. Sound

ANIMALS IN SUMMER
Shows insects, frogs, snakes, squirrels, foxes, and bears exploring the woods and hunting for food. Reveals the natural adaptive coloring of animals and observes the life cycles of insects during the summer.
ENCYC. BRIT. 11 min. Color. Sound

AT YOUR FINGERTIPS— FLOATS
Explains how air in a tightly corked bottle will keep it buoyant, and that in order for things to float they must be waterproof. After exploring what things float and why, the children in the film make their own floating playthings. A floating man is made out of cork and wire; balloons and milk cartons become boats, as do plastic meat-packing trays and styrofoam objects like water-paint trays.
ACI FILMS. 10 min. Color. Sound. 1969

AT YOUR FINGERTIPS—GRASSES
A ladybug on a blade of grass leads to an exploration of grasses and how they can be used. Different kinds of grass are compared to weeds. A fishing pole of bamboo is grass. A stalk of corn is grass. Fresh grass is held into the sun and forms artful patterns on paper. A print is made by placing paper on grass and rubbing with a crayon. Grass is used to decorate boxes, to make collages, grass skirts, masks, and in weaving.
ACI FILMS. 10 min. Color. Sound. 1969

AUDITORY RESPONSES OF NEWBORN INFANTS
Shows various kinds of observable responses in newborn infants when

they are exposed to sudden, controlled noises. These responses suggest methods for the early diagnosis of hearing impairments.
THORNE FILMS. 3 min. Color. Silent. 1965

BABY RABBIT
The sound track is a song with a foot-tapping rhythm. The story told by the song is about three central-city children who are raising a family of rabbits in a cage on their apartment house roof. It tells how all of them—rabbits, girls, and boys —need food and sleep and a warm home in order to live and grow.
CHURCHILL. 11 min. Color. Sound. 1971

BANG!
Students see and hear a boy making "music" in the timeless ways of children: by banging on cans, hitting pots and pans together, striking bottles, and dragging a stick along a picket fence. Contains broad science implications. Magic Moments series.
ENCYC. BRIT. 3 min. Color. Sound. 1969

BIRDS OF THE FOREST
A nature hike into the mixed deciduous and coniferous forests east of the prairies. Five entirely different birds, all living in a common natural habitat: song sparrow; slate-colored junco; chestnut-sided warbler; white-throated sparrow; mourning warbler. Available with study guides. Birds of the Forest series. (A Dan Gibson production)
A-V EXPLOR. 5½ min. Color. Sound. 1967

BIRDS ON A SEA SHORE
The world's largest bird colony, on the mainland and offshore islands of Peru and Chile. Here are millions of large sea birds (cormorants, gulls, dippers, flamingoes, boobies, and pelicans) nesting in densely packed colonies. They feed on the rich marine life of the Humboldt Current, in the shallows, the surface,

and in the ocean. No narration; just the sound of the birds. See 'n Tell series. (Institut fur Film und Bild)
FILMS INC. 10 min. Color. Sound. 1970

BLACKBIRD FAMILY
The story of a pair of birds, incubating and rearing their young. The eggs are laid and incubation begins. The eggs hatch in two weeks, and the young are fed throughout the day. Soon the babies are so big they crowd each other to the rim of the nest. Here they exercise their wings that will carry them out of their cradle. No narration; music and natural background sounds. (Institut fur Film und Bild)
FILMS INC. 12 min. Color. Sound. 1969

BRINE SHRIMP
Brine shrimp (Artemia salina), a tiny salt lake crustacean, is shown from hatching to adulthood, including larval stages and molting. Activities of the adults are shown, including swimming, action of the appendages, mating, egg laying, and live birth. Close-ups of the head and abdomen demonstrate differences between male and female.
MOD LEARNING. 7 min. Color. Silent

THE BUILDERS
A building . . . and the workers who lift it into the sky. Welders in dark pits, giant cranes, intricate cross-sections of steel and pipe, the quiet amidst the confusion during the lunch break. How a building is constructed, from the great foundation trenches to the last girder on the top floor. A modern building's great complexity . . . how tiny elements, seemingly unimportant engineering details, all finally fit together to form a complete landmark. No narration.
AMERICAN ED. 20 min. B&W. Sound

BUILDING A BRIDGE (Tajik)
At 10,000 feet in northeastern Af-

ghanistan, 100 Tajik men and boys from one village work together to re-build their hand-constructed bridge —their lifeline to market and their only means of contact with the out-side world. These 100 Tajiks, in just three days of actual construction, bridge the river with a remarkable cantilever span of 120 feet. Mountain People of Central Asia series. IFF (BRYAN) 10 min. B&W. Sound. 1968

BUILDING ATOM MODELS—ISOMERISM
The 60 films in the series, many of them produced under a grant from the National Science Foundation, are examples of the style of teaching where the films may be utilized as part of a series or treated as a sin-gle unit. The method is left entirely in the hands of the instructor. De-tailed information on film content will be sent upon request. Contact CCM Films. Yale Chemistry Films series. CCM FILMS. 6 min. B&W. Silent

BUTTERFLY
Using close-up photography, this film shows the life cycle of the swallow-tail butterfly. The film begins with the laying of the egg, then follows the hatching and growth of the caterpil-lar, its pupation, and the emergence of the butterfly. Finally the butterfly lays eggs, beginning the life cycle again. (A Gakken Co., Ltd. Film) BFA ED. MEDIA. 9 min. Color. Sound

BUTTERFLY
A picture story of the development of a butterfly. Close-up photography provides shots of the insect as it goes through the stages of its life from egg to butterfly. The cycle be-gins with the laying of the eggs, shows the hatching and growth of the caterpillar, the pupa stage, and finally the emergence of the butter-fly. No narration; natural sounds and background music. See 'n Tell ser-ies. (Institut fur Film und Bild) FILMS INC. 8 min. Color. Sound. 1970

THE CANADA GOOSE
Here is a sight-and-sound documen-tary on the Canada goose. Close-ups and natural sound combine to provide a study of the courtship, nesting, young, flight, and behavior of this in-teresting bird. Award: American Film Festival. Birds of American series. (Produced by Dan Gibson) A-V EXPLOR. $6\frac{1}{2}$ min. Color. Sound. 1967

CARP IN A MARSH
The struggle for survival in the tiny world of the marsh. Ponds and marshes are the home of the carp, for they like standing water and higher temperatures. In winter they live beneath the ice, moving into spots that do not freeze to the bot-tom. The film was made without nar-ration so that viewers could make their own interpretations. See 'n Tell series. (Institut fur Film und Bild) FILMS INC. 7 min. Color. Sound. 1970

CATERPILLAR
A boy and his dancing caterpillar travel all over, giving concerts and performances. One day the cater-pillar disappears—but at the sound of a familiar tune, a dancing butter-fly appears. No narration. Ani-mated. (Produced by Ceskosloven-sky Filmexport) LEARN. CORP. 16 min. Color. Sound. 1971

CHICKENS
Most chickens live in what we might call "egg factories." This film shows chickens in a more familiar habitat. The camera gives us glimpses of chickens' daily lives. How do chickens interrelate? How do chickens communicate? Do they have a "language"? Inquiry and statement are accomplished without narration. AIMS. 13 min. Color. Sound. 1970

CHICKS AND CHICKENS
This is a story of life on a chicken farm. A hen incubates a clutch of

eggs and hatches a brood of chicks. She guards her babies and shows them how to find food. When a dog approaches, the chicks scatter and the adult birds attack the intruder. When the danger is gone, the babies return. See 'n Tell series. (Institut fur Film und Bild)
FILMS INC. 10 min. Color. Sound. 1970

CLAY (Origin of the Species)
A variation on Darwin. Beginning with simple motions on a clay "sea," forms of life emerge and then play, devour one another, change into worms, gorillas, mermaids, clams, lions, whales, and other animals, climaxing in the creation of man himself. The film does not follow any theory of natural history, but evolves its own kind of freewheeling clay life. A jazz group provides the score. Award: International Animated Film Festival. (A film by Eliot Noyes, Jr.)
McGRAW-HILL. 8 min. B&W. Sound. 1964

CONCERT FOR CLOUDS
Cloud formations and movements ascend, swell, and recede under the influence of air currents, change from cumulus puffs to towering thunderheads, then disappear in the upper blue sky. Sun rays bathe the varying formations in myriad colors. No narration. (Portafilms)
PERENNIAL ED. 9 min. Color. Sound

COSMIC ZOOM
This film probes the infinite magnitude of space and its reverse, the ultimate minuteness of matter. Animation art and animation camera achieve this journey to the farthest conceivable point of the universe and then into the tiniest particle of existence—an atom of a living human cell. (National Film Board of Canada)
McGRAW-HILL. 8 min. Color. Sound. 1968

THE COW
A leisurely look at cows: the textures of noses and hides, the shapes and colors of bodies, the ways of the tongue with a blade of grass. Grinding of jaws, chewing of cud, swishing of tails. A new-born calf, licked dry by its mother, tries to stand on collapsible legs, and eventually finds its first meal. No narration; natural sounds. (A Dimension Film)
CHURCHILL. 11 min. Color. Sound. 1968

CROOKE'S TUBES
The 60 films in the series, many of them produced under a grant from the National Science Foundation, are examples of the style of teaching where the films may be utilized as part of a series or treated as a single unit. The method is left entirely in the hands of the instructor. Detailed information on film content will be sent upon request. Contact CMM Films. Yale Chemistry Films series.
CCM FILMS. 8 min. Color. Silent

CRYSTALS
Crystals radiating brilliant prismatic colors grow and merge as if they were dancing to the accompanying soundtrack of electronic tingles and taps.
PYRAMID. 6 min. Color. Sound. 1969

A DAY AT THE BEACH
A self-reliant boy spends a day on the beach by himself. He walks barefoot in the sand, goes for a swim, watches crabs and shorebirds, builds a sand castle, looks for shells, and enjoys his special world. Can be used as an introduction to beach ecology and to stimulate discussion of what it's like to be alone. (A Gordon-Kerckhoff Film)
ACI FILMS. 13 min. Color. Sound. 1971

DIFFUSION ALONG A BAR
A computer-generated random walk model. Part I shows the random

motion of 512 particles in a diffusing group, and Part II shows the random motion of some individual particles in a steady-state concentration gradient. (Made in cooperation with the National Science Foundation)
MOD. MEDIA. 5 min. B&W. Silent

DIMENSIONS
A visual fantasy that displays the relationship of bigness to smallness, height to width. A door is just big enough, a table is just so high, because.... Through the use of the "pixillation" technique of animation many possibilities are investigated.
NAT. FILM BD. $12\frac{1}{4}$ min. Color. Sound. 1968

DUCKS, GEESE AND SWANS
Introduces the student to the beauty, life habits, and importance of waterfowl, and basic concepts about ducks, geese, swans, and their offspring: ducklings, goslings, and cygnets. Depicts birth and hatching. Limited narration.
AIMS. 11 min. Color. Sound. 1970

EARTH: MAN'S HOME
Man's speck of matter in the universe is Earth, yet even the earth is not entirely "home," because most of it is ocean. Of the remaining surface—land—only the green area is suitable for habitation. The rest is covered with deserts, jungle, mountains, and ice. Man's environment is small in relation to the vastness of the universe.
ENCYC. BRIT. 10 min. Color. Sound. 1969

ELECTRICITY
Live action, animated diagrams, working models, and photographs of actual application are combined with original music to answer three basic questions about electricity: Where does it come from? How does it work? How does it get to me? Running water and steam power are selected as two examples of energy sources. Models are used to explain. Narration is kept to a mini-

mum in favor of a teaching song in the style of popular music. (A Trend release by Eric Productions)
WALT DISNEY. 13 min. Color. Sound. 1971

EMBRYO
A wordless dramatization of the basic processes of nature. Pheasants mate, stop-motion photography shows the development of the chick embryo, and birth completes the cycle.
PYRAMID. 10 min. Color. Sound. 1967

ENERGIES
The variable forms of energy manifest themselves into being that of man, through movement and color. Contained herein are experiences in primordial nature. The film is a continuation of the experiment that began with "Becoming," to determine the extent to which stimuli can be summoned without the influence of sound.
FILM IMAGES. 9 min. Color. Silent. 1958

ENERGY
A nonverbal presentation of power systems past, present and future, and the transformation of energy. (By Timothy Huntley)
PYRAMID. 12 min. Color. Sound. 1970

EVENING ACTIVITY
This film is an almost completely unedited observation, showing baboon behavior over a period of a few minutes. Because it is neither structured nor narrated, this film can be used with primate study literature or in training advanced students in recording data.
MOD. MEDIA. $5\frac{1}{2}$ min. Color. Sound

FAST REACTION—
MERCURY AND SILVER NITRATE
The 60 films in the series, many of them produced under a grant from

the National Science Foundation, are examples of the style of teaching where the films may be utilized as part of a series or treated as a single unit. The method is left entirely in the hands of the instructor. Detailed information on film content will be sent upon request. Contact CMM Films. Yale Chemistry Films series.
CCM FILMS. 5 min. Color. Silent

FIRE SAFETY
IN THE LABORATORY
The 60 films in the series, many of them produced under a grant from the National Science Foundation, are examples of the style of teaching where the films may be utilized as part of a series or treated as a single unit. The method is left entirely in the hands of the instructor. Detailed information on film content will be sent upon request. Contact CMM Films. Yale Chemistry Films series.
CCM FILMS. 2 min. B&W. Silent

FOOD
"Food" is intended to demonstrate to farm audiences in developing countries how improvements in farming practice and technology increase the yield of crops and so the farmer's income. An animated color film, without commentary, produced by a filmmaker from India during a period of work-study at the National Film Board of Canada.
NAT. FILM BD. $4\frac{1}{2}$ min. Color. Sound

FROG DEVELOPMENT, Part I:
Fertilization to Hatching
From the naturally laid cluster of eggs, a single egg is taken and placed in the small chamber for time-lapse photography. The egg is seen in side view throughout its development and until it hatches. Then a series of sequences in top view reviews several episodes in this process.
MOD. LEARNING. 12 min. Color. Silent

FROG DEVELOPMENT, Part II:
Hatching through Metamorphosis
The development of tadpoles from hatching through the change into the adult frog is seen. The sequences center on the development during the first week after hatching, the feeding behavior, and many of the changes during metamorphosis.
MOD. LEARNING. $9\frac{1}{2}$ min. Color. Silent

GEIGER COUNTER
The 60 films in the series, many of them produced under a grant from the National Science Foundation, are examples of the style of teaching where the films may be utilized as part of a series or treated as a single unit. The method is left entirely in the hands of the instructor. Detailed information on film content will be sent upon request. Contact CCM Films. Yale Chemistry Films series.
CCM FILMS. 7 min. Color. Silent

GROWING
(A Computer-Animated Film)
A computer-animated approach to the concept of growing. Viewers should see it twice—first to become acquainted with computer animation, and then to consider the concepts of seasonal changes and growth.
ENCYC. BRIT. 7 min. Color. Sound. 1970

GULL ISLAND
Gull Island is a bird sanctuary close to Toronto. Here we observe a colony of ring-billed gulls and some common terns. The nesting cycle is pictured in detail—courtship, mating, incubation, hatching, and development of young. Slow-motion shots capture the flight of both species as well as their headlong dives into the water for food. Available with study guides. Birds of America series.
A-V EXPLOR. 8 min. Color. Sound. 1966

HARMONIC PHASORS
A computer pantomime demonstrating
ideas relevant to the representation
of sinusoidal signals by rotating
"phasors," the addition of vector
quantities, and the description of a
simple periodic function by Fourier
series. (Made in cooperation with
the National Science Foundation)
MOD. MEDIA. 7 min. B&W. Silent

HORSES AND HOW THEY LIVE
Horses, their characteristics, habits,
and behavior. An insight into their
daily life. No narration. (A Cahill
Production)
AIMS. 11 min. Color. Sound. 1968

HYDROGEN FOUNTAIN
The 60 films in the series, many of
them produced under a grant from
the National Science Foundation, are
examples of the style of teaching
where the films may be utilized as
part of a series or treated as a
single unit. The method is left entirely in the hands of the instructor.
Detailed information on film content
will be sent upon request. Contact
CCM Films. Yale Chemistry Films
series.
CCM FILMS. 3 min. Color. Silent

IF YOU COULD SEE THE EARTH
A voyage into space, completely in
animation, reveals that the world is
round and moves in orbit around the
sun, causing day and night. Sequences from a space ship show surfaces of the earth, large areas of
land with different physical characteristics (continents), and gravity as
a force that holds all things on earth.
ENCYC. BRIT. 10 min. Color.
Sound. 1967

INSECTS IN A GARDEN
Photomicrography reveals insects
living on a rose bush: aphids, green
lacewings, ladybird beetles, and
ants. Students observe the intricate
process of insect metamorphosis and
the symbiotic relationship between
ants and aphids.
ENCYC. BRIT. 11 min. Color.
Sound

LE CHATELIER'S PRINCIPLE
The 60 films in the series, many of
them produced under a grant from
the National Science Foundation, are
examples of the style of teaching
where the films may be utilized as
part of a series or treated as a
single unit. The method is left entirely in the hands of the instructor.
Detailed information on film content
will be sent upon request. Contact
CCM. Yale Chemistry Films series.
CCM FILMS. 3 min. Color. Silent

THE LIFE OF A BUTTERFLY
The life cycle of a black swallowtail
butterfly. Begins with an adult
feeding on flowers, then laying eggs.
The eggs hatch, the emerging cater-
pillars eat, crawl about, and molt.
Finally they go through preparations
for pupation, attaching themselves
to a twig with silk threads. The pupa
remains dormant and then the adult
butterfly emerges, and the cycle is
complete.
MOD. LEARNING. 18 min. Color.
Silent

LIFE STORY OF A PLANT
(About Flowers)
Following the life cycle of a flower
helps viewers observe and generalize
about the life processes of one kind
of living thing—the plant. They see
how seeds develop and then are
scattered to make new plants. (National Film Board of Canada)
ENCYC. BRIT. 7 min. Color.
Sound. 1964

LIVING THINGS ARE EVERYWHERE
A boy's discovery of the variety of
living things along a river bank and
in the woods gives viewers an opportunity to test powers of observation,
and to study plant and animal relationships.
ENCYC. BRIT. 11 min. Color.
Sound

LIZARD
An animal often misunderstood is the
common ground lizard, a reptile four

inches long, with a long tail and
scaly skin. Completely harmless, it
feeds on insects and spiders. As it
grows, it sheds its skin several
times. Lizards mate in early summer, and a few weeks later the female lays about ten leathery, oblong
eggs. Baby lizards look like minia-
ture versions of their parents. See
'n Tell series. (Institut fur Film
und Bild)
FILMS INC. 11 min. Color. Sound.
1970

THE MAGNETISM OF MAGNETS
A minimum of concepts for self-
discovery of basic magnetism. An
"open-ended" approach. Minimal
narration. Primary grades.
AIMS. 10 min. Color. Sound. 1966

MAKING GUN POWDER (Tajik)
A Tajik tribesman makes gunpowder
by an ancient technique similar to
that used during the time of the
American Revolution. The tribesman is shown as he grinds a careful
balance of charcoal, potassium nitrate, and sulphur in a stone mortar,
and stores the finished product in a
moisture-proof powder horn. Mountain People of Central Asia series.
IFF (BRYAN). 10 min. B&W.
Sound. 1968

MICE AND HOW THEY LIVE
Uses extreme close-up photography
to reveal basic concepts about
mice—playing, eating, the family,
natural enemies, habitat, etc. Version A—no narration; Version B—
narration. (A Cahill Production)
AIMS. 11 min. Color. Sound. 1969

MILLIKAN'S OIL
DROP EXPERIMENT
The 60 films in the series, many of
them produced under a grant from
the National Science Foundation, are
examples of the style of teaching
where the films may be utilized as
part of a series or treated as a
single unit. The method is left entirely in the hands of the instructor.
Detailed information on film content

will be sent upon request. Contact
CCM Films. Yale Chemistry Films
series.
CCM FILMS. 6 min. B&W. Silent

MR. KOUMAL INVENTS A ROBOT
The subject of this series of episodes, involving an optimistic idea-
man thwarted at every turn, is human nature and man's relationship
to his environment and his fellow
men. Mr. Koumal series. (Produced in Czechoslovakia)
SIM PROD. 1¼ min. Color. Sound.
1969

MODEL FOR WEIGHT RELATIONS
IN CHEMICAL REACTIONS
The 60 films in the series, many of
them produced under a grant from
the National Science Foundation, are
examples of the style of teaching
where the films may be utilized as
part of a series or treated as a
single unit. The method is left entirely in the hands of the instructor.
Detailed information on film content
will be sent upon request. Contact
CCM. Yale Chemistry Films series.
CCM FILMS. 4 min. B&W. Silent

THE NEWBORN CALF
The birth and early development of a
calf. After viewing, students should
be able to discuss the interdependence of living things and to accept a
more detailed biological explanation
of reproduction. Teachers should
preview this film to determine if
its subject matter is appropriate.
Showing the film in segments is recommended for a primary audience.
No narration.
ENCYC. BRIT. 11 min. Color.
Sound. 1971

NOISE
What is the difference between sound
and noise? How much does noise af-
fect the quality of our lives? How
much noise can we tolerate? Are
there ways to limit noise pollution?
These questions are raised in the
film and there are clues to answers—but primarily the film is

designed to promote awareness and
discussion of this growing problem.
(A Don Dickerson Film)
BFA ED. MEDIA. 10 min. Color.
Sound

NUMBERS
An animated film from Czechoslova-
kia, exploring the world of numbers
and their relation to people in a va-
riety of situations. (Produced by
Pavel Prochazka)
McGRAW-HILL. 10 min. Color.
Sound. 1966

NUMERALS EVERYWHERE
An ordinary shopping trip becomes a
description of the concept and use of
numerals. The emphasis is on re-
cognition of symbols, not solution of
problems. Natural sounds and music
serve as background. Teachers can
reinforce youngsters' understanding
of the film by asking them to hunt
for numerals in their classroom, on
objects in their pockets, and at home.
Magic Moments series.
ENCYC. BRIT. 9 min. Color.
Sound. 1969

THE OLDER INFANT:
FOUR MONTHS TO ONE YEAR
(Nairobi Park)
Infant baboons shown at 4, 8, and 12
months of age, indicating stages of
increasing independence, weaning,
and rejection by the mother, and orientation to adult males and peer
group. No narration.
MOD. MEDIA. 8 min. Color. Sound.
1969

OVERTURE/NYITANY
To the score of Beethoven's "Egmont
Overture," time-lapse photography
with a microscopic camera unfolds
the development of a chick embryo.
(A Mafilm production, Hungary)
McGRAW-HILL. 9 min. Color.
Sound. 1965

PHASE DEMONSTRATION
The 60 films in the series, many of
them produced under a grant from

the National Science Foundation, are
examples of the style of teaching
where the films may be utilized as
part of a series or treated as a
single unit. The method is left entirely in the hands of the instructor.
Detailed information on film content
will be sent upon request. Contact
CCM. Yale Chemistry Films series.
CCM FILMS. 1 min. Color. Silent

PHOSPHINE SMOKE RINGS
The 60 films in the series, many of
them produced under a grant from
the National Science Foundation, are
examples of the style of teaching
where the films may be utilized as
part of a series or treated as a
single unit. The method is left entirely in the hands of the instructor.
Detailed information on film content
will be sent upon request. Contact
CCM. Yale Chemistry Films series.
CCM FILMS. 2 min. Color. Silent

PHYSICS IN F-MAJOR
Film artists at the Popular Science
Film Studios in Hungary pose many
questions in this film: How does
sound look? How does light sound?
Starting with the sine curve on an
oscilloscope, the film progresses
through simple lab experiments designed to exhibit the artistic potentials of physics. Colors and sounds
are synchronized with the music of
Scarlatti. (Released in cooperation
with Faroun Films of Canada)
XEROX FILMS. 9 min. Color.
Sound

PREPARATION FOR CHILDBIRTH
AND TWO HOSPITAL DELIVERIES
Outlines prenatal care and preparations for childbirth; shows a father
helping the doctor in the case of a
first child (color); then again (b&w)
for a fourth child, with no anesthesia. Silent, with titles. For nursing
and professional groups, expectant
parents: Free loan/sale at cost.
CLAREMONT. 9 min. C/B&W.
Silent. 1970

PRINCIPLES OF
MASS SPECTROMETER—
Animation Sequences
The 60 films in the series, many of
them produced under a grant from
the National Science Foundation, are
examples of the style of teaching
where the films may be utilized as
part of a series or treated as a
single unit. The method is left entirely in the hands of the instructor.
Detailed information on film content
will be sent upon request. Contact
CCM. Yale Chemistry Films series.
CCM FILMS. 11 min. Color. Silent

THE PRIVATE LIFE OF A CAT
A documentary of cat life in close-up,
produced by cameraman-director
Alexander Hammid. The film shows
the birth of kittens and the manner in
which their parents feed them and
provide them with the social ame-
nities.
CINEMA 16. 22 min. B&W. Silent.
1951

PROPERTIES OF MIXTURES
AND COMPOUNDS
The 60 films in the series, many of
them produced under a grant from
the National Science Foundation, are
examples of the style of teaching
where the films may be utilized as
part of a series or treated as a
single unit. The method is left entirely in the hands of the instructor.
Detailed information on film content
will be sent upon request. Contact
CCM. Yale Chemistry Films series.
CCM FILMS. 4 min. Color. Silent

RABBITS
We are all familiar with rabbits—or
are we? Who has seen a nest of
new-born rabbits ... or wriggling,
silky-white week-old babies? How
many different foods do rabbits eat?
Is a baby rabbit afraid of a kitten?
This film offers a look at one of nature's most gentle and appealing
creatures, the domestic rabbit.
(Films/West)
AIMS. 11 min. Color. Sound. 1970

RESPONSE OF A RESONANT
SYSTEM TO A FREQUENCY STEP
A computer pantomime to be used in
demonstrating fundamental concepts
relevant to: (1) linear system theory;
and (2) frequency modulation. The
role assumed by transients in providing a smooth transition between
initial and final steady-state conditions is illustrated, using rotating
"phasors" to portray the envelope
and phase of modulated signals.
(Made in cooperation with the National Science Foundation)
ED. DEVEL. CTR. 12 min. B&W.
Silent

THE RIVER
Illustrates the ecological history of
a river from a pure stream in the
days when Indians lived on its shore
to its present pollution, as a vastly
larger population uses it as a dump
and sewer. The film follows the
river as it flows from its beginnings
and is steadily polluted on its path to
the sea. There is no dialogue. Live
action.
AIM/ASSN. 9 min. Color. Sound

RIVER: WHERE DO YOU
COME FROM?
Using the lyrics of a folk ballad as
narrative, it follows a river from
its origin in water evaporating from
the ocean to its return to the sea.
The film shows the ways water benefits man and we see its destructive
potential as man battles the fury of
floods. Award: Columbus Film
Festival.
LEARN. CORP. 10 min. Color.
Sound. 1969

THE ROBIN
As if we had powerful binoculars
trained on the robin, the life cycle
unfolds before us from nesting until
the young are independent of their
parents. Songs and calls are examined, as well as plumage and actions. The protective instinct at
nesting time is illustrated. Available with study guides. Award:
American Film Festival. Birds of

America series. (Produced by Dan Gibson)
A-V EXPLOR. $5\frac{1}{2}$ min. Color. Sound. 1966

RYTHMETIC
Norman McLaren's investigation into the relationship of numbers. Even the kindergarten child knows that 2 plus 2 equals 4. But what is the total of 2 plus 2 plus 2 minus 4? The film leads the student into a discovery of the pluses and minuses of "rythmetic." (National Film Board of Canada)
INT. FILM BUR. $8\frac{1}{2}$ min. Color. Sound. 1956

SHEEP AND HOW THEY LIVE
Presents sheep in their natural environment, utilizing varied camera techniques to provide insight and discovery about this important animal. No narration. (Produced by Andrew Janczak)
AIMS. $13\frac{1}{2}$ min. Color. Sound. 1968

SILK MOTH
The life story of the mulberry silk worm moth. Begins with the male attracted to the female. Microphotography reveals the egg-laying process. Metamorphosis begins; finally results in a full-grown caterpillar. The moth emerges, and the cycle begins again. See 'n Tell series. (Institut fur Film und Bild)
FILMS INC. 7 min. Color. Sound. 1970

SLOW REACTION—
IRON AND OXYGEN
The 60 films in the series, many of them produced under a grant from the National Science Foundation, are examples of the style of teaching where the films may be utilized as part of a series or treated as a single unit. The method is left entirely in the hands of the instructor. Detailed information on film content will be sent upon request. Contact CCM. Yale Chemistry Films series.
CCM FILMS. 2 min. Color. Silent

SOLUTION, EVAPORATION, AND CRYSTALLIZATION
The 60 films in the series, many of them produced under a grant from the National Science Foundation, are examples of the style of teaching where the films may be utilized as part of a series or treated as a single unit. The method is left entirely in the hands of the instructor. Detailed information on film content will be sent upon request. Contact CCM Films. Yale Chemistry Films series.
CCM FILMS. 3 min. Color. Silent

SOUND ABOUT
Provides discovery experiences for students in their study of sound. Almost no narration. Open-ended for further inquiry.
AIMS. 11 min. Color. Sound. 1967

THE STORY OF LIGHT
The evolution of the modern light fixture from the very beginning of the world. Shows the torch, the candle, and lamps of several varieties. Traces these developments up to the fluorescent lamp. Animated. No narration. Musical score.
G.E. FILMS. 8 min. Color. Sound

SYMMETRY
The figures in this animated film obey strict mathematical principles—the embodiment of science in art. The music gives the basic rhythm to the movement of the figures. Tone and timing characterize the different symmetries. No narration. Designed and directed by Philip Stapp. (Produced by Sturgis-Grant)
McGRAW-HILL. 10 min. Color. Sound. 1966

TADPOLE TALE
The story of a city boy who wants to own a pet. After rejecting many kinds of pets, he finds a tadpole in a park lake. He brings it home and, as it grows, he begins to understand some of its needs. He decides to return the frog to the lake after he

realizes, to his regret, that its chances for survival are best in its own world. An important feature of the film is the photography of the stages in the maturation of the frog. UNIVERSAL ED. 14 min. Color. Sound. 1967

THE THUNDERSTORM
A boy and his dog play together as thunderclouds gather. Just before the storm breaks, the dog chases a rabbit. His young master searches for him. During the search, the camera allows us to see insects, birds, flowers, trees, and animals carrying on the cycle of life. When the boy and his dog are finally reunited, we have learned something of the interdependence of nature. Useful in stimulating awareness and interest in nature and discussing emotional reactions. (Produced in France)
LEARN. CORP. 9 min. Color. Sound

TRIO FOR THREE ANGLES
This animated film uses the movements of free-swinging angles, synchronized with music, to help make the geometry student aware of the relationships of the triangle's different components. The three sections of the film cover the equilateral, isosceles, and scalene triangles. No narration. Teacher's guide. (Produced by Bruce and Katherine Cornwell)
INT. FILM BUR. 8 min. Color. Sound. 1968

TROUT HATCHERY
The life of the wild fish and the process of assisting nature in the hatchery are shown with a musical accompaniment, in a way that stresses the turn of the seasons and the cycle of nature. No narration.
ACI FILMS. 15 min. Color. Sound. 1970

TUKTU AND HIS ANIMAL FRIENDS
The smaller animals that live in the Arctic, including lemmings, weasels, ducks, and kittiwakes. Includes material on flowers. Tuktu's father climbs the high cliffs in search of gulls' eggs. Stories of Tuktu series. (National Film Board of Canada)
FILMS INC. 14 min. Color. Sound. 1968

VERY FAST REACTION—
AMMONIUM DICTROMATE
The 60 films in the series, many of them produced under a grant from the National Science Foundation, are examples of the style of teaching where the films may be utilized as part of a series or treated as a single unit. The method is left entirely in the hands of the instructor. Detailed information on film content will be sent upon request. Contact CCM. Yale Chemistry Films series. CCM FILMS. 1 min. Color. Sound

WATERS RETURNING
The water cycle from the beginning of clouds as moisture rising upward from water and land, the return of water as rain or snow, and then as streams flowing to the ocean. There is no dialogue. Live action.
AIM/ASSN. $5\frac{1}{2}$ min. Color. Sound

WHAT CAN YOU FIND?
Three children are shown finding shells, rocks, leaves, insects, flowers, and animals as they walk through woods, fields, back yards, and near water. Differences are noted in size, shape, and color. Scenes of fall, winter, spring, and summer show patterns of seasonal change. (Produced by Karl B. Lohmann, Jr.)
THORNE FILMS. $11\frac{1}{2}$ min. Color. Sound. 1967

WHATEVER THE WEATHER
An introduction to wind, rain, snow, and sun, providing an opportunity to use language art skills. A complementary record provides poetry and music for listening, art expression, and rhythmical expres-

sion of the weather. (Produced by
Educational Horizons Films)
ENCYC. BRIT. 10 min. Color.
Sound

WIND
Kite-flying, sailboats, pinwheels, and
tossing trees show the power of the
wind. The accompanying song comments: "Winds blow high and low,
Strong or soft they go . . . ." Starting
to Read series.
ACI FILMS. 8 min. Color. Sound.
1970

WORLD
Through the use of abstract visuals,
the birth of the world is depicted as
a bio-astronomical event. No narration.
PYRAMID. 6 min. Color. Sound.
1970

THE YOUNG INFANT: BIRTH TO
FOUR MONTHS (Amboseli Reserve)
The behavioral development of the
infant baboon and relations of the
troop to mother and infant. Includes
the early development of play, exploration, tasting food, and riding on
the mother's back. Little narration.
MOD. MEDIA. 10 min. Color.
Sound. 1969

YOUR BODY AND ITS PARTS
Defines a system as parts of the
body working together to do a specific job. Introduces the five different systems: muscle, respiratory,
circulatory, skeletal, and nervous.
The interdependence of these systems is also demonstrated.
ENCYC. BRIT. 12 min. Color.
Sound. 1966

4. NATURE

This section might just as accurately have been labelled "Natural Science," "Biology," "Ecology," or "Environment." But a title like that might have frightened away those viewers who are interested in just-plain-outdoorsy scenes of rivers, trees, mountains, and clouds (or any combination thereof). Other viewers may be more concerned with principles of conservation, the interdependence of life-forms, or relationships within nature. So, to accommodate both levels of interest, each of them important, here's where you'll find films that are enjoyable for the intrinsic beauty of their subjects, while also demonstrating, in the most esthetic way possible, natural phenomena in action.

"Nature" also seemed the logical heading for those sure-fire favorites of canvas and camera, animals. In the early days of educational films, there was an almost instant and automatic market for animal films. In fact, black-and-white prints of "Adventures of Bunny Rabbit" and "Grey Squirrel" still circulate briskly, despite their monochrome drabness. Now, of course, these early films suffer by comparison with their modern counterparts. Today's color stock, superior sound, and versatile lenses have bred a celluloid menagerie of species from all over the world.

Sad to say, some of these beasts may already be extinct. Quoth a recent public service ad: "See the animals—while they last!" Yes, see them, show them, and (film can make it happen) save them!

AETNA
Mt. Aetna on the island of Sicily is Europe's highest volcano—a crater and cone that constantly fluctuate. Through close-up photography, extreme slow motion and a musical score, audiences will learn more about our Earth and the forces that shape it. No narration.
AMERICAN ED. 11 min. Color. Sound. 1971

AFRICAN ANIMALS
A day on the African savanna. The approach of elephants to the waterhole disturbs the water buffalo and a rhinoceros. Gnus, antelopes, impalas, and zebras congregate around the waterhole, but are watchful, since life depends upon alertness. Vultures and hyenas await the scraps. A sated lion walks through a herd of gnus, but the animals instinctively know he is not dangerous since he has eaten. (Institut fur Film und Bild)
FILMS INC. 9 min. Color. Sound. 1970

AMERICA THE UGLY
To the musical accompaniment of "America The Beautiful," the camera scans the devastation we've inflicted on our landscape.
G. E. FILMS. 3 min. Color. Sound. 1965

ANIMALS IN AUTUMN
Typical autumn activities of a va-

riety of animals show them searching for food, building warm homes,
preparing to migrate or hibernate.
Includes deer, fox, weasel, cold-
blooded birds, and insects.
ENCYC. BRIT. 11 min. Color.
Sound

ANIMALS IN SUMMER
Shows insects, frogs, snakes, squirrels, foxes, and bears exploring the
woods and hunting for food. Reveals
the natural adaptive coloring of animals and observes the life cycles of
insects during the summer.
ENCYC. BRIT. 11 min. Color.
Sound

AUSTRALIAN ANIMALS
A variety of animals not generally
seen in North America. The absence
of narration encourages youngsters
to make their own interpretations.
Shown are the duckbilled platypus,
an egg-laying aquatic creature, and
the world's only other egg-laying
mammal, the spiny anteater. Also
included are two marsupials (or
pouched animals), the koala bear and
the wombat. Emus, lizards, parrots,
and cockatoos fill out the list. (Institut fur Film und Bild)
FILMS INC. 8 min. Color. Sound.
1970

AUTUMN
A girl discovers the sights and
sounds of fall: the colors of the
foliage; falling leaves and the sound
they make underfoot; bright red berries; the feel of a caterpillar; swing-
ing from a tree; white fluff from bul-
rushes as she wanders through a
marsh. No narration; only natural
sounds and music are heard.
STERLING. 10 min. Color. Sound.
1967

AUTUMN COLOR
A camera study of fall foliage provides an approach to composition,
texture, color, and lighting. The un-
structured progress of this film is

accompanied by a piano improvisa-
tion. No narration.
THORNE FILMS. 7 min. Color.
Sound. 1959

AUTUMN PASTORALE
The changes of autumn are visualized
through the eyes of two children as
they explore the countryside, finding
delight in color transformations and
wonder in the seeds from a milkweed
pod. A blending of visuals and music.
PERENNIAL ED. 10 min. Color.
Sound

BIRDS OF THE FOREST
A nature hike into the mixed deciduous and coniferous forests east of
the prairies. Five entirely different
birds, all living in a common, natural
habitat: song sparrow, slate-colored
junco, chestnut-sided warbler,
white-throated sparrow, mourning
warbler. Available with study
guides. Birds of America series. (A
Dan Gibson production)
A-V EXPLOR. $5\frac{1}{2}$ min. Color.
Sound. 1967

BIRDS ON A SEA SHORE
The world's largest bird colony, on
the mainland and offshore islands of
Peru and Chile. Here are millions of
large sea birds (cormorants, gulls,
dippers, flamingoes, boobies, and
pelicans) nesting in densely packed
colonies. They feed on the rich marine life of the Humboldt Current, in
the shallows, the surface, and in the
ocean. No narration; just the sound
of the birds. (Institut fur Film und
Bild)
FILMS INC. 10 min. Color. Sound.
1970

BLACKBIRD FAMILY
The story of a pair of birds, incubating and rearing their young. The
eggs are laid and incubation begins.
The eggs hatch in two weeks, and the
young are fed throughout the day.
Soon the babies are so big they crowd
each other to the rim of the nest.
Here they exercise the wings that

will carry them out of their cradle. No narration: music and natural background sounds. (Institut fur Film und Bild)
FILMS INC. 12 min. Color. Sound. 1969

BOUQUET
Exploits the potential of film as medium and of flowers as subject. Editing incorporates split screen, kinestatic cutting, and other optical techniques to reveal a manifestation of nature. Original music. (Produced by David Adams)
PYRAMID. 9 min. Color. Sound. 1971

A BOY'S JOURNEY THROUGH A DAY
We follow a boy as he fishes, explores the countryside, and daydreams in the woods. We share beauty around him and his discoveries about nature. No narration. (Produced by Dale Johnson)
CORONET. 16 min. Color. Sound. 1970

BUTTERCUP
An ecology film. Gentle fog, a glistening mountain stream, with a buttercup slipping along the silvery surface. The golden blossom glides past water skippers, a skunk, and a squirrel. It whirls over a waterfall and the stream broadens. The buttercup moves past grazing horses and then is swallowed in the stench, sludge, and garbage of industrial man. No narration. (A Dimension Film)
CHURCHILL. 13 min. Color. Sound. 1971

THE CANADA GOOSE
Here is a sight and sound documentary on the Canada goose. Closeups and natural sound combine to provide a study of the courtship, nesting, young, flight, and behavior of this interesting bird. Award: American Film Festival. Birds of America series. (Produced by Dan Gibson)
A-V EXPLOR. $6\frac{1}{2}$ min. Color. Sound. 1967

CARP IN A MARSH
The struggle for survival in the tiny world of the marsh. Ponds and marshes are the home of the carp, for they like standing water and higher temperatures. In winter, they live beneath the ice, moving into spots that do not freeze to the bottom. The film was made without narration so that viewers could make their own interpretations. See 'n Tell series. (Institut fur Film und Bild)
FILMS INC. 7 min. Color. Sound. 1970

DEEP BLUE WORLD
An underwater adventure-fantasy using a variety of original film techniques. Mood is augmented by multiple music recordings and electronic sound effects. (Produced by David Adams)
PYRAMID. 7 min. Color. Sound. 1971

THE DEER AND THE FOREST—
A Story Without Words
A "life ballet" of deer and other animals moving through a year's cycle. Music by Wagner and Beethoven underscores the rhythm of the seasons. The deer move from the serene days of fall to the dangers of winter. Activity quickens with spring and comes to a climax in late summer as bucks duel for supremacy. The victor stalks to the river, the leaves drift down, and stillness falls again over the forests of Hungary. (Produced by Hungarofilm)
ENCYC. BRIT. 16 min. Color. Sound. 1968

DUNES
Photographer Fred Hudson evokes the aura of this strange world as he follows the activities of the sparse desert. A ground squirrel speckles the sand... a sidewinder leaves eerie waves in its wake... tumbleweeds dance in the wind. Through a wild sandstorm, the ensuing calm, and a final view of the dunes reflecting a sunset, the viewer is involved in a range of desert moods. Award: In-

ternational Film Festival, San Francisco. (Produced by Pyramid Films) HOLT R&W. 7 min. Color. Sound. 1968

THE END OF ONE
The interrelationship of all living things in the "web of life." The camera watches seagulls soar and scavenge for food from a garbage dump. At a distance a lone, frail bird limps haltingly along a polluted stretch of beach, stumbling, dying; his fellows continue their raucous competition, unconcerned, uncaring. An allegory on greed. Winner of Statuette Award, Chicago Film Festival.
LEARN. CORP. 7 min. Color. Sound. 1970

THE ENDLESS CYCLE
A nonnarrative film symbolizing the cycles of man and nature, the movement of a life force, and the persistent flow of nature.
STERLING. 11 min. Color. Sound. 1970

EVASION
French film without words. Pounded by machine, noise and rhythm of the city, man becomes like a marionette, a discarded Pierrot, frozen with anguish. Is discovered by child who leads him to the country where beat and harmony of nature bring him back to life and joy. When he relearns to walk, run and climb trees, Pierrot is overjoyed to find he is still a MAN. He takes the child back to the city and bestows on him a magic spark, symbol of life. (Acromedia)
NAT'L. EDUC. 17 min. Color. Sound

FIRE MOUNTAIN
Searing orange flames of a towering lava fountain; eerie, burned-out tree trunks shrouded in lava and steam; molten lava cascading over a precipice. Close-up views of the second greatest eruption of Mt. Kilauea in

Hawaii. No narration; color, music, and natural sounds. Awards: Trento, Venice, CINE.
ENCYC. BRIT. 9 min. Color. Sound. 1971

FLOWERS AND BEES—
A Springtime Story
Time-lapse photography. Nature moves and changes in a harmonic rhythm—flowers grow, open and close, turn to the sun, droop in the rain. Bees pollinate the flowers and return to their hives. A spring rainstorm disturbs the activity that begins again after the storm. Music synchronizes with the movement of the flowers and bees throughout the film. An edited version of "A Usual Spring." (Produced by Romania Film)
ENCYC. BRIT. 11 min. Color. Sound. 1969

FOREST MURMURS
Reminding the viewer of his responsibility for the problem of littering, the film demonstrates how great natural beauty can be ruined by carelessness. The music of a woodland glade, a sparkling brook, and growing plants becomes discordant and finally rises to a crescendo when broken bottles, tin cans, and trash overpower the loveliness of a public park. (An Interlude Film)
PERENNIAL ED. $8\frac{1}{2}$ min. Color. Sound

FULL FATHOM FIVE
Marine images: brilliantly colored fish, crustaceans, coral trees, kelp, sea grasses, all blending and flashing against blue-black waters.
PYRAMID. 7 min. Color. Sound. 1969.

GENESIS 1-27: UNDERSEA WORLD
An abstract presentation of the Genesis theme, composed entirely of underwater sequences. The "ballet" of the garden eels and the "aquabatics" of the giant manta rays are highlights of this film. No narration; musical accompaniment. The under-

water photography was done by Stanton Waterman in French Polynesia.
PERENNIAL ED. 8¾ min. Color. Sound. 1970

GRAND CANYON
The grandeur of this natural spectacle—including its many moods and its inhabitants (bobcat, jackrabbit, owl, tarantula, Gila monster, and others)—is portrayed to the musical background of Ferde Grofe's "Grand Canyon Suite." No narration.
WALT DISNEY. 29 min. Color. Sound

GRAY GULL THE HUNTER
The struggle for existence among the bird life on a rocky Swedish island, with the gray gull in the role of marauder. Other sea birds—the murre, the ring plover, the merganser duck, the arctic tern, and the sea mew—live in fear of the robber gull. Photographed by Arne Sucksdorff.
ENCYC. BRIT. 19 min. B&W. Sound. 1956

GULL ISLAND
Gull Island is a bird sanctuary close to Toronto. Here we observe a colony of ring-billed gulls and some common terns. The nesting cycle is pictured in detail—courtship, mating, incubation, hatching, and development of young. Slow-motion shots capture the flight of both species as well as their headlong dives into the water for food. Available with study guides. Birds of America series. (Produced by Dan Gibson)
A-V EXPLOR. 8 min. Color. Sound. 1966

HOLY THURSDAY
Based on William Blake's poem, "Holy Thursday." A visual interpretation of nature and Man's interconnection with it and his institutions. No narration except for the poem. Awards: CINE Golden Eagle and first prizes around the world. (Produced by George Hood)
AMERICAN ED. 18 min. Color. Sound. 1969

THE HUNTER AND THE FOREST—
A Story Without Words
Photography, natural sound effects, and original music relate the story of an encounter between a hunter and a family of deer in the forest. Collaborator: Paul Witty, Ph.D., Northwestern University.
ENCYC. BRIT. 8 min. B&W. Sound. 1954

THE HUNTERS
The slow pace of the action, and the silent photography broken only infrequently by narration, slow plucking of native instruments, and song, evoke the peace of the lives of these hunters of the Kalahari Desert. Detailed as to the thought processes, personalities, and techniques of survival of these people. A visual demonstration of the close interrelationship of earth, animal, and primitive man. Also available in B&W. Preview recommended.
McGRAW-HILL. 72 min. Color. Sound. 1958

IMAGES FROM NATURE
Scenes of fall, winter, spring, and summer are interspersed with abstractions inspired by seasonal changes. Animations are created with flowers, colored lights, pressed glass, dye papers, paint, dry ice, and ink. No narration; sounds recorded from nature realistically and abstractly. Selected for exhibition at the American Film Festival and the University of Illinois. (Produced by Karl B. Lohmann, Jr.)
THORNE FILMS. 7 min. Color. Sound. 1962

JANIE SUE AND TUGALOO
This film presents eight-year-old Janie Sue, who lives on a horse farm. Though she has her own pony, Snowball, she dreams of becoming an accomplished rider on Tugaloo, her brother's champion Arabian. Janie Sue explores her environment on Snowball, takes a riding lesson on Tugaloo, helps her brother in preparation for a rodeo. No narration.
CENTRON. 9½ min. Color. Sound. 1970

KANGAROOS
This film shows the kangaroo at home in Australia. The use of natural sound and music, with no narration, enables youngsters to make their own discoveries about these unusual marsupials. See 'n Tell series. (Institut fur Film und Bild)
FILMS INC. 10 min. Color. Sound. 1970

KIDS AND BIRDS
AND EUROPEAN WINTER
Winter is hard on nonmigrating birds. Two youngsters make unusual feed containers, hang them from the snow-covered evergreens in their garden, then watch the different birds respond quickly to their efforts. See 'n Tell series. (Institut fur Film und Bild)
FILMS INC. 10 min. Color. Sound. 1971

LE FARFALLE
This film is a poem about a butterfly—a poem that doesn't use any words to express what it means. Ugo Torricelli orchestrates a complex series of images with musical sounds, songs, and dance melodies that communicate what it is to be a living creature that can fly.
XEROX FILMS. 5 min. Color. Sound

LEAF
Sound, motion, pattern, and color tell the story of one autumn-yellowed leaf—the last to fall from a tree in the mountains. It is blown from tree to rock to water—silhouetted against clouds, sky-reflecting pools, and waterfall mists. The accompaniment employs a combination of strings and woodwinds. (Produced by Pyramid Films)
HOLT R&W. 7 min. Color. Sound. 1962

MARCH-APRIL:
THE COMING OF SPRING
Photographed mostly in forested areas. Opens with a montage of early spring scenes: ice melting, deer running, and snow sculptures melting. Other scenes include rabbits and squirrels, children playing, ice floes breaking up, trees budding, and flowers blooming. (Central Documentary Film Studios, Moscow)
FILMS INC. 9 min. Color. Sound. 1967

MINER'S RIDGE
Filmed in the Glacier Peak Wilderness, adjacent to the North Cascades National Park. With a musical score and very few words, this film states the case for inclusion of the Glacier Peak area in the Park. An open pit copper mine can be put right in the middle of it. (Sponsored by the Sierra Club)
AIM/ASSN. 22 min. Color. Sound

MR. KOUMAL MOVES
TO THE COUNTRY
The subject of this series of episodes, involving an optimistic idea-man thwarted at every turn, is human nature and man's relationship to his environment and his fellow men. Mr. Koumal series. (Produced in Czechoslovakia)
SIM PROD. $2\frac{1}{2}$ min. Color. Sound. 1969

A MOUNTAIN DAY
A "visual poem" about two boys and a girl who set out on horseback to explore and experience the beauties of a mountain environment. The World Around Us series.
ARTHUR BARR. 9 min. Color. Sound. 1970

MULTIPLY AND SUBDUE
A three "movement" treatment, edited to a Bach organ soundtrack, and designed to encourage viewers to reevaluate their attitudes toward man and nature. Part One traces the beginnings of the world. Part Two reexamines the beauties of nature. Part Three examines the Biblical passage in which God commands man to multiply over the earth and

subdue it. Award: Bellevue Film
Festival. (Produced by Eric L.
Hutchinson)
PYRAMID. 8 min. Color. Sound.
1970

NAICA AND THE SQUIRRELS
The photography of a dense forest
covered by snow, and shots of the
many forest animals, combined with
an enterprising little boy, form the
basis of this film. It tells the story
of a child's love for his animal
friends. No narration or dialogue.
Award: First Prize: the plaque of
The Lion of San Marco, Venice Bien-
nale—International Exhibition of
Children's Films. (Produced by
Bucharest Film Studios, Rumania)
McGRAW-HILL. 20 min. Color.
Sound. 1966

NATURE IS FOR PEOPLE
Concept: Living things are inter-
dependent. This treatment contrasts
the peaceful pace of nature with the
daily busyness faced by most of us.
No narration. (Produced by Stuart
Roe)
AIMS. 9 min. Color. Sound. 1969

NIOK
About a jungle boy's devotion to a
baby elephant deserted in the forest
by its parents. Niok's greatest sac-
rifice comes when he sets it free
rather than see it sold into captivity.
This film also depicts living condi-
tions in a small Cambodian village.
Very little narration. (Directed by
Albert Lamorisse)
WALT DISNEY. 29 min. Color.
Sound. 1960

OLD ANTELOPE LAKE
This film begins at the source of the
Navajo lake, then moves around the
lake, showing the unity between natural things and human beings in the
environment. (Made by Johnny Nelson)
CMC/COLUMBIA. 11 min. B&W.
Silent

THE OLD MILL
A bucolic animal community is
threatened by a rampaging storm.
Original music.
WALT DISNEY. 9 min. Color.
Sound

ONE SPRING DAY
A close-up of nature at work. Cameras explore insects and flowers.
We see nature's continual regener-
ation. Interwoven is an ecological
statement about pollution of our environment. An oil-covered ocean
is seen in counterpoint to a smog-
producing refinery. A burnt forest
slowly comes back to life. The
blackened landscape turns gold with
flowers. Nature, left to itself, can
aid man in preserving this planet.
No narration. (An H/K Film)
AMERICAN ED. $8\frac{1}{2}$ min. Color.
Sound. 1970

OUR LIVING FORESTS
Concept: The balance and interdependence of nature. The beauty of
the forest wilderness is portrayed.
A forest fire points up the need for
care and conservation of this basic
natural resource. (Produced by
Dave Estes)
AIMS. 11 min. Color. Sound.
1968

PARADISE LOST
The film suggests the world of nature, where all things live together
in delicate harmony. But into this
earthly paradise drifts an invisible
death, spread by an aircraft, symbolic purveyor of the chemical men-
ace that invades even the most distant places of our globe. Birds of
brilliant plumage, butterflies, and
other creatures of the wild succumb
to it. (National Film Board of Canada)
BENCHMARK. 4 min. Color.
Sound. 1970

THE PERSISTENT SEED
Nature works to preserve her own
beauty as the inevitable process of
civilization would seem to destroy

it. No narrative comment is necessary to see the need of transforming natural beauty to create man's own wonders, or to feel the triumph of a sprig of green pushing its way up through two cement blocks. (National Film Board of Canada)
PERENNIAL ED. 14 min. Color. Sound. 1963

PIGS!
Piglets suckle, explore grass, and wrestle. Faces and personalities: shy, belligerent, sweet. Textures: noses, hoofs, ears, tails. Lazy afternoon—pigs yawn, nap (sometimes in heaps). Momma and piglets gambol out to sniff the world beyond the barnyard. Original music. No narration. (A Dimension Film)
CHURCHILL. 11 min. Color. Sound. 1967

POLLUTION
Satirist Tom Lehrer sings Calypso lyrics while camera exposes evidence of widespread pollution.
NAT. MED. AV. 4 min. Color. Sound. 1968

PORTRAIT OF A HORSE
A nonnarrative, visual impression of a proud, freedom-loving horse and the man who tries to subdue the animal. (A Janus New Cinema Film; filmed by Witold Giersz in animation)
PYRAMID. 8 min. Color. Sound. 1967

THE QUIET RACKET
A tale of a man who feels the common urge to escape the city for a weekend of quiet in the hills. Without words but with a wide range of other sounds, urban and rural, this film tracks our hero to his haven of non-peace. He finds the countryside not so unspoiled and uncrowded as the poets proclaim.
NAT. FILM BD. $7\frac{1}{2}$ min. Color. Sound

RAINSHOWER
The sights and sounds, beauty and rhythm of rain. An experience in the changing moods of a day when a rainshower comes to plants and animals on a farm, and to people at work in a community. Narration is used only for the introduction; the rest is natural sound. (A Dimension Film)
CHURCHILL. $14\frac{1}{2}$ min. Color. Sound. 1965

RAPIDS OF THE COLORADO
A trip down the dangerous rapids of the Grand Canyon's Colorado River. Photographed from a raft, the camera takes in the beauty of the river and the famous canyon through which it flows.
PYRAMID. 15 min. Color. Sound. 1970

REFLECTIONS IN A POND
Music and natural sounds help to describe life on the pond. Our cast is a family of mute swans, six Chinese white geese, and one great blue heron.
JOURNAL. 10 min. Color. Sound. 1969

RICKY'S GREAT ADVENTURE
This story of a blind boy can motivate primary students to become better observers of nature by making greater use of their sense of touch, taste, smell, and hearing. A presentation of the world of nature that can be discovered by every child. No narration; synchronized sound and original music.
ATLANTIS. 11 min. Color. Sound. 1969

THE RISE AND FALL
OF THE GREAT LAKES
A lesson in Canadian geography that concludes that though the Great Lakes have had their ups and downs, nothing has been harder to take than what man has done to them lately. In the film, a lone canoeist lives through all the changes of geological history, through Ice Age and flood, only to find himself trapped in a sea of scum.

Award: Blue Ribbon Award, American Film Festival. (National Film Board of Canada)
PYRAMID. 17 min. Color. Sound. 1969

RIVER
Captures the movement and life-giving force of the river which, flowing out of the ice and snow, roams the meadows and forests of Yosemite, cascades down rocky slopes, and finally leaps over massive cliffs in an earth-shaking plunge to the valley below. Music takes the place of narration.
PYRAMID. 8 min. B&W. Sound

RIVER: AN ALLEGORY
Traces the quickening life of a great river and its eventual absorption into the sea. From a tiny spring the water flows through many strange ways until it joins the ocean. A musical score blends with the movement of the river. (Produced by William M. Harlow)
INT. FILM BUR. 11 min. Color. Sound. 1968

THE ROBIN
As if we had powerful binoculars trained on the robin, the life cycle unfolds before us from nesting until the young are independent of their parents. Songs and calls are examined, as well as plumage and actions. The protective instinct at nesting time is illustrated. Available with study guides. Awards: American Film Festival. Birds of America series. (Produced by Dan Gibson)
A-V EXPLOR. 5½ min. Color. Sound. 1966

SEA SORCERY
The camera dives from 10 to 50 feet to exhibit barracuda, stingray, banded butterfly fish, the hawksbill turtle, porcupine fish, and a juvenile grey angelfish. The camera takes a tour through undersea caves where colorful fish and structures flash in the beam of a diver's light. Filmed in the Caribbean. A guide is avail-able. (Produced by James Dutcher)
McGRAW-HILL. 15 min. Color. Sound. 1970

SHEEP SHEEP SHEEP
Moods, rhythms, and images of sheep. The slowly grazing sheep shuffle, gather, and begin flowing through the valley, a soft, blurry river of wool. They stop, clump together, collect their feet and lie down quietly to chew their cuds. Sleep. Awake! Pressing together, moving to the highlands, hooves thundering, voices high. Natural sounds without commentary. (A Dimension Film)
CHURCHILL. 11 min. Color. Sound. 1970

SKY
From the Rockies of the western plains, this film catches and condenses the spectacle of a day in the life of the sky. Photographed with many lenses and different camera speeds; every changing mood of the sky is registered. Awards: Columbus, Ohio; Swift Current, Saskatchewan. (National Film Board of Canada)
McGRAW-HILL. 10 min. Color. Sound. 1958

SOLILOQUY OF A RIVER
Pictures a river still unspoiled and beautiful, and its surroundings. There is a brief interjection of an antipollution message by the narrator at one point, but the film makes this plea by showing the delights of a clear, clean stream instead of scene after scene of dirty, chemically polluted water. Award: CINE. 26-minute version available from A-V Explorations. (Produced by Robert W. Davison and Mel Hardman)
NATURE GUIDE. 19 min. Color. Sound. 1969

A SPECIAL KIND OF MORNING
Two young girls take an early morning jaunt through the St. Louis Zoo in which only they and the animals are present. The girls, one white, one

black, are seen sharing love, companionship, joy, and sorrow. When
one loses her gas-filled balloon, the
other makes the compassionate sacrifice of voluntarily releasing hers.
The musical score is the only sound
accompaniment to this experimental
film. (Produced by KETC-TV, St.
Louis)
INDIANA UNIV. 27 min. Color.
Sound. 1971

SPRING
Spring in the country, and a little
girl goes for a stroll with her pet
rabbits in a big basket. The film follows her through a field, to a stream,
and to the birch woods. The only
sounds are those of nature.
STERLING. 9 min. Color. Sound.
1967

SPRING COLOR
The colors and forms of spring
flowers (including daffodils, grape
hyacinths, red emperor tulips, Japanese flowering quince, and for-
sythia) are portrayed from a variety
of viewpoints. Original harpsichord
music.
THORNE. 5 min. Color. Sound.
1968

THE STARFISH'S REALM
This film is in two sections. The
first is "Underwater Ballet," in
which original music adds to the
movements by sea animals as they
react to different species of starfish
in their environment. The second
section, "The Crab and the Octopus," portrays events that occur
when a crab and an octopus meet in
an enclosed environment or natural
habitat. Music. Study guide available. (Whitecap Productions)
RARIG'S. 14 min. Color. Sound

STILL WATERS
A combination of carefully chosen
music and revealing under-and-
above-water photography. Unusual
sound and electronic music add to
the total effect. Winner of eleven

national and international awards.
(Elgin Ciampi Production)
PYRAMID. 14½ min. Color. Sound.
1964

SURF!
A film on the beauty and colors of the
sea and the thrills of the surf. An
impression of waves and sun. No
narration. Awards: CINE Golden
Eagle and the National Visual Pre-
sentations Award, Best Musical
Score. (By Homer Groening)
AMERICAN ED. 13 min. Color.
Sound. 1969

TEXTURES OF THE GREAT LAKES
Presents an interpretation of the tex-
tural qualities of the waters, beaches,
sand dunes, and surrounding woods of
the Great Lakes. Visual images synchronized to harp accompaniment.
Award: CINE Golden Eagle. (Produced by Karl B. Lohmann, Jr.)
THORNE FILMS. 6 min. Color.
Sound. 1965

TUKTU AND HIS ESKIMO DOGS
How dogs are used by the Eskimos,
in winter and summer. We see pup-
pies, sled dogs, and dogs being used
as pack animals. Eskimo dogs are
also used for hunting, and we see how
an Eskimo dog sniffs out the seal
blow-holes when snow covers the ice.
Stories of Tuktu series. (National
Film Board of Canada)
FILMS INC. 14 min. Color. Sound.
1968

TUKTU AND THE BIG SEAL
A big seal gets away after being har-
pooned by Tuktu's father. Perhaps
it is the same seal that has, in the
past, escaped the harpoons of other
hunters. But Tuktu's father does
bring home a seal in the end. Stories
of Tuktu series. (National Film
Board of Canada)
FILMS INC. 14 min. Color. Sound.
1968

TUKTU AND THE
TEN THOUSAND FISHES
Tuktu is taken on a fishing trip to the ancient stone weir. He sees his father and other hunters spear fish in great numbers. He sees how his father and his uncle make fire with the Eskimo fire drill. Stories of Tuktu series. (National Film Board of Canada)
FILMS INC. 14 min. Color. Sound. 1968

UP TO THE SEQUOIAS
Begins in the foothills of the Sierra Nevada, where a red-winged black-bird's harsh call contrasts with the fluid tones of a western meadowlark. As we move higher into the mountains, we observe birds and mammals in a constantly changing setting. On the high plateaus, giant sequoia trees (oldest and largest trees in the world) shelter white-headed wood-peckers, fox sparrows, and black-capped chickadees. Available with study guides. Birds of America series. (Produced by Dan Gibson)
A-V EXPLOR. $7\frac{1}{2}$ min. Color. Sound

WATER BIRDS
This film takes you to the shore of a wilderness lake to hear the mournful cry of a loon, to watch the graceful flight of a tern, to listen to the shrill chorus of gulls overhead, to admire the majestic heron in its solitude. An intimate look at these species, their nests, and young. Natural, synchronized sound. Available with study guides. Birds of America series. (Produced by Dan Gibson)
A-V EXPLOR. $5\frac{1}{2}$ min. Color. Sound. 1966

THE WATER SAYS
Clouds creep up the wooded slopes to release their drops with a pleep-bloop-ploop. Gathering, the water begins a curling, cascading race to the sea. In another mood its quiet surface is patterned by water strider, frog, sleek snake. A trout's tail echoes the movement of swaying water plants.
CHURCHILL. 11 min. Color. Sound. 1971

WATER'S EDGE
A camera study of natural water forms, from the quiet of a melting icicle to the pounding of the waves. Set to a musical score by Frank Lewin. A blend of sight, sound, and color. (Ernest Wildi, producer)
FILMS INC. 12 min. Color. Sound

WATERS OF YOSEMITE
One stream—gushing waters at its origins ... raging rapids as it gathers momentum from mists, dews, rains, and tributaries ... powerful calm at its maturity. The musical score is intermingled with sounds of water. Brief commentary by Joseph Wood Krutch. (Produced by Pyramid Films)
HOLT R&W. 10 min. Color. Sound. 1967

THE WAYS OF WATER
Photographed in the wilderness of Washington State's Olympic Peninsula, this nonnarrated film shows the importance of water in nature. Musical background. Teacher's guide available.
ENCYC. BRIT. 13 min. Color. Sound. 1971

WHITE THROAT
The white-throated sparrow is your guide to the forest in this film. Synchronized sound allows the forest to speak for itself as White Throat leads you on a voyage of discovery, to observe and listen to some of the creatures—song-birds, frogs, wolves, beaver, loons, ducks—of a wilderness area. Awards: American Film Festival Honors; Golden Gate Award, San Francisco; Award of Merit, Landers Film Reviews. Available with study guide. Birds of America series. (Produced by Dan Gibson)
A-V EXPLOR. 10 min. Color. Sound. 1965

WILLOW
An aesthetic experience with nature.
Visuals and music were selected to
evoke the qualities of dignity, mass,
intricate structure, strength, solemnity, and cheer—as related to a particular tree. Further dissection of
the film reveals principles of good
cinema composition, which is the
film's primary purpose.
SYRACUSE UNIV. 7 min. Color.
Sound. 1971

WINTER
A little boy sets off to discover the
joys of winter. He finds other children skating, bare trees covered
with ice, and a flock of sheep. At a
zoo, he helps to feed animals. Back
home, he makes patterns on the window before jumping into bed. No
narration; guitar music and natural
sounds.
STERLING. 11 min. Color. Sound.
1967

WINTER COLOR
The beauty of winter color in a se-
ries of photographic studies. Ori-
ginal musical accompaniment.
THORNE FILMS. 5 min. Color.
Sound. 1963

WINTER GEYSER
Yellowstone Park in winter. Opening with shots in late fall, the photographer focuses on random
streams, waters of the geyser area,
bubbling pools—at the same time
changing the scene from autumn to
winter. Suddenly steam, snow, and
water erupt with the first geyser—
initiating sound and motion contrasted with the still, frozen aura
preceding. The remainder of the
film reveals the geyser in its many
aspects, erratic and majestic. No
narration. Award: CINE Golden
Eagle. (Produced by Pyramid Films)
HOLT R&W. 7 min. Color. Sound.
1967

5. EXPRESSION

Under this category you'll find movies that encourage response, be it written, oral, or physical. Their content is independent of any conventional subject. Many of these films are the same ones you used to find catalogued under reading readiness, communications skills, or (that durable favorite) language arts. Like any other good medium, these projections provide a group experience for followup discussion or assignment. Beyond what most pictures accomplish, however, these can stimulate nonverbal reactions such as dancing, rhythmic clapping, and even filming.

These are materials that call for expressive reaction. Naturally, films with similar aims may appear under "The Arts," "Science," or other headings with subject-related foundations. But, in contrast to such subject-oriented materials, "Expression" films are intended to promote expression for the sake of expression. That function covers a lot of ground, as do the films listed herein.

"A"
Animated in fine line pen and ink reminiscent of nineteenth-century engraving. A visual joke based on one of Ionesco's favorite preoccupations, the power of language. The letters also symbolize invasion of privacy, oppression, or one's own problem. (Produced by Jan Lenica)
McGRAW-HILL. 10 min. B&W Sound. 1964

A IS FOR ALPHABET
A blend of animation, rhyme, and song takes us through the alphabet. A book-balancing bear bouncing on a ball, a frog living on a flower farm, a giraffe wearing glasses in the grass, a hippopotamus at home in a hole, and other animals help introduce letters. (Produced by William Peterson Associates)
CORONET. 11 min. Color. Sound. 1971

THE ADVENTURES OF *
Man, represented by the asterisk symbol *, is introduced in this animated film as a baby enjoying the sights of the world about him. As he grows, his ability to see and enjoy life is reduced until he becomes an adult who is unable to react freely. On the birth of his child, he is able to once again discover the world. Award: Venice Film Festival. (Produced by John Hubley)
McGRAW-HILL. 10 min. Color. Sound. 1956

ALPHABET
"A" is apple and ant and alligator. "B" is boat and ball and bounce ... all the way to "Z," which is of course zebra. Such is this film by Eliot Noyes Jr., using pentel and wash to display the letters of the alphabet in a free-flowing, ever-changing panorama of visual examples. (National Film Board of Canada)
NAT. FILM BD. 6 1/4 min. B&W. Sound. 1966

ANIMALS ON THE FARM:
A Film in Song and Rhyme
The world of the barnyard. Nancy
Raven, a young teacher known for her
children's recordings, points out the
sights by singing the "narrative."
Follows each of several animals
through its daily activities.
CLARK BELL. 15 min. Color.
Sound. 1971

BANG!
Students see and hear a boy making
"music" in the timeless ways of
children: by banging on cans, hitting
pots and pans together, striking bottles, and dragging a stick along a
picket fence. Contains broad science implications. Magic Moments
series.
ENCYC. BRIT. 3 min. Color.
Sound. 1969

A BELL FOR URSLI
Ursli's adventures in bringing a bell
from the hills for the annual spring
ritual in his Swiss town. Without
spoken commentary. (Produced with
the cooperation of Faroun Films
[Canada] Ltd.)
XEROX FILMS. $18\frac{1}{2}$ min. Color.
Sound. 1971

THE BOX
What does it "mean"? Perhaps each
to his own thing? No. It means that
when a stranger enters a bar with a
mysterious box, and arouses curiosity about the inhabitant (or contents)
of the box, and when a young lady
enters the same bar with her box,
and the two decide to—but why on
earth should anyone spoil it for you?
Academy Award: Best Cartoon.
(Produced by Murakami-Wolf Films)
CCM FILMS. 7 min. Color. Sound.
1967.

BREATH
An adult cartoon. Without sound,
with outline figures, "Breath"
simply shows a man and a woman
breathing in and out. With each
breath (inhaled and exhaled in concert), the exhalation condenses into

something they want—or something
they don't want. The interpretation
is open to possibilities. Preview.
(Produced by Murakami-Wolf Films)
CCM FILMS. 5 min. Color. Sound.
1967

THE CARNIVAL
The joy and innocence of childhood
are observed in this live-action
film about the adventures of a young
girl at a country fair. (A Richard
Soltys film)
XEROX FILMS. $7\frac{1}{2}$ min. Color.
Sound

CIRCUS IN EUROPE
A one-ring circus arrives in a town
and parades through the streets. The
tent is set up, and the performers
begin their rehearsal. The opening
performance mirrors the glamor of
the animals and the acts that unfold.
The camera picks up the faces of the
children, who watch with excitement. The absence of narration allows viewers to express their reactions. See 'n Tell series. (Institut
fur Film und Bild)
FILMS INC. 10 min. Color. Sound.
1970

CITY IN WINTER
Snow-banked grass; bare trees; a
snowman; ice skating, sledding, and
tobogganing; winter vegetables and
flowers in shop windows. Viewers
who live in warm climates will get a
better understanding of what it's like
to live under these conditions—and
all viewers will have a chance to discuss the differences between summer and winter in the city.
ENCYC. BRIT. 10 min. Color.
Sound. 1969

CLAP!
A boy walks through a park clapping
his hands—and recruits a passerby
to clap with him. A group of school
children yells and claps with abandon. These situations, and others
depicted in the film, may help children better understand clapping as a

way of having fun and a way of expressing appreciation. Magic Moments series.
ENCYC. BRIT. 5 min. Color.
Sound. 1969

CLOWN
A shaggy dog, Clown, lives with a
street urchin in Paris. The two are
inseparable until Clown runs off.
The child searches for the dog and
has nearly given up hope when suddenly he spies his pet. Rushing
over to embrace him, the boy realizes that his dog is tied and held by a
poor old blind man. The boy slowly
walks away, leaving Clown forever.
LEARN. CORP. 15 min. Color.
Sound. 1969

THE COLOSSAL DREAM
OF BLOCKS
Reading is stimulated by setting
selected words within a story-song.
The first time each word is presented, it appears on screen while
being sung. Then it is seen but not
heard. Viewers are encouraged to
sing it, or to think, whisper, or shout
it. Vocabulary is from the first
grade of the Dolch Basic Word List.
Over 20 words appear more than 140
times in this and companion film,
"The Miraculous Dream of Circles."
ACI Films. 15 min. Color. Sound.
1971

COUNTY FAIR
From the Starting to Read series,
with songs and superimposed words
to teach primary vocabulary and
concepts. Also available without
captions. Complete script provided
with purchase. (Produced by Jim
Burroughs, Grace-Metro Enterprises, Ltd.)
ACI FILMS. 7 min. Color. Sound.
1970

DUCKS
Big and little ducks waddle about a
duck farm, eating, drinking, swimming, and quacking. The accompanying song comments: "Duck is a
word that stands for a bird, That

walks with little webbed feet."
From the Starting to Read series,
with songs and superimposed words
to teach primary vocabulary and
concepts. Also available without
captions. Complete script provided with purchase. (Produced by
Jim Burroughs, Grace-Metro Enterprises, Ltd.)
ACI FILMS. 8 min. Color. Sound.
1970

THE FACES OF PATRIOTS
Who are the real Americans? How
broad is the word patriotism? Whom
can it include? Is there only one way
to show love of country? This film
doesn't provide the answers. It does,
however—using no narration, but
only the voices of the people involved
—provide a base upon which to pose
questions.
WOMBAT PROD. 19 min. Color.
Sound. 1971

FLY AWAY
Scenes of birds and kites, gliders and
model airplanes help capture the
feeling of freedom in flight. The
viewer flies away in a small plane
and observes the earth from a detached vantage point. Useful for language art activities. No narration or
dialogue, but with natural sounds and
music. (Produced by Stanton Films)
DOUBLEDAY. 11 min. Color.
Sound. 1967

GETTING ALONG
An old gentleman finds himself em-
broiled in a quarrel between play-
mates, which he smooths over.
Throughout the film the emphasis is
on the placating hands of the man and
the angry hands of the children. Students see how hands show emotions
not expressed in other ways. Magic
Moments series.
ENCYC. BRIT. 2 min. Color.
Sound. 1969

THE GLOB FAMILY
Taking a couple of formless "globs"
resembling ink blots (one red, one
black), this animated film uses the

viewer's imagination to create a tale.
A movement here—a slight change
of shape there—and a gentle, human
theme emerges, recognizable to most
children. No narration.
LEARN. CORP. 8 min. Color.
Sound

GUESSING GAME
This split-screen film shows pan-
tomimists miming an action (e.g.,
pretending to throw a ball). The
blank half of the screen may then
show a ball in the air. But sometimes it will show something different from what the actors are miming.
It's up to the viewers to call out
what matches and what doesn't.
ENCYC. BRIT. 7 min. Color.
Sound. 1969

THE HALF-MASTED SCHOONER
Balladeer Bruce Mackay provides
visual accompaniment for his own
song, "The Half-Masted Schooner,"
as well as musical accompaniment, on his guitar. Song writer,
singer, and filmmaker, this enter-
tainer chooses illustrations that
suggest the same style of commentary as the words of his song.
McGRAW-HILL. 6½ min. Color.
Sound. 1969

HANDS GROW UP
Much of children's play is an imitation of, and a preparation for, adult
activities. Shows children at play
(e.g., children playing with mud) and
then a corresponding adult activity
(in this case, a potter shaping a
vase). Besides giving children the
feeling of being "grown up," the film
shows them the variety of occupations that they are, in a sense, training for every day. Magic Moments
series.
ENCYC. BRIT. 6 min. Color.
Sound. 1969

THE HIDING PLACE
An attractive young woman drives to
a remote area to spend a weekend
alone. After a swim and a meal beside a blazing fireplace, she retires.

Then comes an onslaught of sounds:
the pounding of the surf, the wailing
of the wind as it lashes the creaking
house. Tension builds in the girl.
After a restless night she is still
taut, and goes to the beach. Entering
the disturbed waters, she is seen no
more, until .... No dialogue or narration. (Produced by Tom Scheuer)
FILM IMAGES. 18 min. B&W.
Sound. 1969

HOLDING ON
A boy goes to Fisherman's Wharf and
to a carnival with his father. Suddenly he's lost. What panic and ter-
ror, in the midst of carnival frolic!
What a wonderful feeling to be found
again! Offers students the opportunity of describing usually unspoken
emotions.
ENCYC. BRIT. 4 min. Color.
Sound. 1969

THE HUNTER AND THE FOREST—
A Story Without Words
Photography, natural sound effects,
and original music relate the story
of an encounter between a hunter and
a family of deer in the forest. Collaborator: Paul Witty, Ph.D., Northwestern University.
ENCYC. BRIT. 8 min. B&W. Sound.
1954

IN OUT UP DOWN UNDER
OVER UPSIDE DOWN
A backyard playhouse and a brook
are the centers of activity for a family of children and their pets, including a puppy and a frog. A background chorus sings, "Every day and
every way, Up and down are words
we say." From the Starting to
Read series, with songs and superimposed words to teach primary
vocabulary and concepts. Also available without captions. Complete
script provided with purchase. (Produced by Jim Burroughs, Grace-
Metro Enterprises, Ltd.)
ACI FILMS. 8 min. Color. Sound.
1970

JAIL KEYS MADE HERE
A film essay using contemporary advertising signs as a comment on society. Based on a book of photographs by Lee Boltin. (Produced by Frank DeFelitta)
McGRAW-HILL. 10 min. B&W. Sound. 1965

JUNKYARD
At first glance, the junkyard seems to be a place of untidy wreckage and corrosion. Closer examination, however, reveals the junkyard to be a world of rugged, and sometimes even delicate, beauty. Wild flowers flourish among rusted metals. A summer storm sweeps the junkyard, splattering the old cars, making their dull paint glisten. A snowfall softens the harshness. A junkyard can be a place filled with ever changing shapes, colors, and moods. No narration. (A Nimbus Production)
BFA ED. MEDIA. $9\frac{3}{4}$ min. Color. Sound

LATE FOR DINNER:
Was Dawn Right?
Dawn has disobeyed her mother; she has money that doesn't belong to her; she's late for dinner and gets a scolding. What did she do to get into so much trouble? She simply tried to return a five dollar bill to a woman who dropped it before boarding a bus—with complicating results. This open-ended film helps children understand that conflicting feelings are both common and normal.
ENCYC. BRIT. 8 min. Color. Sound. 1971

LEAVES
A boy watches the leaves fall from the tree in his yard. His imagination moves him to assist nature by making replacements for her casualties. With construction paper, marking crayons, and scissors, he creates his own collection of "leaves." With Scotch tape, the boy fastens his leaves to the naked tree. The next morning he sees the tree once more stripped of its bloom by a whim of nature. He decides to try again. No narration. (A Ronald Phillips Film)
ACI FILMS. 13 min. Color. Sound. 1968

THE MAGIC FRAME—
ADVENTURES IN SEEING
When they jump through a magic frame, children see ordinary things with an exciting sense of heightened perception. They visit a toy shop, play in the park, and taste food at an outdoor market. A repeated song points out that we all have a magic frame if only we open our eyes. (Produced by David Culver)
CORONET. 11 min. Color. Sound. 1971

A MAN'S HANDS
Hands—squeezing, poking, scratching, fixing, zipping, playing, and touching. Alternately funny and informative. Live action. (Produced by Paul Prokop)
PYRAMID. 5 min. Color. Sound. 1970

MATCHING UP
A split-screen film. Here, torsos are projected on the screen, followed by feet. Students must decide which match and which do not. Live action. Magic Moments series.
ENCYC. BRIT. 4 min. Color. Sound. 1969

MATRIX
Design in motion, achieved by computer graphic instrumentation. Horizontal and vertical lines, squares, and cubes move along a closed, invisible pathway. No narration. Original sonata music. (Produced by John Whitney)
PYRAMID. $5\frac{1}{2}$ min. Color. Sound. 1970

ME, TOO?
A boy, alone on the beach, sees other boys building a sand castle, and asks to join them. When the group refuses, the lone boy destroys the castle. Lets children discuss their own

feelings about being rejected and rejecting others. Magic Moments series.
ENCYC. BRIT. 3 min. Color.
Sound. 1969

THE MIRACULOUS DREAM
OF CIRCLES
Reading is stimulated by setting selected words within a story-song.
The first time each word is presented, it appears on screen while
being sung. Then it is seen but not
heard. Viewers are encouraged to
sing it, or to think, whisper, or shout
it. Vocabulary is from the first
grade of the Dolch Basic Word List.
Over 20 words appear more than
140 times in this and companion
film, "The Colossal Dream of
Blocks."
ACI FILMS. 15 min. Color. Sound.
1971

MR. KOUMAL
CRUSADES FOR LOVE
The subject of this series of episodes, involving an optimistic idea-
man thwarted at every turn, is human nature and man's relationship
to his environment and his fellow
men. Mr. Koumal series. (Produced in Czechoslovakia)
SIM PROD. 2 min. Color. Sound.
1969

THE MONKEY AND
THE ORGAN GRINDER
A typical day in the life of three
monkeys and their organ-grinder
master, Bob Jones. As Bob plays
in the shopping section of a large
city, Coco takes coins from passersby and tips his hat. This nonnarrative film suggests what it must
be like to be a gentle man who is
closer to his animal friends than to
other people but who enjoys bringing pleasure to children.
ENCYC. BRIT. 11 min. Color.
Sound. 1971

MY FRIEND THE FISH
Peter, a five-year-old boy, is walking down a hot road when he finds a
fish flopping in the dust. After he
takes it home and puts it in a pail of
water, the fish revives and starts to
swim. Later, close calls with the
family cat and a bully's slingshot
persuade Peter to return the fish,
reluctantly, to its natural habitat in
the lake. Peter sits at the shore at
sunset, waiting for his friend, the
fish, to swim back to him. A wood-
wind score matches the film's
moods.
CCM FILMS. 18 min. Color. Sound.
1966

MY FRIEND THE ROBIN
The story of a young boy's adoption
of a homeless baby robin.
JOURNAL. $9\frac{1}{2}$ min. Color. Sound.
1971

ONE TURKEY, TWO TURKEYS
A counting film, with turkeys who pop
in and out of crates to introduce
numbers one to ten. The chorus
comments, "Eight turkeys, nine turkeys, ten turkey birds, Ten different turkeys, ten different words."
From the Starting to Read series,
with songs and superimposed words
to teach primary vocabulary and
concepts. Also available without
captions. Complete script provided
with purchase. (Produced by Jim
Burroughs, Grace-Metro Enterprises, Ltd.)
ACI FILMS. 6 min. Color. Sound.
1970

ORANGE AND BLUE
Experimental film uses two bouncing
balls as principal characters, inno-
cently exploring their surroundings.
(Directed by Peter and Clare Cher-
mayeff)
McGRAW-HILL. 15 min. Color.
Sound. 1962

THE ORATOR
A man prepares a speech at home,
trying it out on his wife. Pleased
with his ideas, he imagines his
speech a success. But when the
speech is actually delivered, the
audience is bored, misunderstands,

goes to sleep, and plays cards while
he talks on and on. Instead of dialogue, words are visualized by
strings of letters spewing out of
the speaker's mouth. Animated
puppets. Music. Awards: Bergamo,
Oberhausen, Karlovy Vary. (Produced in Czechoslovakia)
McGRAW-HILL. 11 min. Color.
Sound. 1962

PATTERNS
A cinematic experience—an intricate
series of patterns formed by reflections in water as they twist and twirl
in varied shapes and forms to musical accompaniment. No narration.
(A Trend Release)
WALT DISNEY. 6 min. Color.
Sound

PICNIC
A family goes on a picnic to a lake
in the woods, and cooks a meal over
an open fire. From the Starting to
Read series, with songs and superimposed words to teach primary
vocabulary and concepts. Also
available without captions. Complete
script provided with purchase. (Produced by Jim Burroughs, Grace-
Metro Enterprises, Ltd.)
ACI FILMS. 7 min. Color. Sound.
1970

PITTSBURGH MUSICAL COPS
Candid Camera filmed a policeman
directing traffic in Pittsburgh, and
added music to go along with his
motions as he scolds, encourages,
and pleads with pedestrians and
motorists. This sequence is an example of nonverbal communication
and is a training device for showing
creative problem-solving skills.
Available for purchase; no rentals.
CANDID CAMERA. $2\frac{1}{2}$ min. B&W.
Sound

PLAYGROUND
Slides, swings, and lots of games occupy children of all sizes at a playground. From the Starting to Read
series, with songs and superimposed
words to teach primary vocabulary

and concepts. Also available without
captions. Complete script provided
with purchase. (Produced by Jim
Burroughs, Grace-Metro Enterprises, Ltd.)
ACI FILMS. 7 min. Color. Sound.
1970

THE PUFFED-UP DRAGON
Imagination gets free rein in this tale
that combines animated paper cut-
outs with music and sound effects.
The absence of narration permits
the student to create his own story
of what happens between the huge
dragon and the villagers.
STERLING. 10 min. Color. Sound.
1966

RAGAMUFFIN
A visual poem, describing in image
and music the desires, dreams, and
disappointments of a small boy.
Without dialogue. Rental only.
(Produced in Poland)
AUDIO/BRANDON. 10 min. B&W.
Sound. 1947

RAIN
Shows rain in the country and the
city, and how it is enjoyed by plants
and children. A chorus comments,
"The rain is good, it makes things
grow, And every drop will tell you
so." From the Starting to Read series, with songs and superimposed
words to teach primary vocabulary
and concepts. Also available without
captions. Complete script provided
with purchase. (Produced by Jim
Burroughs, Grace-Metro Enterprises, Ltd.)
ACI FILMS. 8 min. Color. Sound.
1970

RAINSHOWER
The sights and sounds, beauty and
rhythm of rain. An experience in
the changing moods of a day when a
rainshower comes to plants and animals on a farm, and to people at
work in a community. Narration is
used only for the introduction; the

rest is natural sound. (A Dimension Film)
CHURCHILL. $14\frac{1}{2}$ min. Color. Sound. 1965

RICKY'S GREAT ADVENTURE
This story of a blind boy can motivate primary students to become better observers of nature by making greater use of their senses of touch, taste, smell, and hearing. A presentation of the world of nature that can be discovered by every child. No narration, only synchronized sound and original music.
ATLANTIS. 11 min. Color. Sound. 1969

A SCRAP OF PAPER
AND A PIECE OF STRING
Creates human aspects of friendship between inanimate objects, while pointing out the importance and utility of paper and string in our economy. Original score of Dixieland jazz. Produced in special string animation by John Korty for the NBC Exploring series.
McGRAW-HILL. 6 min. Color. Sound. 1963

THE SHEPHERD
A day in the life of a shepherd and his two sheep dogs is portrayed without commentary. Serenity exists in the shepherd's daily routine but the stillness is broken as he comes upon signs of a marauder and goes in pursuit. Seven awards, including Ireland, Edinburgh and Johannesburg. (National Film Board of Canada)
INT. FILM BUR. 11 min. Color. Sound. 1955

SHEPHERD DOG AND HIS FLOCK
An account of the day's activities of two German shepherd dogs and the shepherd for whom they work. Both dogs have learned to handle the flock—they move the sheep to the side of the road to let a truck pass, and they keep the sheep out of a grain field. Simple commands by the shepherd to the dogs keep the

flock moving toward their pasture. No narration. See 'n Tell series. (Institut fur Film und Bild)
FILMS INC. 8 min. Color. Sound. 1970

SIGNS, SIGNALS AND SYMBOLS
This film brings an awareness of the multitude of communication tools taken for granted: letters and lights, sirens and sheet music, the hands of an umpire and a traffic officer, and many more. Presented in a manner that reveals the association that signs, symbols and signals stimulate. (Produced by Tony Gorsline)
AIMS. 11 min. Color. Sound. 1970

SKATER DATER
An account of a young boy's emergence into adolescence—when he gives up his skateboard for the company of a young girl. Film festival awards: Cannes, Edinburgh, Moscow, Cortina, and many more. (Produced by Noel Black)
PYRAMID. 18 min. Color. Sound. 1965

SUN
Early morning, the middle of the day, and sunset scenes show sunlight and children. From the Starting to Read series, with songs and superimposed words to teach primary vocabulary and concepts. Also available without captions. Complete script provided with purchase. (Produced by Jim Burroughs, Grace-Metro Enterprises, Ltd.)
ACI FILMS. 8 min. Color. Sound. 1970

TENNESSEE BIRDWALK
Bald birds? Birds wearing underwear? Flying north in winter? Whispering instead of chirping? Can you imagine birds stripped of the very essence of their bird-ness? This fantasy examines these questions—all to the accompaniment of original country music. Animated.
ABC MEDIA. 6 min. Color. Sound. 1970

TIME OF THE HORN
A Negro boy retrieves a discarded trumpet. To his delight, he is able to produce a few strident notes on the battered instrument. Then, oblivious to passersby, the young musician pretends to play the horn as he struts down the busy street, lost in a jazz fantasy of his own imagining. The background is a Duke Ellington composition, interpreted by trumpet virtuoso Jonah Jones. No narration. (Produced by Russell Merritt)
JOURNAL. 7 min. B&W. Sound

TOES TELL
A barefoot girl steps on and feels many textures with her toes: fur, gravel, sand, paint, etc. Viewers may then tell how the textures shown would feel to their feet and what they would do with their own feet (such as pick up a pencil with their toes).
Magic Moments series.
ENCYC. BRIT. 6 min. Color. Sound. 1969

TUKTU AND THE MAGIC SPEAR
Tuktu accompanies his family when fishing is done through the ice during the long cold winter. He sees his father catch fish with a spear during the summer, and he longs to grow up and catch fish, too. Stories of Tuktu series. (National Film Board of Canada)
FILMS INC. 14 min. Color. Sound. 1968

UNE BOMBE PAR HASARD
(The Serendipity Bomb)
A bomb lies unexploded in the middle of a town, and the inhabitants have wisely retreated to a hill some miles away. To their surprise a stranger enters the town, and, paying no attention to the bomb, starts doing what he likes with the abandoned household goods and public places. But some places are holier than others. Can you guess? Indignant, the townsfolk hurry home and cast the stranger from their midst. Guess what happens. More impor-

tant, what does it mean? Animated. Many international awards.
STERLING. 8 min. Color. Sound. 1970

WALKING
The humor and individuality of various styles of walking—and, by extension, various styles of living—are accented by a rock music score, the sole "commentary" of the film. Animated line drawings, color wash, and watercolor sketches capture movement and the personalities behind the walk. Preview recommended. Awards: Academy Award Nominee; film festival awards: Chicago, Toronto, Barcelona, Krakov, LaPlata, Rio de Janeiro. (National Film Board of Canada)
LEARN. CORP. 5 min. Color. Sound. 1968

WE'RE GONNA HAVE RECESS
The schoolyard during recess when, within a space of minutes, hearts are broken, scores are settled, secrets told, and where a bouncing ball or turning rope still tell the future to a chanted rhyme. Filmed without commentary, this is a small world, but a world of childhood that most of us will recognize.
NAT. FILM BD. $9\frac{1}{2}$ min. Color. Sound

WHAT IF?
Here are four situations that are often difficult for children to cope with. These vicarious experiences are ways for children to work out appropriate responses in advance or to better understand why they responded as they did. Two typical situations are: a girl finds a wallet; a boy's ice cream cone is knocked out of his hand. Magic Moments series.
ENCYC. BRIT. 3 min. Color. Sound. 1969

WHAT WOULD YOU DO?
Two children are playing ball. The boy kicks the girl's ball and a car runs over it. There are three al-

ternative endings. The viewer is asked what he would do: (1) accept the ball; (2) give the ball to the other children, even if his parent disapproved; (3) accept the ball with or without parental approval.
ATLANTIS. 8 min. Color. Sound. 1971

WHAT'S HAPPENING?
Five situations are shown, each one a part of a story, for students to complete. In one situation, a group of children is pushing a huge, psychedelically painted box along the sidewalk. What is in the box? Why is it painted that way? Where are they going with it? Magic Moments series.
ENCYC. BRIT. 5 min. Color. Sound. 1969

A WHEEL IS ROUND
A man whose bicycle keeps losing its wheels introduces all the ways that wheels are familiar to children — on bikes, wagons, baby carriages, cars, trucks, and trains. From the Starting to Read series, with songs and superimposed words to teach primary vocabulary and concepts. Also available without captions. Complete script provided with purchase. (Produced by Jim Burroughs, Grace-Metro Enterprises, Ltd.)
ACI FILMS. 8 min. Color. Sound. 1970

WHITE MANE (Crin Blanc)
Written and directed by Albert Lamorisse, director of "Red Balloon." This is a tragic and mythic story of a boy's love for a wild horse, photographed against the watery wilderness of the Camargue region of southern France. Rental only.
MUS./MOD. ART. 39 min. B&W. Sound. 1953

WHOSE SHOES?
A heavy-booted authority figure stands over a child; a child runs after a car, trying to make the driver stop; boys and girls are dancing when something makes them stop and run away. These three incidents, typical of the five shown, motivate students to discuss what might have happened, and to tell how they would feel and what they would do if they were the children in the film. Magic Moments series.
ENCYC. BRIT. 3 min. Color. Sound. 1969

WINTER
A little boy sets off to discover the joys of winter. He finds other children skating, bare trees covered with ice, and a flock of sheep. At a zoo, he helps to feed animals. Back home, he makes patterns on the window before jumping into bed. No narration; guitar music and natural sounds.
STERLING. 11 min. Color. Sound. 1967

Z IS FOR ZOO
For the youngest students, just beginning to read. "Zoo" has a musical score, and introduces words and concepts of Eat, Play, Walk, Clean, and Tail, with glimpses of zoo residents putting the ideas to work.
ACI FILMS. 9 min. Color. Sound. 1970

6. CITY AND SUBURB

This is the topic that made me rethink my original categorizations. Films for "City and Suburb" had originally been listed under "Other Places, Other Customs," which seemed logical enough until the nature and number of these materials practically demanded a grouping of their own.

What is it about cities that attracts so many makers and viewers of films? Every picture you see here will give you a different answer. Some of these motion pictures brag. Others complain. A few try to ignore city locales or at least treat them incidentally. But usually a city will refuse to behave as basic background, and will manage to penetrate (if not dominate) whatever the foreground subject happens to be.

As you'd expect, New York is amply represented in this collection. So are Paris, Tokyo, London, Venice, and other exotic but paradoxically familiar places. But whoever heard of Geelong? Australians, that's who. And because they wanted the rest of the world to know about Geelong, it became one subject in a series of films about the major cities of that island-nation-continent.

Why should Geelong be listed here? Why not? The word "civilized" stems from the Latin word for city. Cities are supposed to represent the highest achievement of collective man. Using that premise, maybe Geelong has more right to the studied than, say, New York.

ADELAIDE
A sight-and-sound story about Adelaide, South Australia's capital city. Without commentary.
AUSTRALIA. 22 min. Color. Sound. 1969

ALLEGRO MA TROPPO
A filmic composition in which we are plunged at high speed into the multitude of experiences comprising the city life of Paris.
PYRAMID. 13 min. Color. Sound. 1962

ARCHITECTURE, USA
Using original music and no narration, presents view of U.S. architecture that reflects America's cultural life. Includes educational and religious institutions, cultural centers, and the skyscraper.
NAT'L AV CTR. 13 min. Color. Sound. 1965

AUTUMN COMES TO THE CITY
Changing weather, new clothes, fall window displays, fall foods, animals moving south or storing food for the winter, cold rains, strong winds, Halloween and Thanksgiving are set without narration against the tall buildings, streaming traffic, and crowded apartments.
CORONET. 11 min. Color. Sound. 1969

AN AUTUMN STORY—
Mrs. Pennypacker's Package
Mrs. Pennypacker forgets her im-

portant package in front of a grocery store. As more and more people try to help return it to her, the viewer becomes aware of the variety of workers in a big city.
ENCYC. BRIT. 11 min. Color. Sound. 1968

BANGKOK
We see Buddhist monks in their saffron robes, street peddlers, a classical dancing school, weavers and dyers of silk, Chinese pharmacy, and the klongs (canals) where people live close to poverty. We visit the home and office of an industrialist who is also a Thai prince. Man and His World series. (Institut fur Film und Bild)
FILMS INC. 18 min. Color. Sound. 1969

BERLIN, BERLIN, BERLIN
A fast-paced view of life in this busy metropolis within East Germany. Has specially composed music and sophisticated camera and sound techniques, but no narration. Sponsored by the City Government of West Berlin. Free loan.
BLUMENTHAL. 20 min. Color. Sound. 1971

BIG, BIG HARBOR
The hustle and bustle of a big port city as seen through the eyes of two children touring with their father. Captured are the sights and sounds of men and equipment loading and unloading ships; tugs moving massive ocean liners; goods arriving from distant places; trains and planes linking markets with the harbor's business activity.
UNIVERSAL ED. 12 min. Color. Sound. 1969

THE BLUE DASHIKI:
Jeffrey and His City Neighbors
This film traces the adventures of a young black boy who wants to earn money to buy the dashiki he has seen in a local African import shop. The cooperation of neighbors and store-keepers, and the cosmopolitan flavor and cultural interests of the Afro-American community, are portrayed as Jeffrey works toward his goal.
ENCYC. BRIT. 14 min. Color. Sound. 1969

BOOMSVILLE
Recreates the process by which man took virgin land and made it a congested "boomsville." The growth of cities, the advent of railroads, cars, and airplanes, the industrial revolution, immigration, the role of wars, the growth of a pleasure-loving society—these are some of the themes sketched in. Animated. No narration. Awards: Columbus Film Festival, American Film Festival. (National Film Board of Canada)
LEARN. CORP. 10 min. Color. Sound. 1969

BRAND NEW DAY
A motion-collage, without narration, showing the architecture, landmarks, and points of interest in San Francisco. U.S. CINE entry at the Brussels Film Festival.
EASTMAN KODAK. $4\frac{1}{2}$ min. Color. Sound. 1969

BRIDGES-GO-ROUND
A camera study of the bridges around New York City; progressive jazz score by Teo Macero. (Directed by Shirley Clarke)
McGRAW-HILL. 5 min. Color. Sound. 1958

CHILDREN ADRIFT
(Les Enfants des Courants d'Air)
A study of foreign slum children on the outskirts of Paris, showing the qualities of a child's environment and of his imagination. It carries neither dialogue nor commentary, except for the child's exclamation at the end—"Wait for me." Award: Prix Jean Vigo. (Les Films d'Art Production)
McGRAW-HILL. 26 min. B&W. Sound. 1958

CHILDREN OF PARIS
Kids—shining faces—Paris in summer! In this little-narration film, the camera catches the excitement of vacation-time in a fascinating city. Faces young and old, rich and poor— in the parks or the "Flea Market," the Louvre or Montmartre, the Sacre Coeur or the back alleys. (Produced by Films/West)
AIMS. 12 min. Color. Sound. 1971

CICERO MARCH
September 4, 1966...a Chicago Negro postal worker, Robert Lucas, leads 300 marchers into Cicero. The attention of the country is focused on the hysteria created by the sight of blacks marching down the main street of an all-white middle-class northern city. Without commentary. The only sounds and sights are those recorded at the scene.
PERENNIAL ED. 8 min. B&W. Sound. 1967

CITIES IN CRISIS: WHAT'S HAPPENING?
Using an original rock-and-roll score and free-form camera techniques, this film exposes the crass and ugly side of contemporary urban life. It deals with traffic jams, smog-filled air, house-smashing bulldozers, cavorting ghetto children, drag-strip racing. These sights and sounds of a pleasure-bent society indict the social, economic, and moral values that have permitted these problems to arise.
UNIVERSAL ED. 21 min. Color. Sound. 1968

CITY AT NIGHT
The sky darkens, lights flash on, cars clog the streets. Dinnertime, warm and friendly. Voices in many accents. Fun and excitement—the amusement part, folk dancing, concert hall, discotheque, movie premiere. Closing down, going home. Lights going off. Cleaning, washing. Workers at night—the bakery, police, television. Dead of night—voice of the disc jockey, the lonely night watchers. No narration. (A Dimension Film)
CHURCHILL. $14\frac{1}{2}$ min. Color. Sound. 1971

CITY IN WINTER
Snow-banked grass; bare trees; a snowman; ice skating, sledding, and tobogganing; winter vegetables and flowers in shop windows. Viewers who live in warm climates will get a better understanding of what it's like to live under these conditions— and all viewers will have a chance to discuss the differences between summer and winter in the city.
ENCYC. BRIT. 10 min. Color. Sound. 1969

CITY...One Day
One day in the life of this nation's largest city. With emphasis on the daily work and the people of the city, this approach is designed to elicit student response and discovery. For use in basic units in geography and community life. Musical score. Two versions available: Version A, no narration; Version B, brief introductory narration.
AIMS. 18 min. Color. Sound. 1969

THE CROWD
What is there about the nature of man that makes him seek out and become part of a crowd? That is one of the questions implicit in this film. The camera moves from crowds in a subway to crowds at a parade, crowds of cattle at a slaughter, crowds at a beach, a nightclub, and a riot. Finally we see a scientist observing the most basic crowd of all—a crowd of human chromosomes. No narration.
LEARN. CORP. 20 min. B&W. Sound. 1970

DAYDREAMING
A day's tour of Daytona Beach, Florida's resort city and site of the annual auto-racing competition, the Daytona International.
MINI FILMS. 11 min. Color. Sound. 1970

EVASION
French film without words. Pounded
by machine, noise and rhythm of the
city, man becomes like a marionette,
a discarded Pierrot, frozen with anguish. Is discovered by child who
leads him to the country where beat
and harmony of nature bring him
back to life and joy. When he relearns to walk, run and climb trees,
Pierrot is overjoyed to find he is
still a MAN. He takes the child back
to city and bestows on him a magic
spark, symbol of life. (Acromedia)
NAT'L. EDUC. 17 min. Color.
Sound

FROM 3 A.M. TO 10 P.M.
Making use of the absence of narration and dialogue, this film is a tri-
bute to the working housewife. It
follows a woman through her work-
day from dawn to dusk. When her
work at the factory ends, her work
at home begins—with worry about
the children, worry about money, and
the attempt to make ends meet. She
toils late into the night, only to get
up early in the morning to get to
her job at the factory on time.
Award: Best Documentary Film at
the Locarno Festival. (Produced by
Zagreb Film, Yugoslavia)
McGRAW-HILL. 15 min. B&W.
Sound. 1967

THE FUGUE
Here we join a group of people in a
church as they listen to an organ
concert of music by Bach. As the
music creates a sense of unity and
peace, we find a brief escape from
the restlessness and noise outside
in the streets. (Produced by
Czechoslovak Television)
McGRAW-HILL. 19 min. B&W.
Sound. 1966

GEELONG
A sight-and-sound story about Gee-
long, a city in Victoria, Australia.
Without commentary.
AUSTRALIA. 22 min. Color.
Sound

GO FASTER
This animated film from France,
created by the Belgian filmmaker
Peter Foldes, focuses on modern
man at the mercy of his conveyances, be they cars, boats, or spaceships. Our hero shaves, dictates
letters, watches TV, and makes love
to his secretary without budging
from behind the wheel. Every day
the routine is the same, increasingly
faster and more perfunctory. At
last he wonders what it's all about.
Preview recommended.
LEARN. CORP. 9 min. Color.
Sound

HAPPY ANNIVERSARY
France's Pierre Etaix directed and
acted in this portrayal of a man trying to reach home to celebrate his
wedding anniversary. Etaix presents, without words, the humorous
but frustrating plight of the husband
who encounters delay after delay in
Paris traffic. Awards: First Prize
at the West German Short Film Festival and an Academy Award for
Live Action Short.
INT. FILM BUR. 13 min. B&W.
Sound. 1961

HARBOR RHYTHM
Award-winner at several festivals,
this film presents the rhythm of
life in Hamburg Harbor. The structure of the film is a day of work,
beginning at dawn, pausing at noon,
and finishing after dark as the
workers seek recreation. Beneath
this action are the natural sounds of
the harbor, occasional electronic
sounds, and a continuous beating
rhythm. (Filmed by Wolf Hart;
original released in Europe as
"Hafenrhythmus.")
INT. FILM BUR. 13 min. Color.
Sound. 1970

HAVE I TOLD YOU LATELY
THAT I LOVE YOU?
Typical weekday of a modern family, as its members use radio-
clocks, electric coffeemakers,
autos, elevators, phones, television,
and even cigarette lighters. Their

reliance on machinery and automation seems to be paralleled by (and possibly related to) the absence of communication among them.
U. OF SO. CAL. 16 min. B&W. Sound. 1959

HEY DOC
About Dr. Ethel Allen, a black physician who is medical adviser, confessor, and friend to North Philadelphia's ghetto. Cameras follow her to the schools, through the streets, and into her office. Spotlights the lives of the addicted, the aged, the angry. Presented without narrators, scripts, actors, or staged interviews. (Produced by WCAU-TV, Philadelphia)
CAROUSEL. 25 min. Color. Sound. 1970

HIGH SCHOOL
The Frederick Wiseman film of the educational process at a "good" white, middle-class high school. As with all Wiseman films, the synchronous sound recording is the only accompaniment to the visuals, and no editorial opinion is narrated. Made in suburban Philadelphia.
ZIPPORAH. 75 min. B&W. Sound. 1969

HOBART
A sight-and-sound story about Hobart, Tasmania's capital city. Without commentary.
AUSTRALIA. 22 min. Color. Sound

HOSPITAL
A night in the emergency ward at Metropolitan Hospital in New York, and indirectly, an essay on the ills of large metropolitan areas. Graphic demonstration of the work done in our hospitals, with a sequence on the effect of drugs on a lost young college student. Not for the squeamish. Awards: Emmy for Best News Documentary and for Best Director; Columbia School of Journalism; Catholic Film Workers;

Mannheim, West Germany. Preview. (Produced by Frederick Wiseman)
ZIPPORAH. 85 min. B&W. Sound. 1970

IN PARIS PARKS
Explores the park, the people, and the games in the famous Tuileries Gardens of Paris. (Directed by Shirley Clarke)
McGRAW-HILL. 14 min. Color. Sound. 1955

A KEY OF HIS OWN
What are the feelings of a child whose parents work late, leaving him alone? This question is explored in the story of Jeff. The nonnarrated open-ended treatment involves the viewer in Jeff's balancing of his independence against his loneliness.
BFA ED. MEDIA. $9\frac{1}{4}$ min. Color. Sound. 1971

KEY PEOPLE
Seven everyday city people and their activities. This essay without words was produced by a filmmaker who selects moments during which individuals perform the daily routine of entering and leaving their homes, and so give an impression of their modes of life. Music. (Produced by Gerald Plano)
FILM IMAGES. 5 min. Color. Sound

L.A. TOO MUCH
The long life and violent death of a handsome Victorian house makes a statement about the probable shape of a dehumanized environmental future. Without commentary.
BERKELEY. 12 min. Color. Sound. 1968

LAUNCESTON
A sight-and-sound story about life in Launceston, Tasmania, Australia. Without commentary.
AUSTRALIA. $19\frac{1}{2}$ min. Color. Sound. 1967

LAW AND ORDER
A Frederick Wiseman production, filmed in Kansas City over a five-week period in 1969. Shows in detail (but without commentary or narration) daily police routine, mostly in the black ghetto. Open-ended. Winner of the Emmy Award for the Best News Documentary of 1969-70. ZIPPORAH. 81 min. B&W. Sound. 1969

MELBOURNE
A sight-and-sound story about Melbourne, Victoria's capital city. Without commentary. AUSTRALIA. 20 min. Color. Sound. 1966

MIKE AND STEVE VISIT THE SHOPPING CENTER
With his friend Steve, Mike tours the shopping center before buying a baseball. This is a chance to see the advantages and disadvantages of large shopping centers and the effect they have on small, individually owned stores, and also to view how two boys—one black and one white—learn about their own community. ENCYC. BRIT. 14 min. Color. Sound. 1969

MINT TEA
A cinematic study of loneliness. As he sits in a glass-enclosed Parisian cafe, life moves all around and seemingly through the young man who is trying to make contact with another human being. (Produced and directed by Pierre Kafian) McGRAW-HILL. 20 min. B&W. Sound. 1962

MORNING, NOON, AND EVENING
These are the sights and sounds of one day, which no narrator needs to interpret. Following two families provides a window to a wider world—a mountain sunrise—first light in the city. From their rest, people move to countless places and duties, not in a world of drudgery but one of productive effort with

moments of warmth and charm. (Produced by Films/West) AIMS. 13½ min. Color. Sound. 1970

N.Y., N.Y.
A highly personal, visual interpretation of the temper and personality of New York City. Awards: Cannes, London, Edinburgh, and New York. (Produced by Francis Thompson) PYRAMID. 16 min. Color. Sound. 1959

PERTH
A sight-and-sound story about Perth, Western Australia's capital city. Without commentary. AUSTRALIA. 19 min. Color. Sound. 1967

PETS: A BOY AND HIS DOG
The companionship between a boy in the inner city and his pet. During daily activities, the boy carries out his responsibilities while the dog patiently awaits the next tumble session. The boy enters his shaggy friend in a pet show. Another animal wins, but the love between the boy and his dog continues to enrich their lives. No narration. (A Gabor Kalman Film) BFA ED. MEDIA. 11 min. Color. Sound. 1969

PIGEONS! PIGEONS!
Ground level camera shots provide close-ups as the birds peck at crumbs, preen their feathers, and settle down for a rest. This nonverbal film can help viewers become aware of sounds and different forms of motion. ENCYC. BRIT. 9 min. Color. Sound. 1969

PORT MORESBY
A day in the major city of New Guinea, the trust territory north of Australia. Without commentary. AUSTRALIA. 9 min. Color. Sound. 1971

PURSUIT OF HAPPINESS
THE MATERIALISTIC WAY
A kaleidoscopic array of colors and symbols of materialistic plenty reinforced by honky-tonk piano. Images of bulging consumer markets flash by in contrast to brief stark visuals suggesting hunger, want, and waste. Without narration, the film uses music, sound effects, and visuals.
THORNE FILMS. 4 min. Color. Sound. 1965

RAIN (Regen)
Joris Ivens, active in the first film club in Holland, filmed in the streets of Amsterdam for three months to produce this impression of a rain shower in the city. Released in 1929 as a silent film; 1931 sound version with music. No narration.
FILM IMAGES. 12 min. B&W. Sound. 1931

RAIN IN THE CITY
The activities of a city as a gentle rain storm comes and goes. The film then shifts to a wooded area where raindrops fall from flowers to the sound of bells, and a solitary walker with an umbrella disturbs a toad and a lizard. (Filmed in Germany by Wolf Hart; originally released in Europe as "Regen")
INT. FILM BUR. 14 min. B&W. Sound. 1970

SAN FRANCISCO
A quick whirl through one of the world's most cosmopolitan cities. With acid-rock music in the background, scenes of famous San Francisco landmarks and scenic spots flash by in staccato sequence. Award: CINE. (Fred Calvert Production)
PYRAMID. 4 min. Color. Sound. 1969

SHIBAM
This film is a wordless study of life among the ancient ten-story buildings of Shibam, a city in Saudi Arabia—a city where water plays a central role in the life of the people. Presents the essential commodity—water—and the city. (Produced by International T.V. Trading Corporation)
McGRAW-HILL. 14 min. B&W. Sound. 1970

THE SINGING STREET
This film, which is without commentary, consists entirely of songs and games sung and played by Edinburgh children in their native city. Phrases of ancient ritual, myth, and lost language are mingled with symbols of present-day life—taxis, telephones and powder-puffs—the favorite themes being of love and death.
BRITISH. 20 min. B&W. Sound

SIRENE
The story of a mermaid in the harbor of a modern city. This creature is charmed by a man playing a flute, and she attempts to flee with him. But the machines that surround the harbor destroy her. The investigation of the mermaid's death provides a satirical look at the bureaucratic institutions of modern society. Told entirely through the animated paintings and a background of contrasting sounds. (Produced by Raoul Servais)
INT. FILM BUR. 10 min. Color. Sound. 1970

SIU MEI WONG—WHO SHALL I BE?
Is a Chinese-American "Chinese" or "American" or both? Siu Mei Wong is a Chinese girl who yearns to be a ballerina. Her father is proud of their Chinese heritage, and insists his daughter attend a Chinese school as well as the American school. When Siu Mei's ballet lessons conflict with her Chinese education, a painful choice must be made. Eventually, her father decides that he must not let his own deep ties to tradition prevent his daughter from having a chance to pursue her own goal. The minimal dialogue in this film is in Chinese, with subtitles.
LEARN. CORP. 18 min. Color. Sound. 1970

SKYSCRAPER

Dramatization of all the human beings who create the modern skyscraper, and reflection of a city's
unending transformation, through a
story of the construction, from blue-
print to occupancy, of the Tishman
Building at 666 Fifth Avenue, New
York. (Produced by Shirley Clarke,
Irving Jacoby, and Willard Van Dyke)
CCM FILMS. 20 min. Color.
Sound. 1960

SOMEDAY

Presents four simple trip ideas—
supermarket, sailboat ride, zoo,
and baseball game. Suggests nonverbal ways for young children to
express their experiences, stretches
awareness of time, and prepares
them for specific trips and new experiences. (A John Korty film)
STERLING. 9 min. Color. Sound.
1967

SPRING IN THE CITY

Youngsters fly kites, skip rope, dye
Easter eggs, and dream of baseball.
Adults start clean-up and paint-up
work, seed and water lawns, plant
flower boxes. Buds appear on trees,
baby birds chirp hungrily in their
nest. The sights and sounds of a new
season in a film without words.
ENCYC. BRIT. 11 min. Color.
Sound. 1969

STATE OF THE EARTH

Mountains, swimming pools, skid-
row bums, superhighways, and music
are contributing elements to a nonverbal essay on the quality of American life. This piece uses vignettes
of life woven together to make
statements, to evoke moods, and to
bring up questions about existence in
a complex society.
NBC. 18 min. Color. Sound. 1969

SURVIVAL

A man, in medieval armor and a gas
mask, mounts his "noble steed," a
Volkswagen, and sets off to do battle
with the smog, traffic, and pollution.
He gives up, and escapes to the
countryside. He is confronted by a
naked couple who offer him an apple
and, in the only spoken line in the
film, ask, "Care to join us?" Perhaps, as this film suggests, our
many achievements have done
little to improve the quality of life.
Live action. (Produced by Tony
Schmitz)
ACI FILMS. 3 min. Color. Sound.
1971

SYDNEY

A sight-and-sound story about Syd-
ney, capital city of New South Wales,
Australia. Without commentary.
AUSTRALIA. 21 min. Color.
Sound. 1967

SYRINX/CITYSCAPE

Two different themes—one ancient,
one modern—are presented without
narration. "Syrinx" depicts the
Greek fable of the goat-god Pan set
to Debussy's music. "Cityscape"
conveys the agitated rhythm of city
life. Awards: New York, San Francisco, Canada, Ethiopia. "Syrinx"
(B&W, 3 minutes) and "Cityscape"
(B&W, 1 minute) are mounted on
one reel.
LEARN. CORP. 4 min. B&W.
Sound. 1966

TERMINUS

A candid study of a day's activities
in a railway station. Scenes in the
film, coupled with a natural soundtrack, run the gamut of situations
that people confront in a large railway station. The deliberate elimina-
tion of a narrative permits students
to develop oral and written versions
of what was seen.
STERLING. 24 min. B&W. Sound.
1964

THIRD AVENUE EL

The film explores the train and its
mechanical environment—reflections in the water, distortions
through glass, patterns of steel and
concrete, switches, coupling devices, and awesome forms of lifting
drawbridges. Relies for its effect

not on words but on the presentation and joining of images. Awards: Academy Award Nomination, Golden Reel, Edinburgh, Columbus. (A Carson Davidson Film)
ACI FILMS. 9 min. Color. Sound. 1956

THIS IS THE HOME OF
MRS. LEVANT GRAHAM
"Cinema verite" piece centering on a Washington, D.C. mother and her large family in the black ghetto. No narration. Awards: Monterey, New York, White House. (Produced by the New Thing Flick Co.)
PYRAMID. 15 min. B&W. Sound. 1970

TOKYO INDUSTRIAL WORKER
Through a day with the O-ga family, we visit Tokyo. Here we see a society in transition—holding to the old customs and adopting new ones. Mr. O-ga, his wife, and three children sleep on mats, but eat breakfast at a high table, and dress in Western fashion for school and work. Mr. O-ga works in a nearby factory and rides a motorbike to work. When he arrives home in the evening, the family dines at a low table, Japanese fashion, then reclines on mats to watch television. Man and His World series. (Institut fur Film und Bild)
FILMS INC. 17 min. Color. Sound. 1969

URBANIA
The struggle for existence in an environment so hostile that even the air is poisonous. Impressionistically it approves civic planning and action to deal with urban blight.
THORNE FILMS. $7\frac{1}{4}$ min. Color. Sound. 1971

VENICE, ETUDE NO. 1
Color and motion pervade this personal visualization of Venice. Dimensional planes, each depicting familiar sights of this famous city, are juxtaposed. Music. (Produced by Ian Hugo)
FILM IMAGES. 8 min. Color. Sound. 1961

VIVALDI'S VENICE
Venice, queen of Italian cities, is photographed by Life photographer Carlo Bavagnoli. There is no spoken commentary. Six eighteenth-century concerti of Vivaldi sustain the camera as it reflects Venice's glories and variety of moods through four seasons. Award: Venice Film Festival Silver Medal.
TIME-LIFE. 27 min. Color. Sound. 1968

WHAT IS A COMMUNITY? (Second edition of "Our Community")
Documentary on a small town and a big city; communities' needs, functions, differences, and similarities; housing, schools, shopping centers, factories, and other elements.
ENCYC. BRIT. 14 min. Color. Sound. 1969

WINTER COMES TO THE CITY
An urban winter is seen through the eyes of Jackie Lee Hibbard, who moves to Chicago from the South. Arriving before Christmas, the boy revels in the window displays, buys warm clothing, makes new friends, observes city plants and animals, and enjoys snow and ice for the first time.
CORONET. 11 min. Color. Sound. 1969

7. VALUES

Thanks to the Britannica Humanities series, that well-worded and hardly non-narrative program, educators were able (for the first time since McGuffey's Reader) to introduce ethical concepts into public classrooms. Spiritual themes went to school disguised as lessons in art, architecture, literature, or history. Prior to the Humanities, producers had tried gamely to accommodate the market for morality with hundreds of guidance films. Coronet titles like "Right or Wrong? (Making Moral Decisions)" had the right idea: concepts were acted out rather than narrated; solutions were suggested, not imposed; issues were secular instead of denominational. But, because guidance itself was outside the curriculum proper, exposure to give-and-take discussion was not built in to the daily cycle of teaching and learning.

Showings of "Right or Wrong," for example, were often limited to auditorium assemblies—not exactly fertile ground for followup. The Humanities approach, though, brought questions of value and vice back into the classroom for examination under the neutralizing light of Plato, Shakespeare, Dickens, or Hemingway. Even as blatant a spiritual symbol as Chartres Cathedral could now be studied in detail, under the aegis of art and architecture, without arousing the fears of church-state separatists. The films listed here are neither Guidance nor Humanities films. But they are reflections of values and relationships uniquely common to the human condition. Questions are presented; answers are withheld; discussion is guaranteed.

THE ABANDONED
An essay in film and electronic music on the final days in the life of many a faithful family car. These cars, once cherished family members, now old and forgotten, are abandoned at the rate of eight million per year—most to rust away, strewn across the countryside.
NBC-TV. 10 min. Color. Sound. 1970

ALF, BILL AND FRED
The friendship of a man, a dog, and a duck dissolves when the man comes into an inheritance and forgets his humble companions. This fable, told in simple animation, concludes with the reunion of the trio. The moral: "It's easier to sell happiness than to buy it." A Contemporary Films release. (Produced by Bob Godfrey)
McGRAW-HILL. 8 min. Color. Sound. 1964

AMBLIN
A prize-winning film about the young, created by the young. Not a word of dialogue is spoken, yet the film speaks of where today's youth is at. Two hitchhikers, a boy and a girl, are making their way across the desert to the Pacific. They meet, join forces, share experiences, make love, and then part when she discovers he is more establishment than he had seemed. Backed by an original score. Preview recommended.
UNITED PROD. 24 min. Color. Sound. 1969

THE BEGINNING
Poses questions about the creative
individual in relation to his society.
Music. Animated with "Wigglemen"
characters. No narration. First in
the series entitled The Wigglemen
Tales.
BOSUSTOW. 4½ min. Color. Sound.
1971

THE BIRD
The hard-working hero has slowly
saved enough money to buy a bird.
Eventually succeeding, he cannot
commit the bird to a captive life like
his own, and sets it free.
STERLING. 10 min. B&W. Sound.
1970

BLESSINGS OF LOVE
A nonverbal film that follows a
couple from courtship to marriage
to old age, to the time when the man
loses his wife and imagines her back
with him, as young and lovely as she
was long ago. This animation is accompanied by Martini's "Plaisir
d'Amour."
CCM FILMS. 9 min. Color. Sound.
1970

BLOSSOM
Without even mentioning race relations, this film goes right to the
heart of the question. The camera
simply watches two children—one
white and one black—at play on a
summer afternoon. Tony and Me-
lissa are totally unaware that race
can be a barrier to good relationships. This is their story—how they
meet, become friends, and build a
sidewalk soft-drink stand. A study
guide, written by the Rev. Don Hall,
is available.
CATHEDRAL. 10 min. Color.
Sound. 1970

THE BRAND-NEW BASKETBALL
Story about two boys—one self-contained and sure of himself, the other
constantly trying to prove himself—
who become involved with a group of
older schoolmates in an afternoon
basketball game. As the film

evolves, the character of each boy in-
evitably influences his behavior and
his capacity to make and keep new
friends. No narration. Music.
UNIVERSAL ED. 9 min. Color.
Sound. 1969

CHOICE
A basic introduction to the drug problem, preventive in nature and designed for discussion on all levels.
No narration.
CORONET. 8 min. Color. Sound.
1970

CLOWN
A shaggy dog, Clown, lives with a
street urchin in Paris. The two are
inseparable until Clown runs off.
The child searches for the dog and
has nearly given up hope when suddenly he spies his pet. Rushing over
to embrace him, the boy realizes that
his dog is tied and held by a poor old
blind man. The boy slowly walks
away, leaving Clown forever.
LEARN. CORP. 15 min. Color.
Sound. 1969

DAY AFTER DAY
Documents and reflects the boredom
of production-line work in a small
papermill town in Quebec. A Con-
temporary Films release. (National
Film Board of Canada)
McGRAW-HILL. 30 min. B&W.
Sound. 1962

DOUGLAS, JAMES, AND JOE
On human relations. Three boys,
one black, the others white, display
natural unbiased bents and joy in just
being with each other and playing together. An object lesson for adults.
No narration or dialogue. (Produced
by Grover Dale)
FILM IMAGES. 6 min. B&W. Sound

DUET
Two men enjoy each other's company
in gardening, fishing, and playing
duets. One brings home a phonograph and in his excitement forgets
his date with his friend. Hurt, the

other obtains his own phonograph.
Friendship ends as each man allows
machines—phonographs, radios, and
television—to replace social activities. Each watches television in his
own home—alone. On the screen
they see two friends doing the very
things they used to enjoy. No narration. Animated puppets. (A Beaux
Arts/Vita Film)
BFA ED. MEDIA. 9 min. Color.
Sound. 1969

ELEGY
The symbolic tale of a prisoner who
passes his days staring longingly at
a pretty red flower outside his cell
window, desperately wishing he could
reach out and touch it. When finally
released from prison, however, he
completely forgets about the flower.
As the film ends, the viewer is left
wondering what new unobtainable desires are running through the main
character's mind. Animated. (Produced by Zagreb Film)
McGRAW-HILL. 5 min. Color.
Sound. 1965

EXCHANGES
An encounter between two train pas-
sengers—a black man and a white
girl. An exchange of glances leads
them into an imagined sequence in
which fantasies and prejudices are
exposed, explored, and finally abandoned. We return to reality and to
the couple still isolated from one
another. A note of hope is sounded
in the final shots: the rails of the
train running parallel, yet seeming
to merge in the distance. Award:
CINE Golden Eagle. (A John Camie
Film)
ACI FILMS. 10 min. B&W. Sound.
1969

THE FAMILY—
THE BOY WHO LIVED ALONE
A 9-year-old runs away because of
imagined mistreatment by his family. The film records his feelings of
being alone, his reactions to people
on the streets. To get out of the
rain, he spends a night in an abandoned house. Flashbacks of home

contrast with present discomforts.
The film also follows the family as
they wait for his homecoming the fol-
lowing morning.
ENCYC. BRIT. 11 min. Color.
Sound. 1967

FAMILY TEAMWORK AND YOU
Concept: Attitudes and relationships
with family and friends. Almost free
of narration, this film provides a
comparison of two families. One
family works successfully as a
team—the other has a "let Mom do
it" attitude. Original musical score.
AIMS. 13 min. Color. Sound. 1966

THE FENCE
This animated allegory illustrates
the consequences of a single incon-
siderate act. A man throws rubbish
into his neighbor's yard. Retaliatory
exchanges follow until house and yard
are demolished. A flashback to the
original scene portrays an alterna-
tive—instead of rubbish, a flower is
thrown over the fence. No narration.
(An Omega Film)
BFA ED. MEDIA. 7 min. Color.
Sound. 1969

FINE FEATHERS
Evelyn Lambart, longtime associate
of Norman McLaren, has created a
fable about two birds who exchange
their plumage for brightly colored
leaves. They admire themselves and
each other; their vanity knows no
bounds. But when the wind blows the
leaves away the moral is told, only
by the visual action. No narration.
NAT. FILM BD. 5½ min. Color.
Sound. 1970

GETTING EVEN
A group of boys disrupts a girls'
soccer game. To get even, the girls
"ambush" the boys, squirting them
with water pistols. The film provides an opportunity for children to
talk about revenge. When, if ever,
is it justified? What are the results?
ENCYC. BRIT. 3 min. Color.
Sound. 1969

GO FASTER
This animated film from France, created by the Belgian filmmaker Peter Foldes, focuses on modern man at the mercy of his conveyances, be they cars, boats or spaceships. Our hero shaves, dictates letters, watches TV, and makes love to his secretary, without budging from behind the wheel. Every day the routine is the same, increasingly faster and more perfunctory. At last he wonders what it's all about. Preview recommended.
LEARN. CORP. 9 min. Color. Sound

GOOD GOODIES
The second in the series entitled The Wigglemen Tales, that poses questions about the creative individual in relation to his society. This film is a satiric lesson on the Gross National Product. Music. No narration. Animated with "Wigglemen" characters.
BOSUSTOW. 4½ min. Color. Sound. 1971

GUIDANCE...DOES COLOR REALLY MAKE A DIFFERENCE?
This film presents several sequences wherein ethnic origins are unidentified, but different colors are presented in varying hostile actions. The viewer is led to believe that these actions have no bearing or relationship to ethnic origin. Conclusions are left completely to the audience. Minimal narration.
AIMS. 11 min. Color. Sound. 1969

GUIDANCE...LET'S HAVE RESPECT
Topic: Respect for country and property. First and fourth episodes: 1. Two boys forget to be respectful during a school flag-raising ceremony. Decision: What should the other boys and girls do about it? 4. One girl mishandles a library book by dropping it and coloring in a picture. Narrator: "What has this girl forgotten about the care of books? What should she do now?"
AIMS. 10 min. Color. Sound. 1969

GUIDANCE...WHAT'S RIGHT?
Topic: Morals and manners. Sample episodes: 1. A primary grade boy has lost his ice cream money. Another student drops a dime. He picks up the dime. Narrator: "What should he do with the dime? What would you do?" 2. A girl catches her best friend cheating on a test. Decision: What should she do about it? What would you do?
AIMS. 10 min. Color. Sound. 1969

GUIDANCE...WORKING WITH OTHERS
Topic: Respect for other races, the opposite sex, the handicapped. "Becoming involved." Sample episode: A Negro boy tries to enter an all-white children's game. He is pushed and told to go away. Another boy leaves the game to talk to the Negro boy. Narrator: "How do you think this boy can help?"
AIMS. 10 min. Color. Sound. 1969

HAVE I TOLD YOU LATELY THAT I LOVE YOU?
Typical weekday of a modern family, as its members use radio-clocks, electric coffeemakers, autos, elevators, phones, television, and even cigarette lighters. Their reliance on machinery and automation seems to be paralleled by (and possibly related to) the absence of communication among them.
U. OF SO. CAL. 16 min. B&W. Sound. 1959

THE HOARDER
A bird-land fantasy by animation artist Evelyn Lambart, about a bluejay who takes whatever his beak can carry. Into his secret cache go berries, birds' eggs, nests and all. Even the sun in the sky is unsafe from his consuming greed. But there is a moral tucked away. The bluejay learns a lesson, and bird-land returns to normal.
NAT. FILM BD. 7½ min. Color. Sound. 1970

HOPSCOTCH
An animated tale about a boy who
wants to make friends but tries too
hard. He desperately wants to join
a boy and girl playing hopscotch. He
parades his possessions, shows off
his athletic prowess, is noisy and
disruptive, acts tough, flatters by
imitation, all to no avail. At last he
gives up playing roles—and is accepted!
CHURCHILL. 12 min. Color.
Sound. 1971

HOW'S SCHOOL, ENRIQUE?
The answer to this simple question
will stimulate provocative discussion and promote increased cultural
awareness. In order to be accepted
as a full citizen and be assimilated
into an alien Anglo society, the Mex-
ican-American is expected to give
up his language and his cultural
identity. The resulting conflicts are
emphasized by examining a young
Chicano's environment—the family,
the barrio, and most importantly,
his school. Minimum narration.
Awards: American Film Festival and
Columbus. (Produced by Stanley
Frager, Ph.D. Released by Cahill &
Assoc.)
AIMS. 18 min. Color. Sound. 1970

IS THIS OUR FATHER'S WORLD?
Pictures the warm relationship between a father and his young son.
Against their simple, happy excursions to the beach, the park, the
zoo, and window shopping, the film
sets another picture of the world—a
polluted world in which technology
runs unchecked. It makes a statement, with a positive note, about
man's stewardship responsibilities
for his environment. The soundtrack
contains no dialogue, but consists of
original rock music and lyrics.
(Paul Kidd, producer)
FAMILY FILMS. 10 min. Color.
Sound. 1971

JOSHUA IN A BOX
This film deals with man's needs,
emotions, and values. Joshua's predicament, his attempts to escape, and

his emotional responses to frustration
can be interpreted in many ways and
on various levels. Animated. No
narration.
BOSUSTOW. 5 min. Color. Sound.
1970

THE JUMP and +PLUS - MINUS
In "The Jump," a little man,
clutched in the grasp of mechaniza-
tion, incessantly performs monoto-
nous series of movements in a world
that is void of humanity and warmth.
Live action is combined with painting
on film and music. No dialogue.
"+Plus - Minus" is a boy-meets-
girl story with an antiwar theme.
Hand painting over photographed
silhouettes against intense background colors. (Produced by Eino
Ruutsalo)
CCM FILMS. 11 min. Color.
Sound. 1966

THE LEMONADE STAND:
WHAT'S FAIR?
A "values" film on the meaning of
commitment, obligations, and responsibility. Three boys open a
lemonade stand. After an unsuccessful morning, business picks up,
but one boy has gone off to play. His
return leads to an argument about
his share of the profits—and the
film ends. What's fair?
ENCYC. BRIT. 14 min. Color.
Sound. 1970

LIFE CYCLE
A red dot symbolically portrays a
man's life from the womb until he
ultimately returns to the earth, to be
succeeded by generations to come.
His birth, growth, schooling, marriage, the birth of his children, and
eventual old age and death are presented. The musical score takes
the place of narration. Animation.
(Produced by Joe Zinn)
ACI FILMS. 7 min. Color. Sound.
1971

MAMMALS
The fourth and last of Roman Polanski's early short films. This is a

story of two men tramping in the
snow with only one sled between
them. They both try to take advantage of each other in order to spend
the most time riding and the least
walking. Though this film uses slapstick, sight-gags, and visual puns,
it is primarily an allegory on the unending conflict and precarious balance between the exploiter and the
exploited—showing how easily roles
can switch. Awards: Tours, Oberhausen, Melbourne, and American
Film Festival.
McGRAW-HILL. 10 min. B&W.
Sound. 1959

MIME OVER MATTER
A humorous treatment of man's relationship to the material objects
that make his life more comfortable.
It stars Ladislav Fialka, Czechoslovakia's leading mime artist.
(Produced by Kratky Films)
SIM PROD. 12 min. Color. Sound.
1970

MR. KOUMAL FACES DEATH
The subject of this series of episodes, involving an optimistic idea-
man thwarted at every turn, is human nature and man's relationship
to his environment and his fellow
men. Mr. Koumal series. (Produced in Czechoslovakia)
SIM PROD. 2 min. Color. Sound.
1969

MROFNOC
Alone in a crowd of people, an individual finds himself doing the exact
opposite of what they consider normal—walking backwards! Surprised
and confused, he tries to "go against
the crowd," only to find it is easier
to give up and conform by learning to
walk backwards himself. Filmed
without dialogue or narration, with a
jazz score. Awards: Independent
Film-Makers' Festival; Edinburgh,
San Francisco, Crakow. (Produced
by Josef Sedelmaier)
FILM IMAGES. 7 min. B&W.
Sound. 1965

THE NAUGHTY DUCKLING
Animated puppets pantomime an important lesson—independence without preparation can lead to trouble.
Duckling's troubles start when he refuses to join his brothers in their
first swimming lesson, and end only
when he escapes from a fox. The
absence of narration makes the film
a medium for learning how to arrange events in sequence, discussing behavior, dramatizing the story,
identifying story clues in the musical
score. (Omega Productions)
ENCYC. BRIT. 9 min. Color.
Sound. 1970

THE NAUGHTY OWLET
The baby owl lives in a hollow tree
with his brothers. They work hard
at learning to fly, but he spends his
time looking at television. A crisis
comes when he has to fly to escape
from a fox, and he finds the value of
learning one's lessons. Animated.
(Produced in Hungary)
ACI FILMS. 8 min. Color. Sound.
1970

ONLY BENJY KNOWS:
SHOULD HE TELL?
Is tattling ever justified? Benjy
goes to a store and sees some boys
he knows slipping toys into their
pockets. They don't see him and he
doesn't say anything to his mother.
But should he tell someone?
ENCYC. BRIT. 4 min. Color.
Sound. 1970

PAVE IT AND PAINT IT GREEN
On ecology and man's capacity for
spoiling his natural environment.
Contrasts the grandeur of Yosemite with the chaos caused by hordes
of tourists. Transitions from black -
and-white to color, time-lapse, and
speeded-up sequences are used for
esthetic and satiric effect. No narration or commentary.
BERKELEY. 27 min. B&W/Color.
Sound. 1970

A PLACE IN THE SUN
Tale of two figures competing for
that important "place in the sun,"

noting human foibles as they win or lose their place. Satire in simple, stylized animation. (Ceskoslovensky Filmexport)
FILMS INC. 7 min. Color. Sound. 1960

THE PROBLEM
An animated puppet film that centers on the question of what color the trash box in a large organization should be painted. As this decision is passed upward through employees, officers, and finally the chairman of the board, it grows larger and more important. The film examines the dehumanizing effect of bureaucracies, and raises questions on the nature of responsibility and the individual. No narration. Music and sound effects. (Produced by Jan Dudesek)
CCM FILMS. 12 min. Color. Sound. 1966

PURSUIT OF HAPPINESS
THE MATERIALISTIC WAY
A kaleidoscopic array of colors and symbols of materialistic plenty reinforced by honky-tonk piano. Images of bulging consumer markets flash by in contrast to brief stark visuals suggesting hunger, want, and waste. Free of a narrated soundtrack, the film uses music, sound effects, and visuals.
THORNE FILMS. 4 min. Color. Sound. 1965

THE PUSHER
A biography of an egocentric "pusher" who elbows his way from babyhood, through adolescence, to adulthood. Pushing himself onward and upward, he finally achieves an executive job, but at the end is elbowed out by his rival who has taught himself to be aggressive too. Pantomimed against white backgrounds. No dialogue. (Produced in Yugoslavia)
CCM FILMS. 17 min. B&W. Sound. 1962

QUEER BIRDS
Two odd-looking pelicans, one large, one small, make their way across the landscape. They meet and conquer imposing obstacles and situations that are reminiscent of the traditional Hollywood cartoon. (Directed by Vladimir Lehky; drawn by Jiri Toman)
McGRAW-HILL. 10 min. B&W. Sound. 1965

THE RED KITE
Adapted from Hugh Hood's story, "Flying a Red Kite." A young father is preoccupied with questions about life, death, and God. An answer is provided in the freedom and joy of the human spirit—as symbolized by the red kite he flies with his little girl. An examination of modern man, society, and the search for security and faith.
NAT. FILM BD. 17 min. Color. Sound. 1966

THE REFINER'S FIRE
By three high-school students; an animated abstract ballet about conformity. The characters are squares and circles that take on human characteristics, as they portray the conflict between an established society and its idealistic members. Intended to demonstrate the fate of pioneers of social change, it retains some optimism.
DOUBLEDAY. 6 min. Color. Sound. 1969

A ROCK IN THE ROAD
A man trips over a rock and plunges into a hole. Fuming, he spots someone coming. He replaces the rock and hides. The second man also falls into the hole. The second man sets up the accident for a third, and the third for a fourth. But the fourth man removes the rock, fills in the hole—and goes away happy. Animated. No narration. (A Beaux Arts/Vita Film)
BFA ED. MEDIA. 6 min. Color. Sound

ROMEO
A story of an elementary classroom
during exam period. A girl doesn't
know some of the answers and a boy
tries to get them for her. He bribes
the teacher's pet and gets the answers. Then he tries desperately to
complete his own test, falling further
and further behind as the others finish theirs. No dialogue or narration.
Music by Prokofiev. (Institute of
Cinematography, Moscow)
CCM FILMS. 9 min. B&W. Sound.
1962

THE SATIRIC EYE
At a funeral, the corpse laughs at
everyone's grief; when a bridge is
dedicated, it is impossible to cut the
red tape; at a circus the lion eats the
tamer; a man attempts to appease
two dogs and is turned on by both of
them. This collection of short, animated works from Hungary and Germany turns a satiric eye on society,
without a word of narration. "Inau-
guration," "Either/Or," "Success,"
and "Funeral" are the selections.
LEARN. CORP. 13 min. Color.
Sound. 1970

THE SHOOTING GALLERY
Mechanical targets in a shooting gallery are the protagonists in an allegory of freedom repressed and love
violently destroyed. Raises questions about the degree of man's freedom, the nature of conformity, and
the power of love. Live action.
(Produced by Kratky Film Studio,
Prague)
SIM PROD. 6 min. Color. Sound.
1970

SIU MEI WONG—WHO SHALL I BE?
Is a Chinese-American "Chinese" or
"American" or both? Siu Mei Wong
is a Chinese girl who yearns to be a
ballerina. Her father is proud of
their Chinese heritage, and insists
his daughter attend a Chinese school
as well as the American school.
When Siu Mei's ballet lessons conflict with her Chinese education, a
painful choice must be made. Eventually, her father decides that he

must not let his own deep ties to tradition prevent his daughter from
having a chance to pursue her own
goal. The minimal dialogue in this
film is in Chinese, with subtitles.
LEARN. CORP. 18 min. Color.
Sound. 1970

A SPECIAL KIND OF MORNING
Two young girls take an early morning jaunt through the St. Louis Zoo in
which only they and the animals are
present. The girls, one white, one
black, are seen sharing love, companionship, joy, and sorrow. When
one loses her gas-filled balloon, the
other makes the compassionate sacrifice of voluntarily releasing hers.
The musical score is the only accompaniment to this experimental
film. (Produced by KETC-TV, St.
Louis)
INDIANA UNIV. 27 min. Color.
Sound. 1971

STATE OF THE EARTH
Mountains, swimming pools, skid-
row bums, superhighways, and music are contributing elements to a
nonverbal essay on the quality of
American life. This piece uses
vignettes of life woven together to
make statements, to evoke moods,
and to bring up questions about existence in a complex society.
NBC. 18 min. Color. Sound.
1969

THE STRING BEAN (Le Haricot)
Story of an old woman who culti-
vates a potted bean plant. Sunning
and watering her green friend is
her sole diversion in the tiny Paris
lodging in which she sews handbags
for her livelihood. Concerned for
the future of the plant, the fragile
lady plants it in the Jardin des
Tuileries. The fate of the plant, and
the faith and optimism of its guard-
ian, form the story line. In black-
and-white and in color. No narration
or dialogue. Award: Cannes Film
Festival. (Directed by Edmond
Sechan)
McGRAW-HILL. 17 min. B&W/
Color. Sound. 1964

SURVIVAL
A man, in medieval armor and a gas mask, mounts his "noble steed," a Volkswagen, and sets off to do battle with the smog, traffic, and pollution. He gives up, and escapes to the countryside. He is confronted by a naked couple who offer him an apple and, in the only spoken line in the film, ask, "Care to join us?" Perhaps, as this film suggests, our many achievements have done little to improve the quality of life. Live action. (Produced by Tony Schmitz) ACI FILMS. 3 min. Color. Sound. 1971

TEA FOR ELSA
Weaves the tense violence of a murder-robbery in an art museum with the slow and deliberate pace of the museum charwoman, to create an expression of apathy and noninvolvement.
COUNTERPOINT. 10 min. B&W. Sound. 1971

THE TENDER GAME
An exercise in free association of popular music and popular images to the tune of "Tenderly" sung by Ella Fitzgerald, accompanied by Oscar Peterson. Animated by John Hubley and Faith Elliot.
McGRAW-HILL. 7 min. Color. Sound. 1958

THAT ALL MAY BE ONE
This multi-scene-image film is designed as a discussion starter. It concerns man's unity with his fellowmen against alienation, the arms race, poverty, prejudice, indifference, and inhumanity under the guise of some noble cause. Previewing is recommended for maximum success of discussion. (Produced by the United Churches of Canada)
SYRACUSE UNIV. 32 min. Color. Sound. 1970

THE TOP
A cartoon satire on man's pursuit of material wealth, by fair means and

foul. (Written, designed, and directed by Teru Murakami)
McGRAW-HILL. 8 min. Color. Sound. 1965

THE TRENDSETTER
A man strives for individuality by doing something different, and is continually imitated by a mindless crowd. In desperation he fakes his suicide. The crowd follows, and the man realizes that once the crowd is gone, the concept of individuality is meaningless. (Produced by Vera Linnecar)
PYRAMID. 6 min. Color. Sound

THE TRIP
Concerns the use of drugs. There is the purveyor—the exploiter—on one hand. And there are the users on the other—in this instance, a group of teenagers. They wonder if they should go on a "trip." They try to reassure themselves that there's nothing to fear, everything will be all right. At first they are enthused, but then the "trip" ends in disaster—although not for the purveyor; he goes scot-free. (Produced by Filmscope)
PERENNIAL ED. $3\frac{1}{2}$ min. Color. Sound

TUKTU AND THE BIG KAYAK
Tuktu impatiently watches his father and the kayak man build a kayak. He longs to cut wood and use the bow drill, but he is told to watch and learn. In the end, the kayak is finished, and Tuktu takes a ride on the kayak with his father. Stories of Tuktu series. (National Film Board of Canada)
FILMS INC. 14 min. Color. Sound. 1968

WHAT IF?
Here are four situations that are often difficult for children to cope with. These vicarious experiences

are ways for children to work out appropriate responses in advance, or to better understand why they responded as they did. Two typical situations are: a girl finds a wallet; a boy's ice cream cone is knocked out of his hand. Magic Moments series.
ENCYC. BRIT. 3 min. Color. Sound. 1969

8. FUN

Maybe it's time we stopped pretending that movies aren't fun. Some sort of guilt or hypocrisy seems to keep us from enjoying "educational" films fully and freely. There seems to be an unwritten proviso that some measure of learning must precede, accompany, or follow a nontheatrical picture, and that learning and enjoyment are mutually exclusive. (That's what gave "sugar-coating" a bad name!) Where or how that mentality originated, I won't venture answering. But I will recommend these 50-odd (the dash is optional) films as therapy for "the blahs." These are films for fun's sake ... films that any group can share and enjoy.

Isn't communal experience one of the strengths of the medium? And maybe a few minutes of guided dreaming will help ghetto children to do some dreaming of their own. Fun and games aren't part of the curriculum (yet), but they are part of life—a part that's been neglected too long. Only in recent years has "fun" become an adjective, e.g., a fun person, a fun place, Fun City. "Fun" is really not just short for "funny." It's closer to "surprising," "relaxed," "different." With those synonyms in mind, see the following films. See why they're called fun.

ART EXPERT
Three Candid Camera men are commenting on an abstract painting. They point out hypothetical boats, and onlookers always agree with these "experts." The Candid Camera men then notice that they have the wrong painting, or that it is upside down. The subjects change their opinions very readily, once the "experts" do. Demonstrates conformity and social influences on perception. Available only for purchase; no rentals.
CANDID CAMERA. 8 min. B&W. Sound

THE BELL (La Cloche)
A man waits for his girl beside a bell that is on display. A storm breaks out, and the man takes shelter under the bell. A barking dog brings the bell down on top of him, and when the girl arrives, he is nowhere to be seen. Annoyed, she walks off, leaving the man to extract himself from the bell, which proves more difficult than it looks. Some dialogue, in French. (Les Films de la Colombe) McGRAW-HILL. 15 min. B&W. Sound. 1964

A BOWL OF CHERRIES
A featurette in the style of the silent comedies. Relates the adventures of a cowboy in present-day Greenwich Village. "Our hero" arrives in the city anxious to become a good, if not great, artist. Will he find love, happiness, and fulfillment in this colorful but impoverished way of life? Some scenes are in color. Music. (Produced by George Edgar) McGRAW-HILL. 24 min. B&W/ Color. Sound

BOYNNG!
The aftermath of a two-car collision seems to be universal, as illustrated

in this French cartoon. The drivers
(represented by colored circles)
start to argue. A crowd gathers and
begins to quarrel. An ambulance
(white rectangle) carries away a witness who has fainted. The police
(black) arrive, and the witnesses
suddenly disappear. And so it goes.
Sound effects only; no narration or
dialogue. Rental only. (Artistic
direction by Jules Engel)
AUDIO/BRANDON. 8 min. Color.
Sound

CADET ROUSSELLE
Two-dimensional puppets animate
the old French folk song that origi-
nated as a satire on the affectations
of the period between the French
Revolution and the Napoleonic Era.
Cadet Rousselle falls down a ladder,
trips on battlements; even his dogs
will not obey him. (National Film
Board of Canada)
INT. FILM BUR. 6 min. Color.
Sound

A CHAIRY TALE
A fairy tale in the modern manner,
told without words by Norman
McLaren. This film is a kind of
ballet of a youth and a kitchen chair.
The young man tries to sit, but the
chair declines to be sat upon. The
ensuing struggle, first for mastery
and then for understanding, forms
the story. The music is by the
Indian musicians Ravi Shankar,
Chatur Lal, and Modu Mullick.
Seven awards, including British
Film Academy. (National Film
Board of Canada)
INT. FILM BUR. 10 min. B&W.
Sound. 1957

THE CLOWN
Nonverbal and with a musical score,
this film shows a clown trying to get
himself and his props together to
perform a trick. One of the props,
a fish, won't cooperate and the trick
doesn't come off until the fish takes
over everything, including the clown,
and rearranges it all to his own
liking. (Produced in Czechoslovakia)
CCM FILMS. 7 min. Color. Sound.
1969

CURIOSITY
A store window has been covered
except for a small open spot with
a sign over it saying, "Please do
not peek in here." Nobody resists
the temptation to look. Demonstrates curiosity and approach-
avoidance conflict. Not available for
rental; purchase only.
CANDID CAMERA. 6 min. B&W.
Silent

THE CURIOUS HABITS OF MAN
By their animal-like behavior,
adults at a cocktail party startle an
imaginative young boy. A woman's
hysterical laughter suddenly mingles
with the laughing call of a loon. A
human wolf is compared to a howling
wolf in the wild. A charging rhinoceros, a croaking frog, raucous
crows, a sloppy hippopotamus, are a
few of the animals that dramatize
some of the effects of excessive
drinking. (Produced by Dan Gibson)
A-V EXPLOR. 13 min. Color.
Sound. 1968

THE CURIOUS MOUSE
Paper collage animation is used in
this film to tell the story of a mouse
who sets out to explore the world.
He discovers Swiss cheese, eats
everything but the holes, and is
carried by them (turned into wheels)
to a mother duck who kicks him into
another adventure, which leads him
to another, and then a surprising
finale. (Produced by Seko Animations, Czechoslovakia)
CCM FILMS. 5 min. Color. Sound.
1969

DAY DREAMS
Charles Laughton and Elsa Lan-
chester, in a satire on a servant
girl's dream of glory, based on a
story by H. G. Wells. It introduces
the student to the characteristics
that distinguish film from the other
arts. Contains illustrations of the
essentials of montage, and illustrates
the advantages and disadvantages of
silent film. Sound speed: 23 min.

Silent speed: 34 min. (Directed by Ivor Montagu)
CCM FILMS. 34 min. B&W. Silent. 1928

DAY OF THE PAINTER
The "biography" of a work of modern art. A painter who knows how to make good in the contemporary market spends the day hurling, dripping, splashing, and spray-gunning paint onto a board. An art dealer chooses one segment that the painter has sawed off. The other parts of the masterpiece float down the stream with some puzzled gulls and swans. No narration. Awards: Academy Award, Best Live Action Short Subject; Best Fiction Short Subject, San Francisco. (A Little Movies, Inc. Prodution)
CCM FILMS. 14 min. Color. Sound. 1959

EAST LYNNE
Candid Camera hires messengers to deliver goods to a specific address. When a messenger comes to the door, he is pulled through the door and finds himself in the middle of a stage where a play is in progress. Some messengers pretend they are characters in the chorus, so as not to create embarrassment before the audience. Demonstrates role-playing and compliance. Purchase only; not available for rental.
CANDID CAMERA. 5 min. B&W. Sound

ENTER HAMLET
With questionable relevance, each word of Hamlet's soliloquy is given its own picture. A multitude of visual puns. Pop art. (A New Janus Cinema Film by Fred Mogubgub)
PYRAMID. 4 min. Color. Sound. 1967

ERSATZ
This film by the Yugoslav animator Dusan Vukotic is about a man whose whole world, even his woman, is inflatable. One of the Yugoslav shorts chosen for inclusion in the Museum of Modern Art's program of films. (Produced by Zagreb Animation Studios)
McGRAW-HILL. 8 min. Color. Sound. 1961

FACE THE REAR
Subjects in an elevator watch three Candid Camera employees enter and face the rear of the car. When a majority of three face the rear, the pressure on the subject to conform is overwhelming. The last subject turns in unison with the group, and even removes his hat when the others do. Demonstrates conformity to group pressure. Available for purchase; no rentals.
CANDID CAMERA. 4 min. B&W. Sound

FIDDLE-DE-DEE
A film of dancing music and dancing color. To "Listen to the Mocking Bird" by an old-time fiddler, patterns ripple, flow, flicker, and blend. The artist, painting on film, translates sound into sight. Five awards, including Brussels and Rome. (National Film Board of Canada)
INT. FILM BUR. $3\frac{1}{2}$ min. Color. Sound. 1948

FILM
Written by Samuel Beckett, starring Buster Keaton. Beckett's only venture into the film medium. It is a one-character production without dialogue, based on Berkeley's theory that "to be is to be perceived."
As in all of Beckett's work, elements of comedy surround the philosophical foundation.
GROVE PRESS. 22 min. B&W. Sound

FIXED BOWLING
A bowling alley is rigged to produce strikes regardless of where the ball is thrown. Candid Camera sees to it that wives and children get strikes all the time, while husbands and parents watch with disbelief. Facial expressions denote surprise and mirth in the beginning, but grad-

ually change to contempt as the event
keeps recurring. Demonstrates
reaction to an apparent but false
cause-effect relationship. Purchase
only; not available for rental.
CANDID CAMERA. 5 min. B&W.
Silent

FOOTBALL FOLLIES
The humorous side of pro football,
captured in slow motion with appropriate sound effects and music.
NFL FILMS. 25 min. Color. Sound

THE GENERAL
The title refers to a locomotive, and
the story is essentially a true one—
the tale of the daring Civil War raid
led by Capt. Anderson, a Northern
spy who penetrated Southern lines to
steal a locomotive and to wreck communications. Massive chases,
counter-chases, and a climactic
battle scene that intermingles humorous situations. One of the last
great silent comedies. Starring
Buster Keaton and Marion Mack;
directed by Keaton.
MANBECK. 31 min. B&W. Silent.
1927

THE GREAT TOY ROBBERY
A Western cartoon starring the
world's most wanted good guy—Santa
Claus, alias Father Christmas, alias
Kris Kringle, alias St. Nicholas.
When he is ambushed, the very
cactus wilts for shame and the dry
gulch gulps. But a hero heaves into
sight. His guitar proves more
potent than his pistol, and Santa's
snatched toy is returned. Award:
American Film Festival. (National
Film Board of Canada)
McGRAW-HILL. 7 min. Color.
Sound. 1963

HAPPY ANNIVERSARY
France's Pierre Etaix directed and
acted in this portrayal of a man trying to reach home to celebrate his
wedding anniversary. Etaix presents, without words, the humorous
but frustrating plight of the husband
who encounters delay after delay in

Paris traffic. Awards: First Prize
at the West German Short Film
Festival and an Academy Award for
Live Action Short.
INT. FILM BUR. 13 min. B&W.
Sound. 1961

INTERNATIONAL SUITCASE
This film (made in America,
France, Germany, and England)
involves a suitcase filled with materials weighing several hundred
pounds. A Candid Camera woman
asks men passing by to assist her
by carrying it to the corner. The
men try desperately to carry the
valise but few of them can even lift
it. Demonstrates cross-cultural
differences in gallantry. Available
only for purchase; no rentals.
CANDID CAMERA. 5 min. B&W.
Silent

JAZZOO
Photographed at the St. Louis Zoo,
this version for children joins images and jazz to create moods,
shapes, and textures. Here is the
beauty of the zoo, and the grace,
dignity, and humor of its denizens.
Awards: CINE, American Film
Festival, Atlanta, Venice, San Francisco, Teheran. Library version:
18 min.; classroom version: 13 min.
ACI FILMS. 13/18 min. Color.
Sound. 1968

JOACHIM'S DICTIONARY
(Le Dictionnaire de Joachim)
In a rhythm of one gag for each
idea, one idea for each drawing,
and one drawing for each word,
Walerian Borowczyk, animated-
film creator, makes good on the
film's subtitle, "Un film distractif,"
whether you translate it "disturb-
ing" or "diverting." Highly sophisticated adult alphabet. No
dialogue or commentary. Music.
CCM FILMS. 9 min. Color. Sound.
1965

JOIN HANDS, LET GO!
A group of children joins hands,
skips, and sings a catchy game song,

"Join Hands, Let Go!" Each time the children let go, the scene cuts to a comedian performing an action that ends unexpectedly. For instance, a "conductor" waving a baton turns out to be directing not an orchestra, but a phonograph. Magic Moments series.
ENCYC. BRIT. 8 min. Color. Sound. 1969

KEY PEOPLE
Seven everyday city people and their activities. This essay without words was produced by a filmmaker who selects moments during which individuals perform the daily routine of entering and leaving their homes, and so give an impression of their modes of life. Music. (Produced by Gerald Plano)
FILM IMAGES. 5 min. Color. Sound

THE KIND-HEARTED ANT
Based on a traditional Yugoslavian children's song, this cartoon tells the story of a kind-hearted ant who unintentionally disrupts the harmony and order of the ant hill. Animated. Award: First Prize, Venice Film Festival. (Produced by Zagreb Film)
McGRAW-HILL. 10 min. Color. Sound. 1965

KOSMODROME 1999
The year is 1999 and interstellar travel has become so common-place that every family has its own rocket ship. The ships, however, are no more dependable than today's automobiles. The family we view trying to set off to visit Grandma in (or on?) another planet has all the same Rube Goldberg problems that the modern, auto-driving public faces. Animated. (Produced by Short Films Studios, Prague)
CCM FILMS. 12 min. Color. Sound. 1969

LE MERLE
Norman McLaren imparts activity to an old French-Canadian nonsense song. Simple white cutouts on pastel background provide illustrations as the song relates how a blackbird loses parts of his body one by one and then regains them two- and three-fold. The folk song, "Mon Merle," is sung in French. Awards: Brussels, New York, Spain, Uruguay. (National Film Board of Canada)
INT. FILM BUR. 4 min. Color. Sound. 1958

MAITRE
A satire on the problems faced by the artist in contemporary society. Our protagonist is rejected by art galleries, is chased by dogs and by gunshot. Concludes with applause, photographs, and cash-register sounds as our artist is finally recognized. Original music instead of narration. Animated.
SIM PROD. 12 min. Color. Sound. 1970

A MAN'S HANDS
Hands—squeezing, poking, scratching, fixing, zipping, playing, and touching. Alternately funny and informative. Live action. (Produced by Paul Prokop)
PYRAMID. 5 min. Color. Sound. 1970

MR. KOUMAL CARRIES THE TORCH
The subject of this series of episodes, involving an optimistic idea-man thwarted at every turn, is human nature and man's relationship to his environment and his fellow men. Mr. Koumal series. (Produced in Czechoslovakia)
SIM PROD. 2 min. Color. Sound. 1969

ORPHEON
Animated circles and the use of voice-tone and inflection convey images and the idea of words. The basic idea is nonverbal communication. The background is a park; the circles represent musicians

and a drum major. A minor mishap
and many situations occur. (Produced in France)
McGRAW-HILL. 8 min. Color.
Sound. 1966

THE PENNY ARCADE
(Captain Flash vs. The Bat)
A "pop" divertissement, alternat-
ing realistic scenes and comic-book
adventures with dialogue in balloons.
An unsuccessful cartoonist, who
works as a portrait artist in a penny
arcade, lives a fantasy life through
his comic strip. There is interplay
between his real world and his
comic strip. No dialogue. Music.
(Produced by H. Hurwitz)
CCM FILMS. 45 min. B&W. Sound.
1965

PITTSBURGH MUSICAL COPS
Candid Camera filmed a policeman
directing traffic in Pittsburgh, and
added music to go along with his
motions as he scolds, encourages,
and pleads with pedestrians and
motorists. This sequence is an example of nonverbal communication
and is a training device for showing
creative problem-solving skills.
Available for purchase; no rentals.
CANDID CAMERA. 2½ min. B&W.
Sound

POLLUTION
Satirist Tom Lehrer sings Calypso
lyrics while camera exposes evi-
dence of widespread pollution.
NAT. MED. AV. 4 min. Color.
Sound. 1968

POOL SHARKS
W. C. Fields' first film. Centers on
the comic rivalry between two men
for the hand of the heroine. (A Janus
Film)
PYRAMID. 14 min. B&W. Silent.
1915

POP SHOW
Originally made as a pilot for a TV
series, this is an assemblage of
animated snatches, live-action se-

quences, old film clips, and stills—
all depicting what is and is not "hip"
in New York's jet set. Includes
Harlow, Cagney, the Peppermint
Lounge, Statue of Liberty, Ringo
Starr—punctuated by scenes of a
smiling model, sampling her bever-
age commodities. (Produced by
Fred Mogubgub)
PYRAMID. 8 min. Color. Sound.
1966

POPPYCOCK!
The story of Everyman, a portly hero
locked in combat—struggling to re-
gain his girl from the clutches of a
handsome aristocrat. The actors are
live, but the rules are those of the
cartoon. With music. Awards: CINE
Golden Eagle; Edinburgh Film Festival; Venice Film Festival. (Produced by Carson Davidson)
McGRAW-HILL. 16 min. Color.
Sound. 1965

POW WOW
Using long-focus lenses in concealed
cameras, two photographers on the
faculty of the University of Minne-
sota filmed this record of a rainy
rehearsal of the university band.
Result: a document of contemporary campus mores, with moments
of surrealism and others of Mack
Sennett. Award: San Francisco;
Robert J. Flaherty. (Photographed
and edited by Allen Downs and
Jerome Leibling)
CCM FILMS. 7 min. B&W. Sound.
1960

THE PROBLEM
An animated puppet film that centers
on the question of what color the
trash box in a large organization
should be painted. As this decision
is passed upward through employees,
officers, and finally the chairman
of the board, it grows larger and
more important. The film examines
the dehumanizing effect of bureaucracies, and raises questions on the
nature of responsibility and the individual. No narration; music and

sound effects. (Produced by Jan
Dudesek)
CCM FILMS. 12 min. Color. Sound.
1966

QUEER BIRDS
Two odd-looking pelicans, one large,
one small, make their way across
the landscape. They meet and conquer imposing obstacles and situations that are reminiscent of the
traditional Hollywood cartoon. (Directed by Vladimir Lehky; drawn
by Jiri Toman)
McGRAW-HILL. 10 min. B&W.
Sound. 1965

THE RAILRODDER
Buster Keaton, as "the railrodder,"
crosses Canada on a railway track
speeder. The film is full of sight
gags as Keaton putt-putts his way to
British Columbia. Not a word is
spoken, and Keaton is as spry and
ingenious as he was in the days of
the silent slapsticks. Awards: Canadian; Berlin; Brussels; Venice;
New York. (National Film Board of
Canada)
McGRAW-HILL. 25 min. Color.
Sound

RED AND BLACK
A parody of a bullfight provides the
setting for children to let their
imaginations run wild. Animation
and live action, plot twists, and
Spanish music create a springboard
to activities in art, writing, and oral
expression.
STERLING. 7 min. Color. Sound.
1965

THE RIDE
A slapstick comedy in the manner of
the old favorites. Directed and acted
by Gerald Potterton, a film animator
who plays chauffeur to a portly, eccentric business tycoon. Filmed in
the winter playground of the Laurentians, this tale moves faster than
life itself. (National Film Board of
Canada)
McGRAW-HILL. 7 min. Color.
Sound. 1965

A SCRAP OF PAPER
AND A PIECE OF STRING
Creates human aspects of friendship between inanimate objects,
while pointing out the importance and
utility of paper and string in our
economy. Original score of Dixieland jazz. Produced in special
string animation by John Korty for
the NBC Exploring series.
McGRAW-HILL. 6 min. Color.
Sound. 1963

THE SCRIBE
The last film made by this genius of
pantomime uses the Buster Keaton
comic style to drive home a serious
message for construction safety and
accident prevention. Lively slapstick when he visits a big construction job as a "newspaper reporter"
to do a story on construction safety.
AIM/ASSN. 30 min. Color. Sound

SQUARES
Candid Camera puts up a sign read-
ing "Please Walk on Black Tiles
Only" in a shoe store with a black
and white tile floor. People go out
of their way to avoid stepping on the
white tiles. Some of them seem to
enjoy it; others look annoyed.
Demonstrates obedience to authority.
No rentals; purchase only.
CANDID CAMERA. 3 min. B&W.
Silent

SUNDAY LARK
What happens when a little girl gets
into a large office on Sunday? Six-
year-old Stella Sun wanders into a
skyscraper and into the silent offices of a New York stock brokerage.
With an original score (appropriate
electronic music accompanies the
big IBM sequence) and no dialogue,
this adventure of a child in the world
of business turns into a romp.
Awards: Berlin Film Festival;
CINE Golden Eagle; U.S. Official
Entry, Edinburgh Film Festival.
(Produced by Sanford Semel)
McGRAW-HILL. 12 min. B&W.
Sound. 1963

TILLIE'S PUNCTURED ROMANCE
Based on "Tillie's Nightmare" by
Edgar Smith. With Charles Chaplin,
Marie Dressler, and Mabel Nor-
mand in the film that marked Chaplin's debut as a major star. One of
the earliest feature comedies, this
Keystone contains both slapstick and
sentiment. With insert titles. (Produced and directed by Mack Sennett)
CCM FILMS. 43 min. B&W. Silent.
1914

TWO
Antonioni and Fellini "art films" are
attacked in this parody. A man and a
woman meet on a classic ocean
beach, he rather suave and she at-
tired in a flowing gown. After some
symbolic (?) horseplay, they engage
in conversation—in ersatz Italian
(with a word or two of Yiddish)
rendered succinctly in English subtitles. Preview recommended. (Directed by Robert Bean, written by
Renee Taylor)
CCM FILMS. 9 min. Color. Sound.
1967

WALKING
The humor and individuality of various styles of walking—and, by extension, various styles of living—
are accented by a rock music score,
the sole "commentary" of the film.
Animated line drawings, color wash,
and watercolor sketches capture
movement and the personalities behind the walk. Preview recommended. Awards: Academy Award
Nominee; Film Festival Awards:
Chicago, Toronto, Barcelona, Krakov, LaPlata, Rio de Janeiro. (National Film Board of Canada)
LEARN. CORP. 5 min. Color.
Sound. 1968

9. ACTION

"Lights! Camera! Action!" The chief characteristic of a motion picture—the something that separates it from all other media—shows up in its name: motion. Even the word "cinema" comes from the Greek word for motion. In this section you'll find films that record, as only films can, man's love of physical motion in the form of sport. The exhilaration people draw from watching or participating in any sport, from individual challenges to team endeavors, from the brutality of buzkashi or bullfighting to the nameless games of children, can be better expressed by films than by any other means short of reality.

And action, like the nonverbal film, is a sort of international language. The games of the Pushtu and Eskimo, of the Russians and Chinese, will in all probability seem more familiar than foreign to their viewers. Sports are a joy common to all the members of the human family. Perhaps sports, rather than war, will finally become the outlet for man's aggressive impulses.

AIRBORN
Uses bilateral configurations of real images such as planes, divers, and birds that alternately diverge and converge, giving the impression of flight or explosion. Begins and ends with the same full-view shot of an approaching plane. Awards: Aspen and National Student Association. (Produced by Charles Windham) PYRAMID. 4 min. Color. Sound. 1970

BOYS' GAMES (Pushtu)
An ancient game known throughout Asia is played by Pushtu boys. The toughness of these rugged young men, as well as the value these tribal people place on physical superiority, is demonstrated. Mountain People of Central Asia series.
IFF (BRYAN). 5 min. Color. Sound. 1968

BUZKASHI (Afghan Tribes)
This once-forbidden sport is performed on horseback by the tribes of Afghanistan. Fierce tribesmen honor the King by competing at the week-long annual festival. Buzkashi is one of the toughest sports in the world, requiring incredible riding ability. The intense pride and rivalry of a tribal society, as well as the role of physical superiority and competition, are implicit. No narration; natural soundtrack. Festivals Around the World series.
IFF (BRYAN). 8 min. Color. Sound. 1968

CATCH THE JOY
Filters and slow-motion photography add a subjective mood as dune buggies speed over desert sands. No narration. Awards: winner of Atlanta and Hemisfilm Festivals. PYRAMID. 14 min. Color. Sound. 1970

CHOOSING UP
The children in this film choose up for different games in different ways.

After each choosing sequence, the game involved is shown in a speeded-up version. The film provides a variety of discussion topics: the reasons for choosing up, the fairest ways to do so, how the ways that class members use are similar to or different from the ways shown on the screen. Magic Moments series.
ENCYC. BRIT. 6 min. Color. Sound. 1969

CLAP!
A boy walks through a park clapping his hands—and recruits a passerby to clap with him. A group of school children yells and claps with abandon. These situations, and others depicted in the film, may help children better understand clapping as a way of having fun and a way of expressing appreciation. Magic Moments series.
ENCYC. BRIT. 5 min. Color. Sound. 1969

CORRAL
The film uses close-up scenes to show the unharnessed dignity of an animal running free, its instinctive protest when haltered, and its reluctant submission when man becomes master. Movement and music tell a story without words, as a cowboy performs a task that is part of a centuries-old tradition. Five awards, including First Prize, Documentary Category, International Film Festival, Venice. (National Film Board of Canada)
INT. FILM BUR. 11½ min. B&W. Sound. 1954

CORRIDA INTERDITE
(Forbidden Bullfight)
A slow-motion study of the majesty, precision, grace, and danger of the Spanish bullfight. (Denys Columb de Daunant)
PYRAMID. 10 min. Color. Sound. 1958

THE EMPTY HAND
Karate, which means "empty hand" in Japanese, is the subject. Photo-graphed at a karate school in New York, "The Empty Hand" shows black-belt instructors demonstrating the art of defending oneself without weapons, but by striking an attacker with hands, elbows, knees, or feet. Sound track comprised of the traditional karate yells and the grunts and blows of physical impact. (A Stephen Verona Film)
ACI FILMS. 10 min. B&W. Sound. 1968

FANTASY OF FEET
Feet walk, dance, run, jump, hop, wear sandals, flippers, slippers, boots, wooden shoes, and no shoes at all. A pair of cowboy boots does a lively square dance. About the kinds of shoes there are, why there are so many, how feet serve different functions. Magic Moments series.
ENCYC. BRIT. 8 min. Color. Sound. 1969

FLY AWAY
Scenes of birds and kites, gliders and model airplanes help capture the feeling of freedom in flight. The viewer flies away in a small plane and observes the earth from a detached vantage point. Useful for language art activities. No narration or dialogue but with natural sounds and music. (Produced by Stanton Films)
DOUBLEDAY. 11 min. Color. Sound. 1967

FOLLOW ME
Shows children playing follow-the-leader along the streets of their neighborhood and through a playground. Follow-the-leader is a rewarding game, since it involves children first in following unquestioningly and then being barred from the game for not following exactly. Magic Moments series.
ENCYC. BRIT. 5 min. Color. Sound. 1969

FOOTBALL FOLLIES
The humorous side of pro football,
captured in slow motion with appropriate sound effects and music.
NFL FILMS. 25 min. Color. Sound

GATE 73
A collage of airports, hangers, and
airplane interiors and exteriors is
complemented by jet engine noise,
terminal hubbub, and communications between pilots and ground control. Traffic streaming into the airport, baggage transported on con-
veyor belts, engineers checking instruments ... all suggest the complex, technological efficiencies required for operation of modern
planes. Climaxes with shots of the
Boeing 747 jet. (Produced by Michael Bloebaum for Pyramid Films)
HOLT R&W. 13 min. Color. Sound.
1970

THE GENERAL
The title refers to a locomotive, and
the story is essentially a true one—
the tale of the daring Civil War raid
led by Capt. Anderson, a Northern
spy who penetrated Southern lines to
steal a locomotive and to wreck communications. Massive chases, counter-chases, and a climactic battle
scene that intermingles humorous
situations. One of the last great silent comedies. Buster Keaton and
Marion Mack. Directed by Keaton.
MANBECK. 31 min. B&W. Silent.
1927

GET WET
Water—limpid, cool, enticing, and
effervescent—and the people who
enjoy it. Music and photography
highlight the splashing, bubbling,
foaming water as it responds to
swimmer, diver, and water skier.
(National Film Board of Canada)
PYRAMID. 9 min. Color. Sound

THE GOAL
A French basketball team in action.
An impressionistic interpretation of
the game itself, almost a basketball
ballet. Employs slow motion, jump

cutting, and angles to convey the
poetry and drama of the game.
Award: International Competition of
Athletic Films, Cortina, Italy. (Pro-
duced by Dominique Delouche)
McGRAW-HILL. 10 min. Color.
Sound. 1969

GYMNASTIC FLASHBACKS
Through photography of the Olympic
Games and the United States World
Cup, milestones in gymnastics are
shown from over fifty years ago
through the present day. The simple
gymnastics of the 1920s are contrasted with today's sophisticated
techniques. Men and women perform
their specialties—acrobatics, floor
exercises, vaulting, rings, parallel
and horizontal bars, and balance
beam. Musical accompaniment and,
where appropriate, slow-motion
photography. (Produced by David
Adams of Pyramid Films)
HOLT R&W. 9 min. Color. Sound.
1970

HANG TEN
A surfing ballet, cut to an original
rock score. Film editor Ken Rudolph
finds a congruity between the ballet
dancer and the surfer. Techniques
include split screen, back motion,
looping, variable speeds, and posi-
tive-negative intercutting. Award:
CINE Golden Eagle. (Produced by
David Adams)
PYRAMID. 10 min. Color. Sound.
1970

HIGHWAY
Hilary Harris photographed this film
from the wheel of an automobile. It
evokes a sense of exhilaration one
might receive when driving, using
every tempo from slow to fast. Rock
music. Award: Prize-winner, Brussels Experimental Film Festival.
FILM IMAGES. 6 min. Color.
Sound

IF KANGAROOS JUMP
WHY CAN'T YOU?
The film is motivational, showing the
value of jumping rope for anyone,

any age, any place, any time. Useful
for physical education, health and
recreation courses; useful, also, to
stimulate creative writing. A nonnarrative film, containing a rhythmic original musical score.
ATLANTIS. 8 min. Color. Sound.
1971

IMAGE OF A RACE
The slalom course provides the setting for an exploration of a competi-
tive event. Cinematic devices such
as multiple printing, freeze-framing,
and single frame editing provide the
approximation of a racer's mental
activity during prerace equipment
preparation, spectator interactions,
starting-gate trauma, and finally, the
race itself. (Produced by Lenny
Aitken)
THORNE FILMS. $3\frac{1}{2}$ min. Color.
Sound. 1971

JEFF SETS SAIL
A 10-year-old boy rigs his sailboat
and sets out on a voyage in a Florida
bay. No narration. (Filmed by
Ronald Floethe of Gordon-Kerckhoff
Productions)
ACI FILMS. 10 min. Color. Sound.
1971

L'HOMME VITE
This study of auto racing includes a
ride under race conditions—eyes
glued to the road, engines roaring,
cars gripping the curves. Begins
with preparations and the start in
Montreal. The film has no commentary but has French titles.
Award: International Competition of
Films on Sports, Cortina d'Am-
pezzo, Italy.
NAT. FILM BD. 9 min. Color.
Sound

MOEBIUS FLIP
Skiers find the world has flip-flopped
onto the other side of reality, and
they have to do this flip ski maneuver
to flop it back again. Awards: Edinburgh, Kranj, Trent, Venice, U.S. Industrial Film Festival. (A Summit
Production)
PYRAMID. 25 min. Color. Sound.
1969

MOODS OF SURFING
An exploration of the sensual de-
lights, humor, and danger of the
sport. Awards: International Sports
Film Festival in Cortina, Italy;
Photographic Society of America.
PYRAMID. 15 min. Color. Sound.
1967

NEUF MINUTES
Nine minutes of wrestling, filmed at
the Quebec Winter Games. In this
tangle of legs and arms and twisted
torsos, viewers will see the dex-
terity with which the two contenders
are able to extricate themselves
from seemingly impossible holds.
Though the title appears in French,
the film is without commentary and
requires no interpretation.
NAT. FILM BD. 9 min. Color.
Sound

1968 WOMEN'S OLYMPIC
COMPULSORY ROUTINES
Featuring Olympic star Linda Meth-
eny. Presents the Japanese and
French interpretation of the 1968
women's Olympic compulsory rou-
tines.
ATHLETIC. 10 min. Color.
Silent. 1968

POPSICLE
The film has no narration. Its moods
and purpose come from the motorcycles themselves. Music: a blend of
rhythm and sound effects played
through the Moog Synthesizer.
Award: CINE Golden Eagle. (Produced by Rohloff)
AMERICAN ED. 11 min. Color.
Sound. 1969

POW WOW
Using long-focus lenses in concealed
cameras, two photographers on the
faculty of the University of Minne-

sota filmed this record of a rainy rehearsal of the university band. Result: a document of contemporary
campus mores, with moments of surrealism and others of Mack Sennett.
Award: San Francisco; Robert J.
Flaherty. (Photographed and edited
by Allen Downs and Jerome Leibling)
CCM FILMS. 7 min. B&W. Sound.
1960

PSYCHEDELIC WET
Water—on top of it, in it, under it—
is the setting for an experience that
can be used in a class on "involve-
ment." The visual patterns may
stimulate expression in writing or in
graphic arts. The film can be shown
with its sound track first, and then
students can select other music that
they feel fits. Awards: American
Film Festival; CINE Golden Eagle;
Milan Trophy, Best Film. (A Homer
Groening Film)
ACI FILMS. 8 min. Color. Sound.
1967

QUEBEC WINTER CARNIVAL
The traditional activities of this annual event in French-speaking Canada. Includes scenes of recent
parades, ice sculpture contests, and
toboggan races.
CANADA. 10 min. Color. Sound.
1969

RAPIDS OF THE COLORADO
A trip down the dangerous rapids of
the Grand Canyon's Colorado River.
Photographed from a raft, the camera takes in the beauty of the river
and the famous canyon through which
it flows.
PYRAMID. 15 min. Color. Sound.
1970

THE RIDE
A slapstick comedy in the manner of
the old favorites. Directed and
acted in by Gerald Potterton, a film
animator who plays chauffeur to a
portly, eccentric business tycoon.
Filmed in the winter playground of
the Laurentians, this tale moves fas-

ter than life itself. (National Film
Board of Canada)
McGRAW-HILL. 7 min. Color.
Sound. 1965

THE RINK
A visit to a typical Canadian open-
air skating rink to watch children of
all ages learning and enjoying the
fun of skating. No narration; background music adds to the rhythm
and color of the skaters. (National
Film Board of Canada)
McGRAW-HILL. 10 min. Color.
Sound. 1963

SAHARA FANTASIA:
A DESERT FESTIVAL
As nomadic desert tribes converge
in Southern Morocco to celebrate
their "moussem," the viewer is immersed in this unique Saharan festival—its tribal dancing and frenzied
music, colorful tents of trade, and
the celebration of the "fantasia,"
a traditional event combining the
precision of ancient musketry with
skilled horsemanship.
IFF (BRYAN). 9 min. Color. Sound.
1970

SAILING
The beauty and drama of nature as
experienced through the sport of
sailing. A visual essay. (Produced
by Hattum Hoving [The Netherlands];
photographed by Pim Heytman)
McGRAW-HILL. 15 min. Color.
Sound. 1963

SKATER DATER
An account of a young boy's emergence into adolescence—when he
gives up his skateboard for the company of a young girl. Film festival
awards: Cannes, Edinburgh, Moscow, Cortina, and many more. (Produced by Noel Black)
PYRAMID. 18 min. Color. Sound.
1965

SKI FEVER
Skiing is beauty, sport, and folly.
The scenes in this nonnarrated film

include ski jumping by children, after-ski "swimming" on skis, slalom racing, tracking in deep powder, and even a small avalanche. After seeing the film, both skiers and nonskiers will be engaged by the question, "Why do people do it?" (A Terril LeMoss Film)
BFA ED. MEDIA. 9 min. Color. Sound. 1971

SKI THE OUTER LIMITS
Photographed at key ski spots, it shows the style, control, and balance required to push toward the outer limits of one's ability. Downhill racing, slaloms, ski dancing, and acrobatics are some of the limit-pushing demonstrations of this aerial ballet. Winner of numerous awards here and abroad. (Produced by Summit Films)
PYRAMID. 25 min. Color. Sound. 1968

SKY CAPERS
The graceful gymnastics of a group of daredevil skydivers during many thousands of feet of free fall. As the ground rushes up, the gaily colored parachutes open and safe landings are made. Filmed by Carl Boenish who jumped with the divers and fell alongside them, photographing their "capers" all the way to the ground. Awards: Prize of the President of the Republic, Grenoble; Diploma of Honor, Cortina, Italy.
PYRAMID. 15 min. Color. Sound. 1968

SOLO
Filmed from Mexico to Canada, this film shows the joys of solo mountain climbing—the rhythm of persistent physical effort, the scenes of beauty, and the joy that comes with each solution to a difficult situation. (Produced by Mike Hoover)
PYRAMID. 15 min. Color. Sound. 1971

STUDY IN WET
A film in which all the pictures and all the sounds come from water. The sound track is a musical score made by drops of water; the photography is of still water, ripples, waves, great breakers. Surfers, swimmers, water skiers appear and disappear. Awards: American Film Festival; CINE Golden Eagle. (Homer Groening)
ACI FILMS. 7 min. Color. Sound. 1965

SUMMER RENDEZVOUS
Using aspects of a track and field meet, this film makes some unspoken observations about the nature of human endeavor and achievement. Background music, ranging from Handel to the Swingle Singers, enhances the camera work. Excerpts of spoken French. Award: Chicago International Film Festival.
UNIVERSAL ED. 30 min. Color. Sound. 1969

SURF!
A film on the beauty and colors of the sea and the thrills of the surf. An impression of waves and sun. No narration. Awards: CINE Golden Eagle and the National Visual Presentations Award, Best Musical Score. (Homer Groening)
AMERICAN ED. 13 min. Color. Sound. 1969

SURFBOARDS, SKATEBOARDS, AND BIG, BIG WAVES
From Ala Moana to Anaheim, this film moves with the speed of surfers and skateboarders, flashes from action to action, from wave to wheelie. (Homer Groening)
AMERICAN ED. 10 min. Color. Sound. 1970

T'AI CHI CH'UAN
The Chinese art of "T'ai Chi Ch'uan" is a series of orderly, balanced exercises in a definite and traditional sequence. Philosophically comparable to the Yoga system of seeking inner peace with the universe; physically analogous to boxing or the dance. Performed by Professor Nan Huau-Chin. Filmed in

Taiwan (Formosa). Nonverbal, with
electronic sound effects and music.
Approved by the American Federation of Art.
DAVENPORT. 9 min. Color. Sound.
1970

TAKE-OFF
A condensed version of "Ski the
Outer Limits." A tightly edited mosaic of mid-air acrobatics, fast-
motion shenanigans and slow-motion
somersaults.
PYRAMID. 10 min. Color. Sound.
1969

TUKTU AND THE CARIBOU HUNT
When the caribou cross the small
lakes to reach new grazing ground,
the Eskimos hunt the animals from
their kayaks. Tuktu's father has bad
luck with his hunting and a caribou
escapes his spear. But we see him
bringing home a caribou. The film
ends with an outdoor fire and everyone enjoying a feast. Stories of
Tuktu series. (National Film Board
of Canada)
FILMS INC. 14 min. Color. Sound.
1968

TUKTU AND THE MAGIC BOW
Eskimos in far-off times used bows
and arrows for hunting. We see a
bow being made and how the Eskimos
practice their shooting skill by aim-
ing arrows at snow men and snow
bears. Tuktu's father proves himself the best at this test of hunting
skill. Stories of Tuktu series. (National Film Board of Canada)
FILMS INC. 14 min. Color. Sound.
1968

TUKTU AND
THE TRIALS OF STRENGTH
Strong and hardy Eskimo hunters

demonstrate and test their strength
in Eskimo boxing, tug-of-war, and
other strenuous activities. We see
and hear the Eskimo drum dance, a
demonstration of Eskimo poetry and
rhythm. Stories of Tuktu series.
(National Film Board of Canada)
FILMS INC. 14 min. Color. Sound.
1968

TURNED ON
With each high point synchronized to
a drum beat, this film is a quick-cut
montage of dune buggies, speedboats,
snowmobiles, and motorcycles. Im-
plies that the capabilities of the human body in motion are the greatest
"turn-on" of all. Edited by Ken Rudolph. (Produced by David Adams)
PYRAMID. 7 min. Color. Sound.
1969

VOLLEYBALL
An encounter between Russian and
American teams, presented more as
an essay in the choreography of
movements than a play-by-play report of a sports event. Camera
tricks dramatize the action, notably
through stop-motion that freezes the
ballet-like leaps and postures of the
players. Jazz background music.
Award: Moscow. (National Film
Board of Canada)
UNIVERSAL ED. 10 min. B&W.
Sound. 1967

WORKOUT
An impressionistic study of the relationship between horse and rider
during an early morning workout in
training for the Olympics. Electronic music.
AUSTRALIA. 9 min. B&W. Sound.
1967

10. WAR AND PEACE

Don't expect to find conventional "war films" here. Far from it. In fact, most of these messages treat their subject allegorically. You'll see very little, if any, "stock footage" from World Wars I, II, their interim blood-sheddings or sequels. Such documentation is now so familiar that we've become almost immune to its impact. The heroes and villains of such reports are usually in uniform, right in the thick of things, and somehow seem resigned to (if not enthusiastic about) the lethal role their government has assigned them.

Other war films—these "War and Peace" films—show us a different set of protagonists: the noncombatant women, children, and old men on both sides of the figurative DMZ. Still another style of screen war, like many listed here, regards war as interpersonal rather than international. These films study one-to-one polarizations ("Neighbors," for example) and nonmilitary confrontations ("Police Power: Right to Assembly"). Technicalities aside, these productions are about war in its broadest sense. It should surprise no one to find that all of them are antiwar. It has been said that war is too important to be left to the generals. Clearly, filmmakers agree.

THE ADMIRAL
An old admiral imagines he is in command of a sea battle. However, all his ships are defeated, and nothing is left for him but to commit suicide. After the shot, sea water gushes out through the armchair admiral's head.
STERLING. 6 min. Color. Sound. 1970

AI! (Love)
Shows the man-woman relationship as a bitter struggle, with the male in the underdog position. Animated by Yoji Kuri. (A Janus New Cinema Film)
PYRAMID. 4 min. Color. Sound. 1964

THE BALLAD OF CROWFOOT
Made by a member of National Film Board of Canada film crew composed of Canadian Indians, this film recalls some of the tragic incidents their people suffered at the hands of the white man. Illustrations and photographs are from private and public archives. Words and music of the song that forms the film's commentary are by Willie Dunn, the filmmaker. (National Film Board of Canada)
McGRAW-HILL. 10 min. B&W. Sound. 1970

BASIC TRAINING
Opens with a group of army recruits arriving at Fort Knox, Kentucky, dressed in a diversity of styles and with a variety of attitudes. The film ends with the same group, nine weeks later, marching smartly in a parade for their graduation exercises. Without commentary. (Produced by Frederick Wiseman)
ZIPPORAH FILMS. 98 min. B&W. Sound. 1971

THE CHESS GAME
A wordless film about the futility of
violent revolution. Utilizing stop-
motion technique, the film brings
chess pieces to life. The battles that
take place illustrate massacre, revolt, and change in position, with
pawns replacing aristocracy in
power. The message—the new
regime is autocratic, oppressive,
and violent; seizure of political
power by force is not the answer.
CENTRON. 7 min. Color. Sound.
1970

CHICKAMAUGA
This adaptation of Ambrose Bierce's
short story creates a symbolic world
of the horrors of war as a little boy
wanders away from home, reaches a
battlefield, plays soldier among the
dead and dying, and returns home
to find his house burned and his
family slain. Directed by Robert
Enrico. Award: Winner, San Sebastian Film Festival.
McGRAW-HILL. 33 min. B&W.
Sound. 1961

CHROMOPHOBIA
Without words, this film uses animation and music to tell a tale of the
victory of the free spirit. An army
attempts to impose its rule on a free
society. The attempt is symbolized
by the draining of color from everything—converting buildings to pris-
ons, colorful balloons to black balls
and chains, and people to black-and-
white striped prisoners. A girl nur-
tures one red flower, however, and
from this color and spirit the people
restore their free, color-filled
world. (Produced in Belgium)
INT. FILM BUR. 11 min. Color.
Sound. 1968

CHRONOLOGY
A concise survey of western civilization from prehistoric times to the
modern era, allowing viewers to
draw their own conclusions as to
the eventual course of mankind.
Approximately 600 hand-drawn illustrations; shot on fully automated

Oxberry animation stand. Electronic
sound.
DA SILVA. $1\frac{1}{4}$ min. Color. Sound.
1971

CICERO MARCH
September 4, 1966.... A Chicago
Negro postal worker, Robert Lucas,
leads 300 marchers into Cicero. The
attention of the country is focused
on the hysteria created by the sight
of blacks marching down the main
street of an all-white middle-class
northern city. Without commentary.
The only sounds and sights are those
recorded at the scene.
PERENNIAL ED. 8 min. B&W.
Sound. 1967

CONFORMITY
This nonnarrated, animated film
shows that people tend to live their
lives in patterns. It further suggests
that, whether at work or at play,
men are traditionalists and, in effect, actually become part of a large
repetitive pattern. Perhaps war
and fighting of any sort are just another form of conformity. Is it possible that man repeats himself so
much that he cannot put an end to
war? (An Omega Production)
BFA ED. MEDIA. $7\frac{3}{4}$ min. Color.
Sound. 1970

CZECHOSLOVAKIA 1918-1968
Without narration, traces events
from the country's founding in 1918,
through the 1939 Nazi invasion, up
to and including the Soviet invasion
of August 1968. Award: CINE Golden
Eagle. (Produced by Sanders Fresco
Film Makers) Also available in
35mm.
USIA. 15 min. Color. Sound. 1968

THE DAISY
The daisy is the symbol of beauty,
yielding only to those who love and
enjoy it. The "rectangular character" is a boor with a whole arsenal
of weapons to destroy beauty; but his
rudeness and narrowmindedness
only make him ridiculous, and the
daisy is untouched. Animation and

direction by Todor Dinov. Music.
Award: Silver Award, Chicago Film
Festival.
CCM FILMS. 6 min. Color. Sound.
1964

DEAD BIRDS
A study of the tribal life of the Dani,
a people of western New Guinea.
Shows how these people have based
their values on an elaborate system
of intertribal warfare and revenge.
(A Contemporary Films release by
Robert Gardner)
McGRAW-HILL. 83 min. Color.
Sound. 1963

THE DESERT
Young boy, playing imaginatively
among remnants of war weapons,
realizes that his own fantasy has
turned against him, that he has become the target of his own mental
projections. Electronic sound track.
(Produced by Janusz Kubik/Janus
New Cinema)
PYRAMID. 16 min. B&W. Sound.
1966

FIGURES FROM A FABLE
An animated film that charts the rise
and fall of a civilization. Figures
of dwarfs are being destroyed. A
civilization begins to rise out of the
ruins. It develops, increases in
power and in possessions. Eventually, absorbed in its own affluence,
it becomes corrupted and begins its
decline until it too is decayed ruin.
What remains turns into little clay
figures of dwarfs. No narration;
music and sound effects only.
ACI FILMS. 10 min. Color. Sound.
1970

GAME OF WAR
A short film from Poland, using stick
figure animation, and giving a brief
history of war. No narration; musical score.
FILM IMAGES. 7 min. Color.
Sound

GENIUS MAN
A cave man searches his brain for
an invention that will please and help
his fellow man. He devises the
wheel, which they examine and throw
away. With each of his other inventions—the clock, the phonograph,
television—their reaction is the
same. Finally, he offers them a
stone at the end of a stick. When the
group learns it can be used for beating each other over the head, they
are jubilant. The inventor returns to
his rock in disgust.
ACI FILMS. $1\frac{1}{2}$ min. Color. Sound.
1970

THE HAND
There are two main symbols, a man
and a Hand. The man lives alone in
a room. His only pleasure is a
single flower. He makes a flowerpot
for it on a potter's wheel. The Hand
disturbs his peace, changing the form
of the pot on the wheel. The man
protests, defends himself in vain.
The Hand, however, has entered into
his life and keeps returning, compelling him to carry out its wish.
Animated by Jiri Trnka. Awards:
Annecy Film Festival; Bergamo
Film Festival; New York Film Festival. (A Harry Belafonte presentation)
McGRAW-HILL. 19 min. Color.
Sound. 1965

HYPOTHESE BETA
A cartoon with a surprise ending. An
isolated perforation on a punch card
becomes bored between readings.
Looking for action, it manages to
create chaos out of order, and proves
that accident and misunderstanding
can mean disaster. (Produced in
France)
McGRAW-HILL. 7 min. Color.
Sound. 1966

THE INSECTS
A brief story of man's losing battle
against the great and diverse world
of insects (or symbolically, petty
annoyances that eventually win over
us). The economy of line and style

is one of the features of this team of
animators. (Directed by Teru
Murakami)
McGRAW-HILL. 5 min. Color.
Sound. 1963

"THE JUMP" and "+PLUS - MINUS"
In "The Jump," a little man, who is
clutched in the grasp of mechaniza-
tion incessantly performs monoton-
ous series of movements in a world
that is void of humanity and warmth.
Live action is combined with painting on film and music. No dialogue.
"+Plus - Minus" is a boy-meets-
girl story with an antiwar theme.
Hand-painting over photographed
silhouettes against intense background colors. (Produced by Eino
Ruutsalo)
CCM FILMS. 11 min. Color.
Sound. 1966

LAW AND ORDER
Filmed in Kansas City over a five-
week period in 1969. Shows in detail (but without commentary or
narration) daily police routine,
mostly in the black ghetto. Open-
ended. Winner of the Emmy Award
for the Best News Documentary of
1969-70. (A Frederick Wiseman
production)
ZIPPORAH. 81 min. B&W. Sound.
1969

LINES AND DOTS
Blue dashes and red dots are fighting
each other when they are brought in
close contact with an unknown third
power that destroys the embattled
signs and spreads over the screen
like spilled liquid.
STERLING. 7 min. Color. Sound.
1970

LIVING (Vivre)
The shock and impression left by war
on its witnesses is conveyed in
newsreel excerpts of faces from the
family of man. War is never directly shown; it is presented solely
through its consequences. The film
makes its comment, not through
narration, but through the order

and choice of its scenes and music.
(Produced in France)
McGRAW-HILL. 8 min. B&W.
Sound. 1959

THE MAGICIAN
A magician attracts a group of children at a beach. At first, he amuses
them with innocent tricks, but gradually, they are led into playing with
guns, and in the end, the guns are
real.
STERLING. 12 min. B&W. Sound.
1963

MR. KOUMAL GETS INVOLVED
The subject of this series of episodes, involving an optimistic but
frustrated idea-man, is human nature and man's relationship to his
environment and his fellow men.
Mr. Koumal series. (Produced in
Czechoslovakia)
SIM PROD. $1\frac{1}{2}$ min. Color. Sound.
1971

THE MOCKINGBIRD
Based on the short story by Ambrose
Bierce. A private in the Union
Army, standing night guard, sees an
indistinct figure, and fires. The next
day, troubled by the experience, he
goes in search of his victim and
finds the body of his twin brother in
Confederate uniform. The shock
causes the soldier to desert. No
dialogue. "The Mockingbird" is one
of a three-part feature, the other
two segments of which are "Occurrence at Owl Creek Bridge" and
"Chickamauga." Awards: Direction
Prize to Robert Enrico, San Sebastian Film Festival.
CCM FILMS. 39 min. Color.
Sound. 1962

NEIGHBORS
A Norman McLaren film employing
"pixillation," in which principles
normally used to put drawings or
puppets into motion are used to
animate actors. The story is about
two people who come to blows over
a flower that grows on the line
where their properties meet. The

film has neither dialogue nor narration, but is accompanied by synthetic music and sound effects. Awards: eight, including Academy Award. (National Film Board of Canada)
INT. FILM BUR. 8 min. Color. Sound. 1952

AN OCCURRENCE AT
OWL CREEK BRIDGE
Based on a short story by Ambrose Bierce, this French film recreates the atmosphere of the Civil War. A man is about to be hanged. Does he miraculously escape or is his bid for freedom the final paroxysm of a mind ready for death? Award: Grand Prize at the Cannes Festival. (Directed by Robert Enrico)
McGRAW-HILL. 27 min. B&W. Sound. 1963

OFFSPRING
A montage of newsreels, stills, and live-action footage that juxtaposes a healthy American child singing peacefully and the starving and injured young of other countries. Song, "Where Have All The Flowers Gone," sung by Maria (aged 8), written by Pete Seeger. (Produced and directed by Warren Forma)
CCM FILMS. 5 min. Color. Sound. 1968

POLICE POWER AND FREEDOM OF ASSEMBLY: THE GREGORY MARCH
This footage documents demonstrators' reaction to the "Police Riot" of August 1968. Beginning with speeches by Pierre Salinger and Dick Gregory, the film follows the protesters down Chicago's Michigan Avenue as they reaffirm their rights of assembly. They meet the National Guard; gas is used, many are arrested, including Gregory and a number of delegates to the Democratic Convention. Filmed as it happened, in synchronized sound, without narration.
PERENNIAL ED. 7 min. B&W. Sound. 1969

POSTERS: MAY-JUNE 1968
(Revolutionary Art of the French Students)
Documents the anti-DeGaulle posters made by students during the confrontations. It begins with a tour of the schools, from the Sorbonne to the National School of Decorative Arts, where the posters were produced. The very first poster, "Vive la Revolution Creatrice," is shown being printed, and then a steady stream of revolutionary art. Soon they cover every available space on buildings. No narration. Music.
FILM IMAGES. 23 min. Color. Sound. 1968

POTEMKIN
Considered one of the most important films in the history of silent cinema. It brought to world attention Eisenstein's theories of cinema art: montage, intellectual contact, and employment of the masses (instead of the individual) as protagonist. Story is based on an incident that occurred on the ship Prince Potemkin during the 1905 Russian uprising. The sailors themselves and the people of Odessa were used as actors. Musical score. No dialogue; English titles.
CCM. 67 min. B&W. Sound. 1926

THE REVOLUTION
The Head of State is at his desk. One of his subjects enters with a number of complaints. The Dictator falls over dead, but another—looking exactly the same—takes his place. He promises action, but orders his guard to take the complainant for a brainwashing. The citizen is returned a new man; he takes his place next to the Leader at a desk. An assassin enters, shoots citizen and Ruler, and seals himself behind the Dictator's desk. Animated. No narration.
ACI FILMS. 8 min. Color. Sound. 1970

THE ROBBER'S DIRGE
An experimental film that expresses itself symbolically in graphic form

and shows relationships between groups. An aggressive group, represented by robbers who harass peaceful inhabitants, is eventually destroyed by another, representing a community which at first took a passive attitude towards aggression. STERLING. 8 min. Color. Sound. 1970

STOLEN CHILDHOOD
Scenes of childbirth and war-injured children during U.S. bombings of North Vietnam. Theme: "War is not healthy for children and other living things." Without commentary. (Directed by Constantinescu, Bucharest Studios)
AMER. DOCUMENT. 10 min. B&W. Sound. 1967

A STUDY IN PAPER
Puppet-like figures tear themselves from newspapers and move by animation. The film demonstrates that even a simple design can develop a theme without the use of words. By means of tear-outs, the artist expresses the struggle between Peace and War. All the actors and "props" are handmade, and all the action is achieved by single-frame exposures. (Produced by L. Bruce Holman at Syracuse University)
INT. FILM BUR. $4\frac{1}{2}$ min. B&W. Sound

THE SWORD
An open-ended discussion film employing animation. Questions for discussion after seeing this film are: What happens when a sword falls? What swords are falling in today's world, and what do we do when they fall? No narration; music and sound effects only. (Produced by V. Stepanek)
CCM FILMS. 6 min. Color. Sound

A TALE FOR EVERYBODY
The moral of this story is reminiscent of the Aesop and LaFontaine fables. In cartoon form, two friendly beetles discover an egg. Though neither knows exactly what it is, ownership becomes increasingly important. The quarrel becomes so intense that they don't see the egg-shell crack, as a chick is hatched. They are still fighting when the chick decides to have them both for his first meal. No narration. (A Beaux Arts/Vita Film)
BFA ED. MEDIA. 6 min. Color. Sound. 1968

TOYS
Begins with children outside a store window at Christmas. Then the war toys appear and we realize that some games are played for keeps. This film has no commentary but it is easy to see what it aims to show: war toys do not necessarily make warriors, but it is possible that they do give a false glamor to the deadly pursuit. Award: La Plata, Argentina. (National Film Board of Canada)
McGRAW-HILL. 8 min. Color. Sound. 1966

TOYS ON A FIELD OF BLUE
An old man, alone and broken in spirit, watches children playing war games. Through their make-believe war and toy weapons, the old man is forced to remember the painful experiences he has come to know through wars. No dialogue. Music. (Produced by Richard Evans)
CCM FILMS. 20 min. B&W. Sound. 1962

11. FANTASY

What made <u>Gulliver's Travels</u> credible was Jonathan Swift's use of verisimilitude, the ability to create the illusion of truth through attention to detail. If Swift could make sense out of fantasy through mastery of the written word, imagine what can be done with camera and film. Better yet, don't imagine. Instead, see the photo fantasies described herein. Their one common element is unreality. Unreality is their theme. That's why they're grouped separately from "Expression" films. These are, in a way, expression films, but built from elements unreal enough to merit special attention. And, despite the apparent lack of rational substance to these pictures, take comfort, and enjoy. Enjoy them in the assurance offered by another master of verisimilitude, Cervantes: "In a world of madness, it is madness itself to accept reality."

THE ADMIRAL
An old admiral imagines he is in command of a sea battle. However, all his ships are defeated, and nothing is left for him but to commit suicide. After the shot, sea water gushes out through the armchair admiral's head.
STERLING. 6 min. Color. Sound. 1970

BAGGAGE
The mental burdens of a young girl, played by Japanese mime Mamako Yoneyama. Through San Francisco, Mamako carries her "baggage," representing the burden of conscience. In a series of episodes, the girl wrestles with her burden. When she manages to rid herself of it, she feels lost. Reunited with her "baggage," she greets it with resignation. She cannot exist without it, but it weighs so heavily on her mind that it prevents her from enjoying the world around her. In the last sequence, Mamako surrenders her "baggage" in death.
ACI FILMS. 22 min. B&W. Sound. 1969

THE BIG SHAVE
A pleasant young man wakes up one morning, goes into the bathroom, and begins shaving. The camera follows every step, and suddenly an ordinary shaving session turns into a bloodbath—the young man shaves himself to death. Winner, International Awards. (Produced by Martin Scorsese)
McGRAW-HILL. 6 min. Color. Sound. 1968

BILL HAS A HUNDRED FACES
The main characters of this puppet film are two billiard balls who are rivals in love, furiously competing with each other. One of them has a marvelous capacity for transformation and proves—in the end—to be invincible. (Produced by Pannonia Film Studio, Budapest, Hungary)
McGRAW-HILL. 11 min. Color. Sound. 1970

BOILED EGG (L'Oeuf a la Coque)
This French cartoon about the misadventures of an apparently tipsy and overconfident boiled egg could be called one of the first examples of

Animation of the Absurd. Taking
place on a desert of sand and stones,
the film follows the egg as it mysteriously appears out of the ground
and strives to escape the clutches of
an invisible seeker. No narration or
dialogue. (A Cinema Nouveau Production)
McGRAW-HILL. 5 min. Color.
Sound. 1963

CHILDREN'S DREAMS
Paintings by children, aged 6 to 15,
from Austria, France, Germany,
Great Britain, Holland, India, Italy,
Japan, Sweden, Turkey, and the
U.S.A., selected, arranged, super-
imposed, and animated so that a
child's dream of a fantasy journey
may be interpreted by the audience.
No narration. Music. (Produced by
Ervin Alberti for Centropa Film,
with the cooperation of the Austrian
Ministry of Education)
CCM FILMS. 14 min. Color. Sound

COAT FROM HEAVEN
A Czechoslovakian cartoon about a
magic coat that fell from heaven.
Tells about its effect on the dispo-
sition of those who chanced to wear
it. Music; no dialogue. Rental only.
AUDIO/BRANDON. 10 min. B&W.
Sound

DEEP BLUE WORLD
An underwater adventure-fantasy
using a variety of original film techniques. Mood is augmented by multiple music recordings and electronic
sound effects. (Produced by David
Adams)
PYRAMID. 7 min. Color. Sound.
1971

THE DESERT
Young boy, playing imaginatively
among remnants of war weapons,
realizes that his own fantasy has
turned against him, that he has become the target of his own mental
projections. Electronic sound
track. (Produced by Janusz Ku-
bik/Janus New Cinema)
PYRAMID. 16 min. B&W. Sound.
1966

DEVIL'S WORK
When a good-natured man finds out
that each good deed he performs is
repaid with a bad one, he turns into
a little devil and goes about avenging
the injustices done him. An example
of abstract design and painted backgrounds, combined with a figurative
story-telling motif. Animated.
(Produced by Zagreb Film)
McGRAW-HILL. 10 min. Color.
Sound. 1965

DOM
Awarded the Grand Prix at the International Festival at Brussels,
"Dom" is an example of the new
school of experimental Polish films.
"Dom" means house, home. A
woman waits for husband or lover,
whose footsteps she hears outside
(the fighting sequence indicates he
may be having a duel). He comes in,
places his hat on a hatrack, and appears to her as a handsome clothes-
dummy's head, which she caresses
only to see it disintegrate. Music.
McGRAW-HILL. 12 min. Color.
Sound. 1957

DREAM OF THE WILD HORSES
The director utilizes slow motion
against soft-focus backgrounds to
create dream-like effects that evoke
the wild horses of the Camargue in
France. Music. Awards: Award of
Merit, Edinburgh Film Festival;
nominated for Academy Award; other
awards at Berlin, Bilboa (Spain),
Mexico, Tokyo. (A SIMPRI Production by Denys Columb de Daunant)
McGRAW-HILL. 9 min. Color.
Sound. 1959

THE DREAMER
The character in this animation is a
typical man performing his usual
tasks, and becoming caught up in
daydreams. He sees himself as a
sport champion, a famous opera
singer, a general, a conductor, and
a lover. (Produced by Zagreb Film)
McGRAW-HILL. 12 min. Color.
Sound. 1965

ELECTROCUTION OF THE WORLD
A McLuhanistic ritual in which the
dying friend, the word, is sacrificed
(in an electronically equipped graveyard) to the all-embracing love of
the omnipresent TV set. Following
the fire and water ritual of death
comes the rebirth of the new totally
electrified, electrocuted man. Lyrics and music by Canadian song-
writer and poet, Bruce Cockburn.
(Produced by Morley Markson)
PYRAMID. $4\frac{1}{2}$ min. Color. Sound.
1968

ERSATZ
This film by the Yugoslav animator
Dusan Vukotic is about a man whose
whole world, even his woman, is inflatable. One of the Yugoslav shorts
chosen for inclusion in the Museum
of Modern Art's program of films.
(Produced by Zagreb Animation Studios)
McGRAW-HILL. 8 min. Color.
Sound. 1961

EXCHANGES
An encounter between two train pas-
sengers—a black man and a white
girl. An exchange of glances leads
them into an imagined sequence in
which fantasies and prejudices are
exposed, explored, and finally abandoned. We return to reality and to
the couple still isolated from one
another. A note of hope is sounded
in the final shots: the rails of the
train running parallel, yet seeming
to merge in the distance. Award:
CINE Golden Eagle. (A John Camie
Film)
ACI FILMS. 10 min. B&W. Sound.
1969

FAROUN, THE LITTLE CLOWN
This animated film, without words,
but with a musical score, is a child's
dream in which toys and household
objects come to life and put on a circus. It can be used to initiate thought
and discussion on the imaginative aspects of children's lives: feelings,
dreams, magic, mystery, beauty.
(Released by Xerox Films with the
cooperation of Faroun Films, Canada, Ltd.)
XEROX FILMS. 14 min. Color.
Sound. 1970

GENESIS
Czech animators demonstrate the
theory that the genesis of man is not
a mystery, but a mechanical phe-
nomenon. A man is stamped out and
assembled in all his parts—egg-
shaped head, scarlet boutonniere,
implanted heart—on an assembly
line of little box-machines of polished
wood. Just when the wooden head
seems able to act, a guillotine chops
off the head. Award: Grand Prize,
Oberhausen. (Produced by the Studio
for Puppet Films, Prague)
CCM FILMS. 6 min. Color. Sound.
1966

GIRL AND THE SPARROW
A fantasy in which a girl captures a
sparrow and puts it in a cage. She
teases the sparrow, poking at it and
putting the cage up to her dog's face.
Her dream world becomes a cage
from which she cannot escape. She
wakes, runs home with the sparrow
and releases it. She has come to
realize all living creatures have the
right to live free and unfettered.
Musical background; no dialogue or
narration. (Remmler Production)
FILMS INC. 14 min. Color. Sound.
1967

THE GOLDEN FISH
A story film about the adventures of
a little boy's pets, a goldfish and a
canary, and the neighborhood alley
cat. A fantasy situation. No narration. (Produced by Jacques Cou-
steau)
COLUMBIA PIX. 20 min. Color.
Sound. 1959

THE HAND
There are two main symbols, a man
and a Hand. The man lives alone in
a room. His only pleasure is a single flower. He makes a flowerpot for
it on a potter's wheel. The Hand disturbs his peace, changing the form

of the pot on the wheel. The man protests, defends himself in vain. The Hand, however, has entered into his life and keeps returning, compelling him to carry out its wish. Animated by Jiri Trnka. Awards: Annecy Film Festival; Bergamo Film Festival; New York Film Festival. (A Harry Belafonte presentation) McGRAW-HILL. 19 min. Color. Sound. 1965

THE HAPPY PACE OF SWITZERLAND

A truck driver encounters an elegant carriage pulled through the countryside by a white horse. He gazes longingly after the apparition, but continues his drive. At a lakeside he unloads the sailboat his truck has been carrying. He watches as the boat glides away ... and on the other shore of the lake, he again sees the wonderful horse and coach. He leaps into his truck and the chase begins. Rossini's "String Sonata in C Major" sets the pace across the Swiss landscape. Award: American Film Festival. (By Condor-Films) THORNE FILMS. 11 min. Color. Sound. 1963

THE HOUSE

The history of an old house that is being demolished. Out of the fragments grows the mosaic of many lives, the story of a house and its occupants. Half a century is compressed into thirty minutes, interrupted by falling walls, collapsing rooms, and a hailstorm of rubble. As the house is demolished, so the lives of its occupants are constructed. Music. (By Louis van Gasteren) McGRAW-HILL. 32 min. B&W. Sound. 1961

HYPOTHESE BETA

A cartoon with a surprise ending. An isolated perforation on a punch card becomes bored between readings. Looking for action, it manages to create chaos out of order, and proves that accident and misunderstanding can mean disaster. (Produced in France) McGRAW-HILL. 7 min. Color. Sound. 1966

I AM FIVE

And five is a very special age, much different from four or six. Using a felt board and a collage technique, the film-makers have illustrated the whimsy, logic, and imagination of five-year-olds. (Produced by Hristo Topouzanov and Maria Nacheva) CCM FILMS. 10 min. Color. Sound. 1967

THE INSECTS

A brief story of man's losing battle against the great and diverse world of insects (or symbolically, petty annoyances that eventually win over us). The economy of line and style is one of the features of this team of animators. (Directed by Teru Murakami) McGRAW-HILL. 5 min. Color. Sound. 1963

A KITE STORY

A boy comes upon a strange man who makes wonderful kites, and who gives him a small smiling kite of his own. String taut. Flying, swooping, plunging. Mysteriously, the kite acts as though it loves the boy as the boy loves the kite. But on another day the boy forsakes his small kite for a great beribboned, ridiculous kite that the stranger made. There is more. There is even a moral. (Producer: Pieter VanDeusen) CHURCHILL. 25 min. Color. Sound. 1969

KOSMODROME 1999

The year is 1999 and interstellar travel has become so commonplace that every family has its own rocket ship. The ships, however, are no more dependable than today's automobiles. The family we view trying to set off to visit Grandma in (or on?) another planet has all the same Rube Goldberg problems that the

modern, auto-driving public faces.
Animated. (Produced by Short Films
Studios, Prague)
CCM FILMS. 12 min. Color. Sound.
1969

LES ESCARGOTS

A fable of a farmer who discovers
that his tears have the power to
make his crops grow. In the days
that follow, he can be seen using
every means to make himself cry.
One night, snails appear and begin
gobbling up his crops. They grow to
monstrous size and advance towards
town, crushing everything in their
path. After they enter town, however, they become immobilized and
turn to stone. None of this dis-
courages the farmer, though, and as
the film ends, he is watering his new
carrot patch with tears ... under the
watchful stare of three rabbits.
Three international film awards.
Animated. (Produced by Les Films
Armorial)
McGRAW-HILL. 11 min. Color.
Sound. 1966

THE LITTLE AIRPLANE
THAT GREW

Depicts a boy who daydreams his
model airplane is real. In his imagination the plane soars overhead,
performing breath-taking acrobatic
feats. Following his plane into a
field, the boy directs it in a joyous
ballet. When the boy's teacher
scolds him for his reveries and takes
away the plane, his dream is shat-
tered. But as he walks home de-
jectedly after school, he looks up,
and to his delight, sees his plane
again dancing in the sky. (Produced
in France)
LEARN. CORP. 9 min. Color.
Sound. 1970

THE LITTLE BLUE APRON

The meaning of this story depends
upon the interpretation of the symbols. A paper bird meets a little
blue apron on a clothesline. The
bird frees the apron and together
they journey through the sky. They
help one another many times in their
travels, but eventually encounter
attacks that destroy them both,
though not before the apron manages
to outwit their enemy. No narration. (A Beaux Arts/Vita Film, made
in Czechoslovakia)
BFA ED. MEDIA. 8 min. Color.
Sound. 1968

THE LITTLE GIRAFFE

In this puppet film enacted by toys,
a stuffed giraffe is thrown into the
air from a merry-go-round, and
lands on a hedgehog. Stoically he
permits mother giraffe to pluck out
the spines. There follows a ride
across town to reach the gas station
where the deflated toy can be blown
up again. Music and sound effects.
No narration or dialogue. (Puppet
Film Studios, Lodz, Poland)
McGRAW-HILL. 8 min. Color.
Sound

THE LITTLE MARINER

Music and visuals reveal the dreams
and ambitions of a boy as he sails in
his small boat in Long Beach Har-
bor. Without dialogue. Award:
CINE Golden Eagle. (Produced by
Tiger Productions)
ENCYC. BRIT. 20 min. Color.
Sound. 1965

L'OISEAU (The Bird)

About a clockwork bird, bored in his
gilded cage. He dreams of liberty in
a world of birds. Despite his efforts
to become part of that world, he becomes an undesirable and sets in motion a revolt among the birds. But
he becomes their victim. He awak-
ens in his gilded cage, a clockwork
bird with a mechanical song. Animated. Music. (Produced in France)
McGRAW-HILL. 9 min. Color.
Sound. 1965

THE LOST WORLD

Arthur Conan Doyle's adventure
story of Professor Challenger's ex-
pedition to the headwaters of the
Amazon in search of prehistoric remnants. First effort at animating dinosaurs by Willis O'Brien, who later

created the trick photography for
"King Kong." This film stars Wallace Beery, Lewis Stone, and Bessie
Love; directed by Harry Hoyt. Musical score available on tape.
CINE CONCEPTS. 48 min. B&W.
Silent. 1925

MACHINE
An animated allegory on man's inventions and his subsequent destruction through the very machines he
creates. Awards: Prix A La Qualite;
Catholic Film Award. (Produced by
Wolfgang Urchs)
PYRAMID. 10 min. Color. Sound.
1966

THE MAGIC BALLOONS
A lonely boy sells balloons along the
beach. He creates fantasies about
them, thinking of them as friends.
When he falls asleep, a young couple
passes and buys all his balloons,
leaving money in his pocket. When
the boy awakes, he feels he cannot
part with his companions and finally
locates the balloons at a party where
grown-ups are bursting them. The
boy manages to rescue one, and together they escape—back into his
dreams. (Produced in France)
LEARN. CORP. 17 min. Color.
Sound. 1969

MAGIC HANDS
In four situations, four different children are suddenly granted magic
hands that can make frozen cones
multiply, turn bullies into frogs, and
solve other problems magically.
Magic Moments series.
ENCYC. BRIT. 7 min. Color.
Sound. 1969

MAGIC SNEAKERS
A boy finds a wondrous pair of magic
sneakers—but an evil monster wants
to take them away from him. Thanks
to the magic properties of the sneakers, the boy is able to outwit the
monster. Yet he abandons the sneakers. Why? Magic Moments series.
ENCYC. BRIT. 8 min. Color.
Sound. 1969

MAGNOLIA
An episode in pantomime at the
abandoned mine of Magnolia, a ghost
town in the Colorado Rockies.
Through one pathetic flower growing
nearby, Magnolia (a being who inhabits the old mine) makes contact
with Suzie (a little girl who represents human life in the outside
world). Original music.
THORNE FILMS. 7 min. B&W.
Sound. 1963

MAN AND HIS WORLD
We see a group of Negro teenagers
playing with a soccer ball. An African chant is heard as the youths
bounce the ball, toss it, and balance
it. There is no verbal narration. Instead, titles appear on screen, telling of this planet's vulnerable suspension in time and space. (A Homer
Groening Film)
ACI FILMS. 2 min. Color. Sound.
1969

MERBABIES
A blend of musical and visual fantasy. Tiny ocean children evolve
from the bubbling foam, play "follow
the leader" and other underwater
games in their storybook world.
Animated. Original score.
WALT DISNEY. 9 min. Color.
Sound. 1970

THE MERRY-GO-ROUND HORSE
A little ragamuffin adores a merry-go-round horse. One day the horse
is replaced by a merry-go-round
"car" and sold to the fleamarket.
The wooden horse is bought by a
wealthy child who abuses it while
playing cowboy. Infuriated by such
cruelty, the ragamuffin conspires
with friends to rescue the horse. As
he throws his arms around it, the
horse comes to life and the boy rides
away. (Produced in France)
LEARN. CORP. 17 min. Color.
Sound

MR. KOUMAL FLIES LIKE A BIRD
The subject of this series of episodes, involving an optimistic idea-

man thwarted at every turn, is human
nature and man's relationship to his
environment and his fellow men. Mr.
Koumal series. (Produced in
Czechoslovakia)
SIM PROD. 2 min. Color. Sound.
1969

MIXUMMERDAYDREAM

A composer is working out a musical
idea. As he plays his composition on
the piano, his room is invaded by
dancers who appear and disappear,
multiply and divide. Color separa-
tion of the images gives a fantasy atmosphere to the dance as the scene
moves in and out of doors, but finally
back to the composer's studio as he
completes his music. No dialogue or
narration but a musical score. (Produced in Holland)
ACI FILMS. 10 min. Color. Sound.
1971

MOEBIUS FLIP

Skiers find the world has flip-flopped
onto the other side of reality, and
they have to do this flip ski maneuver
to flop it back again. Awards: Edinburgh, Kranj, Trent, Venice, U.S. Industrial Film Festival. (A Summit
Production)
PYRAMID. 25 min. Color. Sound.
1969

OMEGA

Deals with the end of mankind on
earth—not his death, but his rebirth
and his liberation to roam the universe at will. Award: Silver Phoenix
Award, Atlanta Festival. (Produced
by Don Fox)
PYRAMID. 13 min. Color. Sound.
1969

RAILROADED

A railroad guard's confrontation
with a strange little man who arrives in a box thrown from a train.
Each time the guard tries to cross
the tracks that separate them, he is
stopped by the stranger. Finally,
the guard makes one last try—this
time to be repulsed by an onrushing
train. When the train passes, the

little man and his box are gone.
(Produced by Harrison Engle)
McGRAW-HILL. 10 min. B&W.
Sound. 1968

THE RED BALLOON

A boy makes friends with a balloon.
It follows the boy to school, in the
bus, and to church. Boy and balloon
play together in Montmartre, and try
to elude the urchins who want to destroy the balloon. The enemy wins,
and the balloon dies. Then, all the
other captive balloons in Paris come
down to the boy and lift him up into
the sky. No dialogue. Awards:
Academy Award, Cannes, Edinburgh,
French Film Critics' Award. (Directed by Albert Lamorisse)
CCM FILMS. 33 min. Color. Sound.
1956

SAND CASTLES

Children dream they are characters
from "Robin Hood," but their sand
castle is washed out as they play at
the beach. Meanwhile, their parents
are hoping to win a vacation in Hawaii, as their dream is visualized on
the screen. Minimal dialogue, natural sound effects, and a musical
score. (Produced by Graphicom)
AIMS. 6 min. Color. Sound. 1970

SEVEN AUTHORS
IN SEARCH OF A READER

(A Sunday Afternoon
on the Island of La Grande Jatte)
Alluding to the playwright Pirandello
and the painter Seurat, this film develops the theme of the writer and
his public, and presents an idea for
discussing the liberation and adventure of the mind through books.
(Directed by Frans Weisz)
McGRAW-HILL. 21 min. B&W.
Sound. 1965

SIRENE

The story of a mermaid in the harbor of a modern city. This creature
is charmed by a man playing a flute,
and she attempts to flee with him.
But the machines that surround the
harbor destroy her. The investiga-

tion of the mermaid's death provides a satirical look at the bureaucratic institutions of modern society. Told entirely through the animated paintings and a background of contrasting sounds. (Produced by Raoul Servais) INT. FILM BUR. 10 min. Color. Sound. 1970

SUNDAY LARK
What happens when a little girl gets into a large office on Sunday? Six-year-old Stella Sun wanders into a skyscraper and into the silent offices of a New York stock brokerage. With an original score (appropriate electronic music accompanies the big IBM sequence) and no dialogue, this adventure of a child in the world of business turns into a romp. Music. Awards: Prize, Berlin Film Festival; CINE Golden Eagle; U.S. Official Entry, Edinburgh Film Festival. (Produced by Sanford Semel) McGRAW-HILL. 12 min. B&W. Sound. 1963

THRESHOLD
A nonnarrative fantasy on the meaning of life and death. John Carradine plays Death. Teacher's guide is available. Award: Atlanta Film Festival. (Produced by J. Maynard Lovins)
PYRAMID. 25 min. Color. Sound. 1970

TWO MEN AND A WARDROBE
The camera looks out to sea. Suddenly, something breaks water and two men emerge carrying a wardrobe closet. They head for the city.

They try to board a streetcar; no wardrobes allowed. They try to make friends with a girl; when the wardrobe comes, she goes. They walk into a restaurant; sorry, no diners with closets. And so it goes as they move from place to place. Filmed without dialogue or narration, set to a melancholy jazz score. (Directed by Roman Polanski) McGRAW-HILL. 15 min. B&W. Sound. 1957

UMBRELLA
The story of a happy young couple whose lives are changed by a mysterious umbrella that is the outward representation of prosperity. Theme: True happiness exists independently of any striving to attain it. It is a by-product of the right attitude toward life. No dialogue. Awards: Silver Dragon, Cracow International Festival; Prize of the International Society of Film Critics. (Directed by Mikhail Kobakhidze) McGRAW-HILL. 20 min. B&W. Sound. 1967

UN CHIEN ANDALOU
(An Andalusian Dog)
An attempt at pure surrealism (a work of art created entirely from the subconscious). Dream-imagery is used in a free association technique that discards conventional standards of esthetics, in order to shock the viewer. Audiences should be forewarned of content and style. Originally silent; music added. (Produced by Salvador Dali and Luis Bunuel) PYRAMID. 16 min. B&W. Sound. 1929

12. LITERATURE

This bracket consists of about 30 titles that are based on or otherwise related to the written word. Some of us will be disappointed to find literature so sparsely represented in nonnarrated form. It seems there should be more literature films around, but then why? Should a subject whose prime component is words be expected to translate well into nonverbal pictures? Anyway, maybe the low count is evidence that films have developed a literature of their own. Or this scarcity might prove that films have finally broken away from conventions imposed on them by the printed arts. It may further show that only a few styles of linear literature (Ambrose Bierce, for example) are convertible to nonverbal expression.

There are countless other sources from which film-makers might borrow. That they haven't had to is one way they've asserted their new independence from Gutenberg.

By the way, let me anticipate—and, at the same time, sidestep—a moot question: "Which should come first, seeing the film or reading the story?" The answer doesn't matter. Whichever comes first, films help reveal the very things that precede and create both the visual and the graphic... namely, ideas, ideas, ideas.

ACT WITHOUT WORDS
Guido Bettiol's film interpretation of Beckett's one-act mime examines the darker implications of man's condition. "Act Without Words" is the story of a puppet on a desert, taunted and frustrated by an unseen power. When the puppet begins to enjoy the shade of a tree, the bough falls. A pitcher of water is lowered, just out of reach. Boxes slide on stage, but his attempt to reach the water by stacking them is futile. A whistle draws his attention to a rope, which he begins to climb, only to have it fall. Whenever he tries to escape his predicament—even through suicide—he is prevented. At the end, he refuses to be enticed any longer and reclines on the sand, inspecting his nails.
PYRAMID. 10 min. Color. Sound. 1965

AFRICA
Drawings in a book turn into an African adventure for a daydreaming youngster. (Produced by Merlin Dobry)
PYRAMID. 10 min. Color. Sound. 1970

ALEXANDER AND THE CAR WITH A MISSING HEADLIGHT
A boy replaces a headlight on an old junkyard car and then drives around the world with his animal friends. Drawings by kindergarten children.
WESTON WOODS. 13 min. Color. Sound

CHICKAMAUGA
This adaptation of Ambrose Bierce's short story creates a symbolic world of the horrors of war as a little boy

wanders away from home, reaches a
battlefield, plays soldier among the
dead and dying, and returns home to
find his house burned and his family
slain. Award Winner, San Sebastian
Film Festival. (Directed by Robert
Enrico)
McGRAW-HILL. 33 min. B&W.
Sound. 1961

DAY DREAMS
Charles Laughton and Elsa Lanches-
ter in a satire on a servant girl's
dream of glory based on a story by
H. G. Wells. It introduces the student to the characteristics that distinguish film from the other arts.
Contains illustrations of the essentials of montage, and illustrates the
advantages and disadvantages of silent film. Sound speed: 23 min; silent speed: 34 min. (Directed by Ivor
Montagu)
CCM FILMS. 23 min. B&W. Silent.
1928

THE DAY IS TWO FEET LONG
Attempts to visualize the experiences
of the haiku. Using only natural
sounds, director Peter Rubin tries
to make the viewer feel alone in
peaceful contemplation of the natural
world around him, and to free the
mind and the soul in the manner of
haiku poetry.
WESTON WOODS. 8 min. Color.
Sound

DEATH AND SUNRISE
An animated cartoon in stylized form
on the theme of the classic Western
gunfight. No narration. Music.
(Produced by Eyvind Earle)
CCM FILMS. 10 min. Color. Sound.
1963

ENTER HAMLET
With questionable relevance, each
word of Hamlet's soliloquy is given
its own picture. A multitude of visual puns. Pop art. (A New Janus
Cinema Film by Fred Mogubgub)
PYRAMID. 4 min. Color. Sound.
1967

ESTHER
A simple and brief study of a girl
named Esther as she moves, smiling
and softly, through flowers. Visually
comparable to a Japanese haiku
poem. (Produced by Robert Johnson)
PYRAMID. 2 min. Color. Sound.
1970

FILM
Written by Samuel Beckett, starring
Buster Keaton. Beckett's only venture into the film medium. It is a
one-character production without
dialogue, based on Berkeley's theory that "to be is to be perceived."
As in all of Beckett's work, elements of comedy surround the philosophical foundation.
CINEMA 16. 22 min. B&W. Sound

GENESIS
A visualization in animation of the
seven days of creation as written in
the first book of the Old Testament.
The imagery is suggestive rather
than literal. Its abstract approach
makes it useful for all denomina-
tions in the teaching of the Old
Testament. Award: Gran Premio,
Bergamo, Italy.
CMC/COLUMBIA. 13 min. Color.
Sound

HOLY THURSDAY
Based on William Blake's poem,
"Holy Thursday." A visual interpretation of nature and Man's interconnection with it and his institutions. No narration except for the
poem. Awards: CINE Eagle and first
prizes around the world. (Produced
by George Hood)
AMERICAN ED. 18 min. Color.
Sound. 1969

JAIL KEYS MADE HERE
A film essay using contemporary ad-
vertising signs as a comment on so-
ciety. Based on a book of photo-
graphs by Lee Boltin. (Produced by
Frank De Felitta)
McGRAW-HILL. 10 min. B&W.
Sound. 1965

THE KIND-HEARTED ANT
Based on a traditional Yugoslavian
children's song, this cartoon tells the
story of a kind-hearted ant who unin-
tentionally disrupts the harmony and
order of the anthill. Animated.
Award: First Prize, Venice Film
Festival. (Produced by Zagreb Film)
McGRAW-HILL. 10 min. Color.
Sound. 1965

LA POULETTE GRISE
One of Norman McLaren's films, this
illustrates the imagery of a simple
lullaby traditional in France and
Canada. Photographed from pastel
drawings as the artist changed each,
and varied the lighting. Illustrates
how a single drawing can "animate"
a scene. Sung by Anna Malenfant.
(National Film Board of Canada)
INT. FILM BUR. 5½ min. Color.
Sound. 1947

LADY OF THE LIGHT
When the lonely young daughter of a
lighthouse keeper is dejected because no one writes to her, her
father has a novel idea that brings
her lots of mail. No narration. (A
Trend Release)
WALT DISNEY. 19 min. Color.
Sound. 1967

LONG EARS
A European version of an Uncle
Remus fable explaining why rabbits
have long ears. Two young rabbits
get caught in a rainstorm and are
hung up to dry on a washline, their
ears stretching longer and longer
as they wait. No dialogue.
CCM FILMS. 6 min. Color. Sound

THE LOST WORLD
Arthur Conan Doyle's adventure
story of Professor Challenger's ex-
pedition to the headwaters of the
Amazon in search of prehistoric
remnants. First effort at animating
dinosaurs by Willis O'Brien, who
later created the trick photography
for "King Kong." This film stars
Wallace Beery, Lewis Stone, and

Bessie Love; directed by Harry
Hoyt. Musical score available on
tape.
CINE CONCEPTS. 48 min. B&W.
Silent. 1925

THE MOCKINGBIRD
Based on the short story by Ambrose Bierce. A private in the Union
Army, standing night guard, sees an
indistinct figure, and fires. The
next day, troubled by the experience,
he goes in search of his victim and
finds the body of his twin brother in
Confederate uniform. The shock
causes the soldier to desert. "The
Mockingbird" is one of a three-part
feature, the other two segments of
which are "Occurrence at Owl
Creek Bridge" and "Chickamauga."
Awards: Direction Prize to Robert
Enrico, San Sebastian Film Festival.
CCM FILMS. 39 min. Color.
Sound. 1962

NOBI AND THE SLAVE TRADERS—
An African Legend
Animated puppets dramatize a legend
of the time when the slave trade
flourished in Africa. This is the
story of young Nobi, who plays hap-
pily with jungle animals until white
traders attack his village. The film
has no narration—actions of the puppets are accented by sound effects
and African rhythms. Teachers can
use this film to introduce the moral
questions of slavery, to stimulate
study of African history, and to
create interest in puppetry. (Produced by DEFA Studio for Animated
Films)
ENCYC. BRIT. 30 min. Color.
Sound. 1970

THE NOSE (Le Nez)
From the short story by Gogol. Fol-
lows the tale of the nose of Major K
that was found by his barber in a loaf
of bread. The shadow pin-board ani-
mation creates a nightmare quality.
Music. (Produced for Cinema
Noveau, France)
McGRAW-HILL. 16 min. B&W.
Sound. 1963

AN OCCURRENCE AT
OWL CREEK BRIDGE
Based on a short story by Ambrose
Bierce, this French film recreates
the atmosphere of the Civil War. A
man is about to be hanged. Does he
miraculously escape, or is his bid
for freedom the final paroxysm of a
mind ready for death? Award: Grand
Prize at the Cannes Festival. (Directed by Robert Enrico)
McGRAW-HILL. 27 min. B&W.
Sound. 1963

THE RED KITE
Adapted from Hugh Hood's story,
"Flying a Red Kite." A young father
is preoccupied with questions about
life, death, and God. An answer is
provided in the freedom and joy of
the human spirit—as symbolized by
the red kite he flies with his little
girl. An examination of modern
man, society, and the search for
security and faith.
NAT. FILM BD. 17 min. Color.
Sound. 1966

RHINOCEROS
A visual translation from Ionesco's
play on the theme of conformity,
condensed in animation. (Produced
by Boris Borresholm, and animated
by Jan Lenica)
McGRAW-HILL. 11 min. Color.
Sound. 1964

SEVEN AUTHORS
IN SEARCH OF A READER
(A Sunday Afternoon
on the Island of La Grande Jatte)
Alluding to the playwright Pirandello and the painter Seurat, this
film develops the theme of the writer
and his public, and presents an idea
for the discussion of the liberation
and adventure of the mind through
books. (Directed by Frans Weisz)
McGRAW-HILL. 21 min. B&W.
Sound. 1965

SISYFOS
This allegory points up the ludicrous
aspects of blind acceptance of au-
thoritarian rules. It is based on the
ancient Greek myth of Sisyphus, who
was condemned in Hades to roll a
huge stone uphill—only to have it
constantly roll back. In this treatment, a little man is frustrated when
each toothpick he makes, upon being
tested, breaks. (Short Film Studios,
Prague)
McGRAW-HILL. 8 min. Color.
Sound. 1969

SUNFLIGHT
Gerald McDermott's graphic design
combines with animation technique
to depict the ancient but timely Greek
legend of Daedalus and Icarus. Har-
old Zellerbach Award, San Francisco
Film Festival.
IFF (BRYAN) 6 min. Color. Sound.
1968

SYRINX/CITYSCAPE
Two different themes, one ancient,
one modern, are presented without
narration. "Syrinx" depicts the
Greek fable of the goat-god Pan set
to Debussy's music. "Cityscape"
conveys the agitated rhythm of city
life. Awards: New York, San Francisco, Canada, Ethiopia. "Syrinx"
(B&W—3 minutes) and "Cityscape"
(B&W—1 minute) are mounted on
one reel.
LEARN. CORP. 4 min. B&W.
Sound. 1966

TILLIE'S PUNCTURED ROMANCE
Based on "Tillie's Nightmare" by
Edgar Smith. With Charles Chaplin,
Marie Dressler, and Mabel Nor-
mand. The film marked Chaplin's
debut as a major star. One of the
earliest feature comedies, this Keystone contains both slapstick and
sentiment. With insert titles.
(Produced and directed by Mack
Sennett)
CCM FILMS. 43 min. B&W. Silent. 1914

THE TOWN MUSICIANS
From 'The Bremen Town Musicians"
by the brothers Grimm, this film is
a translation of the story of the donkey, dog, cat, and rooster who set

out to become the town musicians. Original music. Award: Silver Reel Winner. (Produced by Piper Productions. Directed by William Tytla)
CCM FILMS. 9 min. Color. Sound

TREES
A combination of poetry by Joyce Kilmer, music by Oscar Rasbach, singing by Fred Waring's Pennsyl-vanians, and depiction by Walt Disney's animators.
WALT DISNEY. 5 min. Color. Sound

THE UGLY DUCKLING
The classic Hans Christian Andersen tale about the cygnet who hatches in a brood of ducklings. Rejected by his "family," he is finally claimed by a beautiful swan and finds his rightful place in the world.
WALT DISNEY. 8 min. Color. Sound

13. MORE

I've purposely avoided the word "miscellaneous" in headlining this segment. "Miscellaneous" seems to suggest odds and ends that are intrinsically trivial or somehow undeserving of their own identity. On the contrary, here's where you'll find some of the most successful nonnarrated films of all. It's just that there aren't enough of them to justify individual categories. Some major subjects listed under "More" are: History, Social Studies, Psychology, Economics, Anthropology, Guidance, Industrial Training, Agriculture, and Medicine. Even topics of a biblical or religious nature had to settle for potpourri grouping here.

I hope your own favorite interest is somewhere in these pages. If not, that's probably because treatment of it is not suited to word-free techniques. Whatever your field, this section is a good place for serendipity, for shopping around for concepts completely outside your specialty. Experiment. Pick out a film, any film—the most unlikely one you can find. Preview it. Spring it on a group or class, to see how they interpret it. Chances are you'll open the way to new combinations of ideas, feelings, and facts that may someday deserve a category of their own.

THE ABANDONED
An essay in film and electronic music on the final days in the life of many a faithful family car. These cars, once cherished family members, now old and forgotten, are abandoned at the rate of eight million per year—most to rust away, strewn across the countryside.
NBC-TV. 10 min. Color. Sound. 1970

ACCEPTANCE
Flowers portray the individual and groups who accept or reject him, showing how most people need a group to be identified with, but that a group does not necessarily accept the individual. Joining a group just to belong is not always satisfying. Animated flowers dance through these experiences in pantomime against a musical background. No dialogue. (Produced by Graphicom)
AIMS. 6 min. Color. Sound. 1970

AN AMERICAN TIME CAPSULE
Two hundred years of U.S. history impressionistically condensed via a visual staccato of hundreds of still pictures. (Produced by Charles Braverman)
PYRAMID. 3 min. Color. Sound. 1967

BAGGAGE
The mental burdens of a young girl, played by Japanese mime Mamako Yoneyama. Through San Francisco, Mamako carries her "baggage," representing the burden of conscience. In a series of episodes, the girl wrestles with her burden. When she manages to rid herself of it, she

feels lost. Reunited with her "baggage," she greets it with resignation. She cannot exist without it, but it weighs so heavily on her mind that it prevents her from enjoying the world around her. In the last sequence, Mamako surrenders her "baggage" in death.
ACI FILMS. 22 min. B&W. Sound. 1969

BAKERY BEAT
The story of night workers racing the dawn to bake their quota of bread and cakes. A small bakery plays in counterpoint to the automation of an "assembly line" bakery—the pride of craftsmanship versus the wonder of mass production. No narration; original music and sound effects.
AIMS. 15 min. Color. Sound. 1965

BARGES
Follows the progress of a cargo of corn from a field in Illinois to an ocean steamer at the port of New Orleans. Along the way, this barge encounters a variety of river vessels, each one playing its part in the complex economic scheme of supply and demand. The highly condensed narration reflects the isolation of the crew members who help to supply the nation and the world with raw materials and consumable goods.
ACI FILMS. 15 min. Color. Sound

BLACK FOREST FAMILY CELEBRATES CHRISTMAS
A modern German family prepares a traditional Christmas celebration— making music, colorful ornaments, and special holiday foods. Father and son play duets on recorder and flute, while mother and daughter bake cookies. The parents trim the tree on Christmas eve, and the children are called in to open the presents. Festivals Around the World series.
IFF (BRYAN). 14 min. Color. Sound

THE CARD CATALOG
Pictures elementary students searching for books, fiction and non-

fiction. The cards for each book are shown and briefly explained. Students then are seen using the call numbers found on the cards to locate their books. Minimal narration.
BFA ED. MEDIA. $8\frac{1}{2}$ min. Color. Sound. 1971

CHANGING OF THE GUARD
An animated fairy tale in which all the characters—the soldier of the Royal Guard, the king's daughter whom he loves, the inhabitants of the castle—are matchboxes. They all go up in flame because they have not learned not to play with fire. No dialogue or narration. Awards: First Prize, Cannes Film Festival; Honorable Mention, Stratford, Canada. (Film Miniatures Studio/Czech)
CCM FILMS. 8 min. Color. Sound. 1959

CHRISTMAS CRACKER
A seasonal pleasantry of three segments by National Film Board of Canada artists and animators, with music. The film contains three parts: Jingle Bells in which paper cut-outs dance; a dime-store rodeo of tin toys; and a new Christmas story. Seven awards, including: Nomination, Hollywood; Rome; Naarden, Holland. (National Film Board of Canada production)
McGRAW-HILL. 9 min. Color. Sound. 1964

CHRISTMAS EVE SERVICE IN THE BLACK FOREST
A traditional Lutheran Christmas Eve service celebrated in a tiny, 600-year-old church in the Black Forest. A study of the faces of villagers at worship, familiar hymns, and the reading of the Christmas story in German. Festivals Around the World series.
IFF (BRYAN). 16 min. Color. Sound

CHRISTMAS LIGHTS
The colorful lights of Christmas— decorations, trees, ornaments, store windows—are photographed to a

background of choral music. The film combines the sights of the season with the singing of some favorite carols: "We Wish You a Merry Christmas," "The Holly and the Ivy," "Hark, the Herald Angels Sing," and "Silent Night."
STERLING. 11 min. Color. Sound. 1965

CONFORMITY
This animated film shows that people tend to live their lives in patterns. It further suggests that, whether at work or at play, men are traditionalists and, in effect, become part of a large repetitive pattern. Perhaps war and fighting of any sort are just another form of conformity. Is it possible that man repeats himself so much that he cannot put an end to war? No narration. (An Omega Production)
BFA ED. MEDIA. $7\frac{3}{4}$ min. Color. Sound. 1970

THE CROWD
What is there about the nature of man that makes him seek out and become part of a crowd? That is one of the questions implicit in this film. The camera moves from crowds in a subway to crowds at a parade, crowds of cattle at a slaughter, crowds at a beach, a nightclub, and a riot. Finally we see a scientist observing the most basic crowd of all—a crowd of human chromosomes. No narration.
LEARN. CORP. 20 min. B&W. Sound. 1970

CURIOSITY
A store window has been covered except for a small open spot with a sign over it saying, "Please do not peek in here." Nobody resists the temptation to look. Demonstrates curiosity and approach-avoidance conflict. Not available for rental; purchase only.
CANDID CAMERA. 6 min. B&W. Silent

THE CURIOUS HABITS OF MAN
By their animal-like behavior, adults at a cocktail party startle an imaginative young boy. A woman's hysterical laughter suddenly mingles with the laughing call of a loon. A human wolf is compared to a howling wolf in the wild. A charging rhinoceros, a croaking frog, raucous crows, and a sloppy hippopotamus are a few of the animals that dramatize some of the effects of excessive drinking. (Produced by Dan Gibson)
A-V EXPLOR. 13 min. Color. Sound. 1968

DAIRY—FARM TO DOOR
The story of milk—from the dairy to the creamery, the retail market, and your home. Minimal narration.
AIMS. 11 min. Color. Sound. 1965

DIALECTICS OF A DROPOUT
The producer of this wordless film, an Oxford graduate student, probes the world of the dropout. If a person finds human society to be hypocritical, is dropping out a solution? Does the dropout always find tranquility and fulfillment in his solitude? Or might he be drowning himself in a dark pool of futility and boredom?
CENTRON. $8\frac{1}{2}$ min. Color. Sound. 1970

DURER: THE GREAT PASSION
Albrecht Durer (1471-1528) grasped the importance of printmaking, the artistic equivalent of printing in his time. His work reflected the faith of the Middle Ages, the restlessness of the Renaissance, and his own striving for knowledge. This film depicts his series of scenes in the life of Christ, from original woodcuts in Vienna. No narration; music by the Vienna Symphony Orchestra. (Produced in Austria)
FILM IMAGES. 14 min. B&W. Sound

EAST LYNNE
Candid Camera hires messengers to deliver goods to a specific address. When a messenger comes to the door, he is pulled through the door and finds himself in the middle of a stage where a play is in progress. Some

messengers pretend they are characters in the chorus, so as not to create embarrassment before the audience. Demonstrates role-playing and compliance. Purchase only; not available for rental.
CANDID CAMERA. 5 min. B&W. Sound.

ECCE HOMO
(Czechoslovakian Art 1400-1600)
The richly painted and gilded wood sculpture of the birth, life, death, and resurrection of Christ were late manifestations of the Gothic influence in Czechoslovakia in the fifteenth and sixteenth centuries. No narration. Award: Bergamo. (From Kratky Film Praka)
TIME-LIFE. 9 min. Color. Sound. 1969

ECONOMICS: NEWSPAPER BOY
A newspaper boy is a businessman. He sells a product, provides a service, and makes a profit. With no narration except for introductory questions, the film allows the viewer to identify basic economic concepts in this familiar situation: initiative, responsibility, saving for a goal, and good relationships with co-workers and customers.
BFA ED. MEDIA. $10\frac{1}{2}$ min. Color. Sound. 1971

ECONOMICS: THE CREDIT CARD
Two children learn about credit cards when their father purchases a present they want to give their mother. The entire credit sequence, from purchase to payment of the monthly bill, is presented, emphasizing the economic function of credit in the family and community. This film explores an increasingly important aspect of our society. Minimal narration. (A Jarvis Couillard Associates film)
BFA ED. MEDIA. $9\frac{1}{2}$ min. Color. Sound. 1971

ECONOMICS: WORKERS
WHO BUILD HOUSES
What economic concepts can be ob-

served by the young child during the construction of houses? This film uses such a commonplace activity to illustrate division of labor, specialization, conversion of materials into products, payment of wages, pride of workmanship, cooperation, supervision, quality control, and use of the product by the buyer. Concepts are described visually with almost no narration, which eliminates the burden of special vocabulary.
BFA ED. MEDIA. $11\frac{1}{4}$ min. Color. Sound. 1970

EYES
An attractive young woman puts on a pair of glasses just as she is hit by a popped champagne cork, a fishing fly, welder's sparks, an exploding firecracker, and other objects. The message: Wear eye protection. Award: Bronze Plaque, National Committee on Films for Safety. (Produced by Crawley Films, Ltd.)
INT. FILM BUR. 4 min. Color. Sound. 1970

FACE THE REAR
Subjects in an elevator watch three Candid Camera employees enter and face the rear of the car. When a majority of three face the rear, the pressure on the subject to conform is overwhelming. The last subject turns in unison with the group, and even removes his hat when the others do. Demonstrates conformity to group pressure. Available for purchase; no rentals.
CANDID CAMERA. 4 min. B&W. Sound.

FEET
A young woman's bare feet dance through broken glass, with booted partners, over construction sites, near a falling kitchen sink, and away from a pursuing lawn mower. The message: Wear safety shoes. (Produced by Crawley Films, Ltd.)
INT. FILM BUR. $3\frac{1}{2}$ min. Color. Sound. 1970

FIRE SAFETY
IN THE LABORATORY
The 60 films in the series, many of
them produced under a grant from
the National Science Foundation, are
examples of the style of teaching
where the films may be utilized as
part of a series or treated as a single unit. The method is left entirely
in the hands of the instructor. Detailed information on film content
will be sent upon request. Contact
CCM Films. From The Yale Chemistry Films series.
CCM FILMS. 2 min. B&W. Silent

FOOD
An animated color film, without
commentary, produced by a filmmaker from India during a period of
work-study at the National Film
Board of Canada. "Food" is intended
to demonstrate to farm audiences in
developing countries how improvements in farming practice and technology increase the yield of crops
and also the farmer's income.
NAT. FILM BD. $4\frac{1}{2}$ min. Color.
Sound

FREIGHTER
Daybreak, gulls, and water ... a
freighter comes to her moorings.
Without words, the camera dwells on
harbor sights and sounds. The work
of the dock crews ... the work of the
seamen ... lunch and a few minutes'
rest ... cargo unloading ... new cargo
aboard. Newly laden, the freighter
is again ready for sea. Award: CINE
Golden Eagle. (Produced by Films/
West)
AIMS. $12\frac{1}{2}$ min. Color. Sound. 1969

FRESCOES IN DANISH CHURCHES
The world of the old frescoes in Dan-
ish village churches is presented
with music in this evocation of Bib-
lical history and art produced by
Luciano Emmer. No narration.
(Produced for Danish Culture
Films)
CCM FILMS. 10 min. B&W. Sound.
1954

GARBAGE
A film without words that suggests
there is a tragic-comic quality about
everything that has to do with man—
even his garbage. People reveal
their characters by the ways they
get their garbage into the can. The
tempo increases as disposal systems struggle to sweep away an
evergrowing flood of garbage created by our affluent society. Strange
mechanical monsters flounder about
in a world where there is nothing
but garbage as far as the eye can
see.
KING SCREEN. $10\frac{1}{2}$ min. Color.
Sound. 1970

GENESIS
A visualization in animation of the
seven days of creation as written in
the first book of the Old Testament.
The imagery is suggestive rather
than literal. Its abstract approach
makes it useful for all denomina-
tions in the teaching of the Old Testament. Award: Gran Premio, Bergamo, Italy.
CMC/COLUMBIA. 13 min. Color.
Sound

GENESIS 1-27: UNDERSEA WORLD
An abstract presentation of the Genesis theme, composed entirely of underwater sequences. The "ballet" of
the garden eels and the "aquabatics"
of the giant manta rays are highlights of this film. The underwater
photography was done by Stanton Waterman in French Polynesia. No narration; accompaniment of musical
score.
PERENNIAL ED. $8\frac{3}{4}$ min. Color.
Sound. 1970

GOIN' HOME
A film on the world around us and
the poetry of song. Singer/poet Arlo
Guthrie sings of home, nature, and
the essence of life and death. No
narration. Awards: CINE Golden
Eagle, Eastman Kodak Best Film of
the Year. (Produced by George
Hood)
AMERICAN ED. 4 min. Color.
Sound. 1968

THE GREATER COMMUNITY ANIMAL
An examination of how the individual, represented by the symbol "I," has to have his idiosyncracies—and his potentialities—processed out of existence in order to be made acceptable to the great community animal, Society. The ornately drawn "I" becomes extinct, replaced by the standard typeface. Animated. No narration. Award: American Film Festival. (A Derek Phillips Film)
ACI FILMS. 7 min. Color. Sound. 1968

HANDS
Hands narrowly escape disaster as they slice carrots, type, work in a machine shop, open drawers, paint, and lift. The message: Beware of hand traps. (Produced by Crawley Films, Ltd.)
INT. FILM BUR. $3\frac{1}{2}$ min. Color. Sound. 1970

HANDS GROW UP
Much of children's play is an imitation of—and a preparation for—adult activities. Shows children at play (e.g., children playing with mud) and then a corresponding adult activity (in this case, a potter shaping a vase). Besides giving children the feeling of being "grown up," the film shows them the variety of occupations that they are, in a sense, training for every day. Magic Moments series.
ENCYC. BRIT. 6 min. Color. Sound. 1969

HAPPY FAMILY PLANNING
Cartoon animation explains contraceptive devices. Captions in English, Spanish, French, Arabic, and Chinese. No narration. Award: CINE Golden Eagle. (Made by Wexler Film Productions for Wyeth Laboratories)
PLAN. PARENT. 8 min. Color. Sound. 1969

IN A BOX
Line drawings suggest the predicament of people who find themselves boxed in by life. A few strokes of the animator's pen show how men's lives are limited by their own view of things. The box they are in may not fit; it may be uncomfortable in many ways, but they rush back to its familiarity, if not security, even though brief sorties outside may show them a bigger world. (National Film Board of Canada)
LEARN. CORP. 4 min. B&W. Sound. 1968

INTREPID SHADOW
Called by Margaret Mead "one of the finest examples of animism shown on film," this film deals with subjective rather than objective aspects of Navajo life. In the film, Al Clah attempts to reconcile the Western notion of God with his traditional Navajo notion of gods. Navajos Film Themselves series.
CMC/COLUMBIA. 18 min. B&W. Silent

IS THIS OUR FATHER'S WORLD?
Pictures the warm relationship between a father and his young son. Against their simple, happy excursions to the beach, the park, the zoo, and window shopping, the film sets another picture of the world—a polluted world in which technology runs unchecked. It makes a statement, with a positive note, about man's stewardship responsibilities for his environment. No dialogue; original rock music and lyrics. (Paul Kidd, producer)
FAMILY FILMS. 10 min. Color. Sound. 1971

LA CHAMBRE (The Room)
In animated form, the camera views the frustration of a confused figure who cannot escape from the room that imprisons him. No dialogue. (Produced by Les Productions Select)
INT. FILM BUR. 6 min. Color. Sound. 1971

L.A. 53
A document that records the sights, the rhythms, the feeling of railroad-

ing. We follow a freight train made
up at dawn in Chicago, and then see
it barrelling through the plains
states, on its way through the south-
west, then up into the mountains, and
finally on its ride to Los Angeles.
JOURNAL. 10½ min. Color. Sound.
1970

LAMBING (Parturition in the Ewe)
Illustrates the techniques and pro-
cedures for delivery of a pregnant
ewe: preparation of the pens, care of
the mother, and obstetrical methods
in normal and abnormal births.
(Presented by The Royal Norwegian
Ministry of Agriculture, Audio Visual
Division)
ENCYC. BRIT. 20 min. B&W.
Silent. 1966

LUCY
The story of an unwed, pregnant
teenager. The brief narrative presents her romantic relationship with
her boy friend, the tensions the preg-
nancy causes in the family, and the
alternatives Lucy faces as an expectant mother. This film has an urban
setting, and the central character is
a Puerto Rican girl. Ten copies of a
correlated booklet are provided free
with film purchase. (Produced by
Alfred Wallace)
PICTURA. 13 min. Color. Sound.
1970

MAN TO MAN
With the view that human problems
are best understood by studying human beings, this film concentrates on
its people, a boy of ten and his father.
There is no narrator, no guide with a
pointer, no charts, no animated sequences. There is nothing but you
and the boy and his father. This film
is a portrait of tomorrow's alienated
young man—the rebel in embryo.
(Produced by Slevin-Peshak)
PERENNIAL ED. 13 min. Color.
Sound

MARY'S DAY 1965
Consists of two reels shown simultaneously on two screens. It is a

contemporary celebration at Immacu-
late Heart College with processions,
Mass, dancing, feasting, flowers,
children, warm faces, brightly hued
constructions, butterflies and drag-
ons (to symbolize the ugly and the
beautiful). For sound, just play
some Beatles records.
GLASCOCK. 11 min. Color. Silent.
1965

MEMENTO
Uses picture and sound contrapun-
tally. Photographed in an automobile
"graveyard," the film presents a
study of cars irreparably smashed in
accidents, while the sound track re-
constructs the voices of the people
involved in three accidents. Montages, single frame images, and
sound effects. Awards: Grand Prix,
Vienna Film Festival (first American
film ever to win this award); CINE
Golden Eagle. (Produced by Sumner
J. Glimcher)
CMC/COLUMBIA. 9 min. Color.
Sound. 1967

MICROSECOND
Animated, experimental, and ab-
stract interpretation of 3,000 years
of recorded history in quick stills.
Awards: Colombo, Cracow, Padua,
Venice, CINE. (Produced by Dan
McLaughlin for IBM)
S-L FILMS. 6 min. Color. Sound.
1969

MR. KOUMAL
DISCOVERS "KOUMALIA"
The subject of this series of episodes, involving an optimistic idea-
man thwarted at every turn, is human nature and man's relationship
to his environment and his fellow
men. Mr. Koumal series. (Produced in Czechoslovakia)
SIM PROD. 2 min. Color. Sound.
1971

ON THE MOVE
Public relations survey of Lockheed
products, plants, and personnel. Includes famous aircraft of the past
and possibilities for the future. Ac-

cepted as U. S. entry, in its category, for the Florence Film Festival. (Produced by Douglas Muir) LOCKHEED. 16 min. Color. Sound. 1969

PARABLE
An allegory of Christ's passion and death. A circus caravan company and a clown traveling through the countryside provide the symbols. A discussion film. No narration. (Produced for the New York City Protestant Council)
NAT. ED. FILM. 20 min. Color. Sound. 1963

PEOPLE
Using documentary technique, this film offers the viewer intimate glimpses of people—all ages, all races—at rest, at work, earning, buying, playing. The film makes a simple statement: Each of us is different, a distinct and separate individual, yet we are all alike. Minimal narration. Award: CINE Golden Eagle.
AIMS. $10\frac{1}{2}$ min. Color. Sound. 1969

THE PERILS OF PRISCILLA
From the viewpoint of a cat, getting food and finding a quiet corner become frightening adventures under the feet of a busy family. When Priscilla gets lost in the city, viewers share her encounter with roaring wheels, pursuing dogs, and flashing night lights. Her final fate is unknown. (A Dimension Film) CHURCHILL. $16\frac{1}{2}$ min. Color. Sound. 1969

THE PHANTOM FREIGHTER
Two hours in the life of a special cargo airplane. This 727 craft arrives, early in the morning, filled with containerized freight; it is then unloaded, converted for commercial use, and departs as a passenger flight. During this speedy changeover, the viewer sees the men and machines that make an airport

function. Commodities shipped by air freight are explored. Minimal narration.
ACI FILMS. 15 min. Color. Sound

PIER 73
Supported by music and sound effects, the camera observes the activities of a busy pier. Freighters, fishing boats, tugboats, sailing vessels, tankers, and passenger liners follow in panorama. Aboard a freighter are a complex radio system, the crew, engine rooms, and equipment. The many tools and types of equipment for unloading cargo come into focus. Some of the cargo itself is scanned: clothes, foodstuffs, grains, ore. (Produced by Michael Bloebaum for Pyramid Films) HOLT R&W. 10 min. Color. Sound. 1970

PREPARATION FOR CHILDBIRTH and TWO HOSPITAL DELIVERIES
Outlines prenatal care and preparations for childbirth, showing the father helping the doctor in this case of a first child (color); then again (B&W) for a fourth child, with no anesthesia. For nursing and professional groups, expectant parents: free loan, sale at cost. Silent, with titles.
CLAREMONT. 9 min. Color/B&W. Silent. 1970

RAIL
A paean to the world of trains. This film catches the pulse, motion, and excitement of rail travel. It creates a blend of past and present—from the nostalgic beauty of the old steam engines to the sleek efficiency of the modern, high-speed electric train. No narration. Awards: Locarno International Film Festival, British Industrial and Scientific Film Association. (A British Transport Film by Geoffrey Jones)
ACI FILMS. 13 min. Color. Sound. 1968

REFLECTIONS OF A COMPANY
The only narration is one line of Robert Burns ("Oh, wad some

power the giftie gie us, to see our-
selves as others see us"). Award:
CINE Golden Eagle. (Produced by
John J. Hennessy for Crown Zel-
lerbach)
ZELLERBACH. 8 min. Color.
Sound. 1969

REMBRANDT'S CHRIST
This film examines drawings in
which members of Rembrandt's
family and the townspeople of Amsterdam are compassionately represented as biblical characters encountering Christ as He fulfilled
His mission on earth. No narration;
music. Awards: Art Documentary of
the Year, Assisi; Columbus. (From
Les Films de Saturne)
TIME-LIFE. $40\frac{1}{2}$ min. B&W.
Sound

THE REPORT CARD:
HOW DOES RICCARDO FEEL?
A scolding instead of praise for a
good report card. How could it happen? Viewers see Riccardo at
school, proud of a report card he
knows will please mother. But she
is having a frustrating day. So when
Riccardo bursts into the kitchen and
knocks over the scrub bucket, he becomes the target of an emotional
tirade. The last scene shows Riccardo clutching his report card in
hurt, confused astonishment. By
using the empathy young viewers may
have for Riccardo, teachers can help
them see that people do not always
control their emotions and that anger
can be misdirected.
ENCYC. BRIT. 5 min. Color.
Sound. 1971

RESURRECTION
From its last resting place the steam
engine rises up to make a final run
past the glass and concrete buildings
that symbolize the age that has cast
it aside. The end of the journey
brings a more permanent destruction as the engineering marvels
that the camera has lingered upon
are reduced to heaps of scrap metal.
An atmospheric short that brings to

life an age now almost past. No nar-
ration.
AMERICAN ED. 9 min. B&W.
Sound. 1970

SAFETY AS WE PLAY
Children on their way to the playground demonstrate safety rules for
pedestrians, bicyclists, and ball
players. The film features basic
words superimposed on the screen,
matched to an original song and
visuals.
ACI FILMS. 7 min. Color. Sound.
1971

THE SCRIBE
The last film made by this genius of
pantomime uses the Buster Keaton
comic style to drive home a serious
message for construction safety and
accident prevention. Lively slapstick when he visits a big construction job as a "newspaper reporter"
to do a story on construction safety.
AIM/ASSN. 30 min. Color. Sound

THE SHALLOW WELL PROJECT
This film by Johnny Nelson is dif-
ferent in style and approach from
"Navajo Silversmith." It illus-
trates the building of a shallow well
to replace an open pond once used
for water supply. Navajos Film
Themselves series.
CMC/COLUMBIA. 14 min. B&W.
Silent

A SHIP IS BORN
A ship is built and launched. This
construction process is filmed from
the standpoint of the emotional relationship between man and his work.
The launching adds another emotional dimension, in which the gaiety
of the holiday crowd on the dock contrasts with the tension of the workers. How would students relate this
to topping out a skyscraper, harvesting a wheat crop, constructing a
bridge? (Produced by Polish Documentary Productions/Film Polski)
ENCYC. BRIT. 9 min. B&W. Sound.
1969

SLEEP WELL
Cut-out animation. A man settles
into an armchair for a nap. His
sleep, however, is interrupted with
troublesome dreams. Each dream
depicts the predicament faced by the
individual in the societies we know
today: bureaucracy, jingoism, to-
talitarianism. The dreams become
nightmares faster than the dreamer
can control them. (A Lasse Lindberg
Film)
ACI FILMS. 9 min. Color. Sound.
1969

SMOKE SCREEN
Antismoking film especially designed
for elementary and secondary school
students. (Produced by Michael and
Mimi Warshaw)
PYRAMID. 5 min. Color. Sound.
1970

SOIR DE FETE
The humor of a celebration—fire-
works, people, events—is suggested
in visual abstractions. Music. Animated. Awards: Prix Emile Cohl;
selected for exhibition at Venice and
Oberhausen film festivals.
CCM FILMS. 6 min. Color. Sound.
1955

SPACE PLACE
From Mercury to Apollo II, Charles
Braverman has produced this
impressionistic collage of American
space efforts. To the electronic music of Mort Garson, he has enhanced
NASA footage through selective
editing, slow motion, color filters,
and polarization. The last section is
devoted to Armstrong's landing of
the Eagle on the moon.
PYRAMID. 10 min. Color. Sound.
1969

THE SPIRIT OF THE NAVAJO
Begins with an old medicine man
looking for roots to use in a ceremony. He prepares for a sand
painting, and part of the actual cur-
ing ceremony is featured in which
the patient appears. Navajos Film
Themselves series. (Made by
Maxine and Maryjane Tsosie)
CMC/COLUMBIA. 21 min. B&W.
Silent

SQUARES
Candid Camera puts up a sign reading "Please Walk on Black Tiles
Only" in a shoe store with a black
and white tile floor. People go out
of their way to avoid stepping on the
white tiles. Some of them seem to
enjoy it; others look annoyed. Demonstrates obedience to authority.
No rentals; purchase only.
CANDID CAMERA. 3 min. B&W.
Silent

STAR OF BETHLEHEM (1700-1750)
Neapolitan craftsmen reflect the refinement of the late Baroque period
in retelling the story of the Nativity
with minute wood-carved religious
figures, dressed in fabrics and styles
of the seventeenth century. No narration; music. (From Film-Studio
Walter Leckebusch)
TIME-LIFE. 12 min. Color. Sound

SUMMER RENDEZVOUS
Using aspects of a track and field
meet, this film makes some un-
spoken observations about the nature
of human endeavor and achievement.
Background music, ranging from
Handel to the Swingle Singers, en-
hances the camera work. Excerpts
of spoken French. Award: Chicago
International Film Festival.
UNIVERSAL ED. 30 min. Color.
Sound. 1969

TEMPTED (Drugs)
A boy (sixth grade age) goes through
an average day, during which he is
exposed to pills, alcohol, and other
temptations in today's permissive
society. At school he picks up an
accidentally dropped bag of mari-
juana, and hides it. The effects of
environmental exposure cause him to
get out the bag, examine it, and be
tempted to experiment. Minimal narration. (Produced by Graphicom)
AIMS. 6 min. Color. Sound. 1970

THAT ALL MAY BE ONE
This multi-scene-image film is designed as a discussion starter. It concerns man's unity with his fellowmen against alienation, the arms race, poverty, prejudice, indifference, and inhumanity under the guise of some noble cause. Previewing is recommended for maximum success of discussion. (Produced by the United Churches of Canada)
SYRACUSE UNIV. 32 min. Color. Sound. 1970

THIS TRAIN
The sights, sounds, and colors of a night train and railroad station. The content is enhanced by the singing of "This Train," a folksong about the underground railroads of pre-Civil War days. (Produced by Frank R. Paine)
THORNE FILMS. 5 min. Color. Sound. 1965

TOMATOES—
FROM SEED TO TABLE
How does food get to our table? In this film, we follow the story of one example—tomatoes—from planting and harvesting to the canning and transportation of familiar products, such as tomato juice, whole tomatoes, and ketchup. With emphasis on economics, people, and machines, this film will illustrate the vital concept of fulfilling our basic, daily needs.
AIMS. 11 min. Color. Sound. 1970

TRACK 73
Early black-and-white still photography is contrasted with recent color sequences. They show how the railroad has evolved from coal-burning engines to diesels and electric trains. Differences in present-day commuter, freight, and passenger services are exhibited in conjunction with the complexity of their operations. Major subjects: economics, history, sociology, and geography. (Produced by Michael Bloebaum for Pyramid Films)
HOLT R&W. 10 min. Color. Sound. 1970

TRAINS
Using live-action techniques, attempts to convey the essence of railroading, without resorting to narration. Employs frame-at-a-time photography to condense time and movement. Quick cuts of fast locomotives are paced by nostalgic steam-engine scenes. Soundtrack includes location sound effects. Specially composed music for banjo, fiddle, and guitar demonstrates the influence of railroads on native American music. (Produced by Communico Films)
ACI FILMS. 15 min. Color. Sound

VERY NICE, VERY NICE
Looks behind the business-as-usual face we put on in everyday life, and shows anxieties we want to forget. Made of dozens of pictures that seem familiar, with fragments of speech heard in passing and, between times, a voice saying, "Very nice, very nice." Awards: Tours, France; Columbus, Ohio; Academy Award nomination, Hollywood. (National Film Board of Canada)
McGRAW-HILL. 7 min. B&W. Sound. 1961

THE WALL
An example of animation from Yugoslavia. This cartoon is a comment on an all too recognizable human type—the people user. Presents two men and a wall. One watches while the other tries to get to the other side. Several times the persistent one tries to get over. Frustration mounts to desperation and the obstinate one makes a breakthrough. It is clear who has come off best. The path is clear for the watcher— at least as far as the next wall. Awards: Golden Pelican, Mamaia Festival of Animated Films; Oberhausen Film Festival. (Produced by Zagreb Film)
McGRAW-HILL. 4 min. Color. Sound. 1965

THE WORLD OF THREE
A typical day of a child whose feeling of security has been undermined

by a new baby sister. Shows the
devastating effects of jealousy on a
child's behavior and personality.
Also shows what causes jealousy and
how, with thought and planning,
parents can prevent it. (Produced by
George Kaczender for the National
Film Board of Canada)
McGRAW-HILL. 28 min. B&W.
Sound. 1967

FILMS
INDEXED BY TITLE

Note that all films listed herein are in color unless otherwise indicated. Numbers in parentheses refer to the number of the section in which a full description of the film's content can be found.

Title and Description	Min.	Year	Distributor
"A". Language as source and symbol of power. Animated. B&W. (5)	10	1964	McGraw-Hill
A IS FOR ALPHABET. The ABC in picture, rhyme and song. Animated. (5)	11	1971	Coronet
THE ABANDONED. Annual scrap of eight million U. S. cars. (7), (13)	10	1970	NBC-TV
ACCEPTANCE. Personal and group relations. Animated. (13)	6	1970	AIMS
ACID BASE REACTION IN ELECTROLYSIS OF WATER. From the Yale Chemistry Films series. Silent. (3)	2	--	CCM Films
ACT WITHOUT WORDS. Beckett's one-act pantomime. Animated. (12)	10	1965	Pyramid
ADAGIO. Antiwar protest in Crayola-style art. (1)	4	1969	Pyramid
ADELAIDE. The capital city of South Australia. (6)	22	--	Australia
THE ADMIRAL. An old sea captain's final defeat. (10), (11)	6	1970	Sterling
THE ADVENTURES OF*. Asterisk symbolizes man. Animated. Award. (5)	10	1956	McGraw-Hill
AETNA. Sicily's volcano, highest in Europe. (3), (4)	11	1971	American Ed.
AFRICA. Picture-book animals in sound and motion. (12)	10	1970	Pyramid
AFRICAN ANIMALS. See 'n Tell series; music and natural sound. (3), (4)	9	1970	Films, Inc.
AI! (LOVE). The male's subservience to woman. Animated. (10)	4	1964	Pyramid
AIRBORN. Symmetry and motion of planes, birds, and divers. (9)	4	1970	Pyramid

Title and Description	Min.	Year	Distributor
AI-YE. Man's evolution and "recycling." Awards. (2)	24	--	Film Images
ALEXANDER AND THE CAR WITH A MISSING HEADLIGHT. Based on the picture-book story. Animated. (12)	13	--	Weston Woods
ALF, BILL AND FRED. A fable on friendship vs. money. Animated. (7)	8	1964	McGraw-Hill
ALLEGRO MA TROPPO. The "quiet desperation" of life, even in Paris. (6)	13	1962	Pyramid
ALPHABET. From A to Z, pictorially. Animated. Awards. B&W. (5)	6	1966	Nat. Film Board
AMAZON FAMILY. Life of a Bolivian latex-gatherer and his family. (2)	19	1963	IFF (Bryan)
AMBLIN. Young couple on the road, on their own. Preview. (7)	24	1969	United Prod.
AMERICA THE UGLY. Coast-to-coast deterioration of landscape. (4)	3	1965	G. E. Films
AN AMERICAN TIME CAPSULE. Instant (almost subliminal) U. S. history. Award. (13)	3	1967	Pyramid
AMMONIA FOUNTAIN. From the Yale Chemistry Films series. Silent. (3)	2	--	CCM Films
ANIMALS IN AMBOSELI. Ecology of a typical region of East Africa. (3)	20	1968	Mod. Media
ANIMALS IN AUTUMN. Deer, foxes, weasels, birds, and insects. (3), (4)	11	--	Encyc. Brit.
ANIMALS IN SUMMER. Foxes, bears, squirrels, frogs, and snakes. (3), (4)	11	--	Encyc. Brit.
ANIMALS ON THE FARM. Subtitle, "A Film in Song and Rhyme." (5)	15	1971	Clark Bell
ANNUAL FESTIVAL OF THE DEAD. From the series African Village Life. (2)	14	1967	IFF (Bryan)
ARCHITECTURE, USA. How buildings reflect our way of life. (1), (6)	13	1965	Nat. AV Ctr.
ARCTIC PEOPLE. How Eskimos hunt, how Lapps farm and fish. (2)	14	1970	Sterling
ART. Split-second scenes of 2,000 masterpieces. (1)	4	1965	Pyramid
ART EXPERT. Example of conforming to "expert" opinion. B&W. (1), (8)	8	--	Candid Camera
THE ART OF SEEING. Finding beauty in common surroundings. (1)	10	1969	ACI Films

Title and Description	Min.	Year	Distributor
ART SCENE, USA. Contemporary painters, sculptors, and dancers. (1)	17	1966	Nat. AV Ctr.
AT THE CARIBOU CROSSING PLACE, Part I. From a series on Net-silik Eskimo life. (2)	30	1969	Mod. Media
AT THE CARIBOU CROSSING PLACE, Part II. From a series on Net-silik Eskimo life. (2)	30	1969	Mod. Media
AT YOUR FINGERTIPS—BOXES. Making toys out of cartons. Awards. (1)	10	1969	ACI Films
AT YOUR FINGERTIPS—CYLINDERS. Tube-like forms from household objects. (1)	10	1969	ACI Films
AT YOUR FINGERTIPS—FLOATS. Examples of things that float and that don't. (1), (3)	10	1969	ACI Films
AT YOUR FINGERTIPS—GRASSES. Relationship of weeds, corn stalks and bamboo. (1), (3)	10	1969	ACI Films
AT YOUR FINGERTIPS—PLAY CLAY. Simple sculptures from flour, salt and water. (1)	10	1969	ACI Films
AT YOUR FINGERTIPS—SUGAR AND SPICE. Party decorations from a sugar and water paste. (1)	10	1969	ACI Films
AUDITORY RESPONSES OF NEW-BORN INFANTS. Diagnosis of hearing impairments. Silent. (3)	3	1965	Thorne Films
AUSTRALIAN ANIMALS. See 'n Tell series; music and natural sound. (4)	8	1970	Films, Inc.
AUTUMN. The colors and events of the season's start. (4)	10	1967	Sterling
AUTUMN COLOR. Seasonal texture, color and lighting. (4)	7	1959	Thorne Films
AUTUMN COMES TO THE CITY. Halloween, Thanksgiving, other fall events. (6)	11	1969	Coronet
AUTUMN FIRE. Early film essay, recently released. Silent. B&W. (1)	17	1930	McGraw-Hill
AUTUMN PASTORALE. Rural changes as seen by two children. (4)	10	--	Perennial Ed.
AN AUTUMN STORY—Mrs. Pennypacker's Package. City workers help find lost article. (6)	11	1968	Encyc. Brit.
BABY RABBIT. City children raise rabbits. "Song-track." (3)	11	1971	Churchill
BAGGAGE. Pantomime of a conscience in conflict. B&W. (11), (13)	22	1969	ACI Films

Title and Description	Min.	Year	Distributor
BAKERY BEAT. Pride of craftsmen vs. speed of automation. (13)	15	1965	AIMS
BAKING BREAD. From a series on the Afghan tribe, the Pushtu. (2)	10	1968	IFF (Bryan)
THE BALLAD OF CROWFOOT. Abuses suffered by North American tribes. B&W. (10)	10	1970	McGraw-Hill
BALLET BY DEGAS. Simulates movement of his dance-paintings. (1)	10	1951	CCM Films
BANG! The "music" of cans, pots, pans and what-not. (3), (5)	3	1969	Encyc. Brit.
BANGKOK. Man and His World series; minimal narration. (6)	18	1969	Films, Inc.
BARGEMEN ON THE RHINE. Man and His World series; minimal narration. (2)	13	1970	Films, Inc.
BARGES. The economics and logistics of river transport. (13)	15	--	ACI Films
BASIC TRAINING. Change from civilian to soldier in nine weeks. B&W. (10)	98	1971	Zipporah
THE BEDOUINS OF ARABIA. Man and His World series; minimal narration. (2)	20	1969	Films, Inc.
THE BEGINNING. Creative person's role in society. Animated. (7)	$4\frac{1}{2}$	1971	Bosustow
BEGONE DULL CARE. Interprets three forms of jazz. Animated. Awards. (1)	8	1949	Int. Film Bureau
THE BELL (La Cloche). Freakish accident keeps man from date. B&W. (8)	15	1964	McGraw-Hill
A BELL FOR URSLI. Swiss boy's contribution to his town. (5)	$18\frac{1}{2}$	1971	Xerox Films
BERLIN, BERLIN, BERLIN. "Chamber of commerce" film on West Berlin. (6)	20	1971	Blumenthal
BIG, BIG HARBOR. Commercial activity of a big city port. (6)	12	1969	Universal Ed.
THE BIG SHAVE. Exaggerates hazards of shaving. Animated. (11)	6	1968	McGraw-Hill
BILL HAS A HUNDRED FACES. Billiard balls' amorous rivalry. Animated. (11)	11	1970	McGraw-Hill
THE BIRD. Man decides to free hard-earned pet. B&W. (7)	10	1970	Sterling
BIRDS OF THE FOREST. Five species in a single environment. (3), (4)	$5\frac{1}{2}$	1967	A-V Explor.

Title and Description	Min.	Year	Distributor
BIRDS ON A SEA SHORE. See 'n Tell series; music and natural sound. (3), (4)	10	1970	Films, Inc.
BLACK FOREST FAMILY CELE-BRATES CHRISTMAS. Modern family in traditional observance. (13)	14	--	IFF (Bryan)
BLACKBIRD FAMILY. Nesting, incubation, feeding, and training. (3), (4)	12	1969	Films, Inc.
BLESSINGS OF LOVE. Story of a courtship, marriage, and widowhood. (7)	9	1970	CCM Films
BLINKITY BLANK. Persistence of vision. Animated. Awards. (1)	6	1955	Int. Film Bureau
BLOSSOM. A modern parable on race relations. (7)	10	1970	Cathedral
THE BLUE DASHIKI. Inner-city boy saves to buy African garb. (6)	14	1969	Encyc. Brit.
BOAT FAMILIES. Contrasts river life in Thailand and France. (2)	14	1970	Sterling
BOILED EGG. Adventures of a Humpty Dumpty hero. Awards. (11)	5	1963	McGraw-Hill
BOOMSVILLE. Unplanned urban sprawl. Animated. Awards. (6)	10	1969	Learn. Corp.
BOUQUET. Flower subject variously edited. Music. (1), (4)	9	1971	Pyramid
A BOWL OF CHERRIES. Modern story in an old-fashioned style. B&W. (8)	24	--	McGraw-Hill
THE BOX. Cartoon riddle on communications. Awards. (5)	7	1967	CCM Films
BOYNNG! The funny side of a two-car accident. Animated. (8)	8	--	Audio/Brandon
BOYS' GAMES. From a series on Afghan tribe, the Pushtu. (2), (9)	5	1968	IFF (Bryan)
A BOY'S JOURNEY THROUGH A DAY. Fishing, daydreaming, and exploring the woods. (4)	16	1971	Coronet
BOZO DAILY LIFE. From the series African Village Life. (2)	16	1967	IFF (Bryan)
THE BRAND-NEW BASKETBALL. Two boys learn capacity for friendship. (7)	9	1969	Universal Ed.
BRAND NEW DAY. San Francisco architecture and landmarks. Award. (6)	$4\frac{1}{2}$	1969	Kodak
BREATH. Animated male-female abstraction. Preview. (5)	5	1967	CCM Films

Title and Description	Min.	Year	Distributor
BRIDGES-GO-ROUND. Bridges of metropolitan New York. Music. (6)	5	1958	McGraw-Hill
BRINE SHRIMP. Crustaceans; hatching to maturity. Silent. (3)	7	--	Mod. Learning
BRONZE. Creating huge Daudelin sculpture. Award. (1)	14	1969	Learn. Corp.
THE BUILDERS. Great complexity of modern skyscrapers. B&W. (3)	20	--	American Ed.
BUILDING A BOAT. From the series African Village Life. (2)	8	1967	IFF (Bryan)
BUILDING A BRIDGE. From a series on Afghan tribe, the Tajik. B&W. (2), (3)	10	1968	IFF (Bryan)
BUILDING A HOUSE. From the series African Village Life. (2)	7	1967	IFF (Bryan)
BUILDING A KAYAK, Part I. From a series on Netsilik Eskimo life. (2)	32	1969	Mod. Media
BUILDING A KAYAK, Part II. From a series on Netsilik Eskimo life. (2)	33	1969	Mod. Media
BUILDING ATOM MODELS—ISOMERISM. From the Yale Chemistry Films series. Silent. B&W. (3)	6	--	CCM Films
BUTTERCUP. Flower is killed by industrial waste. (4)	13	1971	Churchill
BUTTERFLY. Life cycle in time-lapse and closeups. (3)	9	--	BFA Ed. Media
BUTTERFLY. See 'n Tell series; music and natural sound. (3)	8	1970	Films, Inc.
BUZKASHI. Afghan horseback sport, "world's roughest." (2), (9)	8	1968	IFF (Bryan)
CADET ROUSSELLE. Puppets animate pre-Napoleonic folk song. (8)	6	--	Int. Film Bureau
THE CANADA GOOSE. Behavior, migration, offspring, flight. Award. (3), (4)	$6\frac{1}{2}$	1967	A-V Explor.
CANDLEFLAME. The changing patterns of fire and melting wax. (1)	7	1971	ACI Films
CANON. Animated description of the music. Awards. (1)	9	1963	Int. Film Bureau
THE CARD CATALOG. Introductory treatment. Minimal narration. (13)	$8\frac{1}{2}$	1971	BFA Ed. Media
THE CARNIVAL. A young girl's adventures at the fair. (5)	$7\frac{1}{2}$	--	Xerox Films
CARP IN A MARSH. See 'n Tell series; music and natural sound. (3), (4)	7	1970	Films, Inc.

Title and Description	Min.	Year	Distributor
CASTING IRON PLOW-SHARES. From a series on Afghan tribe, the Tajik. B&W. (2)	11	1969	IFF (Bryan)
CATCH THE JOY. Dune-buggies speed across desert. Awards. (9)	14	1970	Pyramid
CATERPILLAR. Musical creature's double life. Animated. (3)	16	1971	Learn. Corp.
A CHAIRY TALE. Man and chair in a ballet-battle. Awards. B&W. (8)	10	1957	Int. Film Bureau
CHANGING GREENLAND. Modernization of an isolated nation. (2)	14	1971	Films, Inc.
CHANGING OF THE GUARD. Fairy tale on fire safety. Animated. Awards. (13)	8	1959	CCM Films
THE CHESS GAME. Is power by force the answer? Animated. (10)	7	1970	Centron
CHICKAMAUGA. Boy's reaction to Civil War slaughter. Award. B&W. (10), (12)	33	1961	McGraw-Hill
CHICKENS. Communication and "pecking order" relationships. (3)	12	1970	AIMS
CHICKS AND CHICKENS. See 'n Tell series; music and natural sounds. (3)	10	1970	Films, Inc.
CHILD OF DANCE. Children, ages 4 to 6, in Bach sonatas. (1)	9	1970	Film Images
CHILDREN ADRIFT. Slum conditions near Paris. B&W. (6)	26	1958	McGraw-Hill
CHILDREN OF ISRAEL. From the How We Live series. With music. (2)	13	1969	IFF (Bryan)
CHILDREN OF PARIS. French children's summer vacation in city. (2), (6)	12	1971	AIMS
CHILDREN'S DREAMS. Interpretive paintings of 6- to 15-year-olds. (1), (11)	14	1960	CCM Films
CHOICE. Introduction to the question of drug-taking. (7)	8	1970	Coronet
CHOOSING UP. Ways of forming teams for various games. (9)	6	1969	Encyc. Brit.
CHRISTMAS CRACKER. Three forms of art and animation. Awards. (1), (13)	9	1964	McGraw-Hill
CHRISTMAS EVE SERVICE IN THE BLACK FOREST. Lutheran ceremony in 600-year-old church. (13)	16	--	IFF (Bryan)
CHRISTMAS LIGHTS. Holiday scenes associated with carols. (1), (13)	11	1965	Sterling

Title and Description	Min.	Year	Distributor
CHROMOPHOBIA. Ultimate victory of free spirit. Animated. (10)	11	1968	Int. Film Bureau
CHRONOLOGY. Questions final fate of mankind. Animated. (10)	$1\frac{1}{4}$	1971	da Silva
CICERO MARCH. Blacks confront Chicago suburb in 1966. B&W. (6), (10)	8	1967	Perennial Ed.
CIRCUS. All scenes based on children's drawings. (1)	8	1961	BFA Ed. Media
CIRCUS IN EUROPE. See 'n Tell series; music and natural sound. (5)	10	1970	Films, Inc.
CITIES IN CRISIS: WHAT'S HAPPENING? Social and esthetic decay of urban U.S. life. (6)	21	1968	Universal Ed.
CITY AT NIGHT. Impressions of recreation and occupations. (6)	$14\frac{1}{2}$	1971	Churchill
CITY IN WINTER. Seasonal events, shopping, and sports. (5), (6)	10	1969	Encyc. Brit.
CITY ...One Day. People of New York and their work. (Two versions.) (6)	18	1969	AIMS
CLAP! Clapping hands for pleasure and appreciation. (5), (9)	5	1969	Encyc. Brit.
CLAY (Origin of the Species). Novel view of evolution. Animated. Award. B&W. (3)	8	1964	McGraw-Hill
CLOWN. Paris boy "loses" dog to blind man. Award. (5), (7)	15	1969	Learn. Corp.
THE CLOWN. Stubborn fish gets and keeps upper hand. (8)	7	1968	CCM Films
COAT FROM HEAVEN. Magic mantle's effect on wearers. Animated. B&W. (11)	10	--	Audio/Brandon
COFFEE PLANTERS NEAR KILIMANJARO. Man and His World series; minimal narration. (2)	14	1969	Films, Inc.
THE COLOSSAL DREAM OF BLOCKS. Story-song words are seen, heard, and voiced. (5)	15	1971	ACI Films
CONCERT FOR CLOUDS. Cloud formations synchronized with music. (1), (3)	9	--	Perennial Ed.
CONFORMITY. Predictability of human behavior. Animated. (10), (13)	$7\frac{3}{4}$	1970	BFA Ed. Media
COOPERATIVE FARMING IN EAST GERMANY. Man and His World series; minimal narration. (2)	15	1969	Films, Inc.

Title and Description	Min.	Year	Distributor
CORK FROM PORTUGAL. Man and His World series; minimal narration. (2)	14	1970	Films, Inc.
CORRAL. Gently taming a spirited horse. Awards. B&W. (9)	11½	1954	Int. Film Bureau
CORRIDA INTERDITE (Forbidden Bullfight). Matador succumbs to intended victim. (9)	10	1958	Pyramid
COSMIC ZOOM. Man as the center of inner and outer space. (3)	8	1968	McGraw-Hill
COTTON GROWING AND SPINNING. From the series African Village Life. (2)	6	1967	IFF (Bryan)
COUNTY FAIR. Captions reinforce song-and-picture story. (5)	7	1970	ACI Films
THE COW. Herd, mother, and calf in meadow home. (3)	11	1968	Churchill
CRASH, BANG, BOOM. Rhythm, melody, and harmony of percussion. (1)	9½	1970	Xerox Films
CREATION: THE ARTIST AT WORK. Glass vase: conception, design and completion. (1)	12	1969	BFA Ed. Media
CROOKE'S TUBES. From the Yale Chemistry Films series. Silent. (3)	8	--	CCM Films
THE CROWD. Man's individuality and his social nature. B&W. (6), (13)	20	1970	Learn. Corp.
CRYSTALS. Microscopic growth and electronic sounds. (1), (3)	6	1969	Pyramid
CURIOSITY. Reverse example of the power of suggestion. Silent. B&W. (8), (13)	6	--	Candid Camera
THE CURIOUS HABITS OF MAN. Parallels party drinkers and certain animals. (8), (13)	13	1968	A-V Explor.
THE CURIOUS MOUSE. Adventures and misadventures. Animated. (8)	5	1969	CCM Films
CURRIER AND IVES. Lithographs accompanied by folk songs. (1)	13	--	Film Images
CUT-UPS. Complex figures from basic forms. Animated. (1)	5	--	Mod. Media
CZECHOSLOVAKIA 1918-1968. Czech history in newsreel format. Award. (10)	15	1968	USIA
DAIRY—FARM TO DOOR. Milk production, processing and distribution. (13)	11	1965	AIMS

Title and Description	Min.	Year	Distributor
DAIRY FARMING IN THE ALPS. Man and His World series; minimal narration. (2)	16	1970	Films, Inc.
THE DAISY. Example of "flower power." Animated. Award. (10)	6	1964	CCM Films
DANCE SQUARED. Symmetries of the square. Animated. Awards. (1)	$3\frac{1}{2}$	1962	Int. Film Bureau
DANZE CROMATICHE. Dance concepts expressed in colors. Awards. (1)	$8\frac{1}{2}$	1969	Xerox Films
DAY AFTER DAY. The dehumanizing tedium of factory work. B&W. (7)	30	1962	McGraw-Hill
A DAY AT THE BEACH. Independent boy explores his private retreat. (3)	13	1971	ACI Films
DAY DREAMS. H. G. Wells' satire on visions of glory. B&W. (8), (12)	34	1928	CCM Films
THE DAY IS TWO FEET LONG. Visual equivalent of haiku poetry. (12)	8	--	Weston Woods
DAY OF THE PAINTER. Spoof on the abstract art market. Award. (1), (8)	14	1959	CCM Films
DAYDREAMING. A day's tour of Daytona Beach, Florida. (6)	11	1970	Mini Films
DEAD BIRDS. Tribal life and war in western New Guinea. (2), (10)	83	1963	McGraw-Hill
DEATH AND SUNRISE. A typical Western "shoot-out." Animated. (12)	10	1963	CCM Films
DEEP BLUE WORLD. Underwater fantasy; varied musical effects. (4), (11)	7	1971	Pyramid
DEEP SEA TRAWLER. Man and His World series; minimal narration. (2)	18	1969	Films, Inc.
THE DEER AND THE FOREST. A "life ballet." Music: Wagner and Beethoven. (4)	16	1968	Encyc. Brit.
DEGAS DANCERS. Painter's technique for simulating motion. B&W. (1)	13	--	Time-Life
DELACROIX (1798-1863). His draftsmanship and romanticism. Awards. B&W. (1)	13	--	Time-Life
THE DESERT. Boy's imaginary weapons attack him. B&W. (10), (11)	16	1966	Pyramid
DESERT PEOPLE. Compares Sahara nomads and East Indians. (2)	14	1970	Sterling
DEVIL'S WORK. Man resorts to evil, for a change. Animated. (11)	10	1965	McGraw-Hill

Title and Description	Min.	Year	Distributor
DIALECTICS OF A DROPOUT. The quality of life in modern society. (13)	$8\frac{1}{2}$	1970	Centron
DIAMOND MINING IN EAST AFRICA. Man and His World series; minimal narration. (2)	9	1970	Films, Inc.
DIFFUSION ALONG A BAR. National Science Foundation-supported lab supplement. Silent. B&W. (3)	5	--	Mod. Media
DIMENSIONS. Introduces relative proportion. Animated. (3)	$12\frac{1}{4}$	1968	Nat. Film Board
DINA IN THE KING'S GARDEN. Maillol's model for classical sculpture. Award. (1)	10	--	Time-Life
THE DIRECTOR. The challenge of feature-film production. (1)	31	1969	Universal Ed.
DISCOVERING THE FOREST. Mood, color, and forms of woodland life. (1)	11	1965	Encyc. Brit.
DOM (The House). Man's unreal homecoming to woman. Award. (11)	12	1957	McGraw-Hill
DOUGLAS, JAMES, AND JOE. Young examples of unspoiled race relations. B&W. (7)	6	--	Film Images
DREAM OF THE WILD HORSES. Spirited stallions in slow motion. Awards. (11)	9	1959	McGraw-Hill
THE DREAMER. Romantic fantasies of typical man. Animated. (11)	12	1965	McGraw-Hill
DUCKS. Captions based on song-and-picture story. (5)	8	1970	ACI Films
DUCKS, GEESE AND SWANS. Concepts on waterfowl and their offspring. (3)	11	1970	AIMS
DUET. Competitive materialism and friendship. Animated. (7)	9	1969	BFA Ed. Media
DUNES. Animals, insects, and a desert storm. Awards. (4)	7	1968	Holt R&W
DURER: THE GREAT PASSION. His series of prints on the life of Christ. B&W. (1), (13)	14	--	Film Images
EARTH: MAN'S HOME. Comparative size of Earth and the universe. (3)	10	1969	Encyc. Brit.
EAST LYNNE. Impromptu role-playing and compliance. B&W. (8), (13)	5	--	Candid Camera

Title and Description	Min.	Year	Distributor
ECCE HOMO (Czech. Art 1400-1600). Period example: Christ's life in wood. Award. (1), (13)	9	1969	Time-Life
ECONOMICS: NEWSPAPER BOY. Familiar example of business in action. (13)	10½	1971	BFA Ed. Media
ECONOMICS: THE CREDIT CARD. The credit cycle, from purchase to payment. (13)	9½	1971	BFA Ed. Media
ECONOMICS: WORKERS WHO BUILD HOUSES. Primary concepts of manufacturing and sales. (13)	11¼	1970	BFA Ed. Media
EGYPTIAN VILLAGERS. Man and His World series; minimal narration. (2)	14	1969	Films, Inc.
ELECTRICITY. Basic concepts in song, action, and animation. (3)	13	1971	Walt Disney
ELECTROCUTION OF THE WORD. Death of the verbal, birth of the visual. (11)	4½	1968	Pyramid
ELEGY. Impossible dream attained but ignored. Animated. (7)	5	1965	McGraw-Hill
EMBRYO. Development and birth of a pheasant chick. (3)	10	1967	Pyramid
THE EMPTY HAND. Karate demonstration by black-belt teachers. B&W. (9)	10	1968	ACI Films
ENCRE. Lithography by three different Paris artists. (1)	20	1971	Int. Film Bureau
THE END OF ONE. Scavenger gulls symbolize greed. Award. (4)	7	1970	Learn. Corp.
THE ENDLESS CYCLE. The constant force and flow of nature. (4)	11	1970	Sterling
ENERGIES. The potential of soundless stimuli. Silent. (3)	9	1958	Film Images
ENERGY. Power systems—past, present, and future. (3)	12	1970	Pyramid
ENTER HAMLET. Pictorial puns based on "To be or not to be." (8), (12)	4	1967	Pyramid
ERNST BARLACH: THE FIGHTER. German sculptor in wood, bronze, and stone. B&W. (1)	14	--	Film Images
ERNST BARLACH: THE VICTOR. Sculpture and woodcuts from his mature period. B&W. (1)	15	--	Film Images

Title and Description	Min.	Year	Distributor
ERSATZ. Plastic almost takes over. Animated. Awards. (8), (11)	8	1961	McGraw-Hill
THE ESKIMO: FIGHT FOR LIFE. Arctic inhabitants. Brief comment. Awards. (2)	51	1970	Ed. Dev. Center
ESTHER. A pretty young woman moving through flowers. (12)	2	1970	Pyramid
ETHIOPIAN MOSAIC. A "people" picture. Punctuated by blackouts. (2)	10	1970	Nat. Film Board
EVASION. City man draws new life from nature. (4), (6)	17	--	Nat. Ed. Film
EVENING ACTIVITY. Unedited record of baboon behavior. (3)	$5\frac{1}{2}$	--	Mod. Media
EXCHANGES. Bias complicates glance between people. B&W. (7), (11)	10	1970	ACI Films
EXERCISES #4. One of five pieces of "visual music." Award. (1)	6	1944	Pyramid
EXPOSITION. Expo '67: sights, sounds, and reactions. (1)	10	1968	Pyramid
EYES. Warns of potential optical hazards. Awards. (13)	4	1970	Int. Film Bur.
EYES ARE FOR SEEING. An exercise in appreciating everyday sights. (1)	9	1967	Sterling
FACE THE REAR. Example of conformity to group pressure. B&W. (8), (13)	4	--	Candid Camera
THE FACES OF PATRIOTS. Pros and cons of protest and dissent in America. (5)	19	1971	Wombat Prod.
THE FAMILY FARM. Modern Danish methods vs. Yugoslavian custom. (2)	14	1970	Sterling
FAMILY OF THE MOUNTAINS: A PERUVIAN VILLAGE. Typical day at home, school, and in the fields. (2)	22	1971	McGraw-Hill
FAMILY TEAMWORK AND YOU. Situational comparison of attitudes and cooperation. (7)	13	1966	AIMS
THE FAMILY—THE BOY WHO LIVED ALONE. Nine-year-old's second thoughts on running away. (7)	11	1967	Encyc. Brit.
FANTASY FOR FOUR STRINGS. Music in tempo with animated visuals. (1)	5	1957	CCM Films

Title and Description	Min.	Year	Distributor
FANTASY OF FEET. Fast-paced study of footwork and footwear. (9)	8	1969	Encyc. Brit.
FAROUN, THE LITTLE CLOWN. Boy's toys and imaginary circus. Animated. (11)	14	1970	Xerox Films
FAST REACTION—MERCURY AND SILVER NITRATE. From the Yale Chemistry Films series. Silent. (3)	5	--	CCM Films
FEET. Hazards of bare feet, benefits of booted ones. (13)	$3\frac{1}{2}$	1970	Int. Film Bureau
THE FENCE. Results of Golden Rule vs. "getting even." Animated. (7)	7	1969	BFA Ed. Media
FIDDLE-DE-DEE. Painted patterns are set to music. Awards. (1), (8)	$3\frac{1}{2}$	1948	Int. Film Bureau
FIGURES FROM A FABLE. Rise and fall of a dwarf civilization. Animated. (10)	10	1970	ACI Films
FILM. A one-character drama with Buster Keaton. B&W. (8), (12)	22	--	Cinema 16
FILM IMPRESSIONS. Film production crew in action. Awards. (1)	5	1969	Mini Films
FINE FEATHERS. Two birds wish away their dearest asset. (7)	$5\frac{1}{2}$	1970	Nat. Film Board
FIRE MOUNTAIN. Second great eruption of Kilauea. Awards. (4)	9	1969	Encyc. Brit.
FIRE SAFETY IN THE LABORATORY. From the Yale Chemistry Films series. Silent. B&W (3), (13)	2	--	CCM Films
THE FIREMAN IS SAD AND CRIES. Life as seen in children's art. Awards. (1)	10	1965	McGraw-Hill
FISHING AT THE STONE WEIR, Part I. From a series on Netsilik Eskimo life. (2)	29	1969	Mod. Media
FISHING AT THE STONE WEIR, Part II. From a series on Netsilik Eskimo life. (2)	27	1969	Mod. Media
FISHING IN ROMANIA. Follows the daily activities of a fisherman. (2)	10	1971	IFF (Bryan)
FISHING ON THE COAST OF JAPAN. The beauty and drudgery of maritime life. (2)	13	1964	IFF (Bryan)
FISHING ON THE DANUBE DELTA. Rumanian fisher's time-honored methods. (2)	15	--	IFF (Bryan)
FISHING ON THE NIGER RIVER. From the series African Village Life. (2)	18	1967	IFF (Bryan)

Title and Description	Min.	Year	Distributor
FIXED BOWLING. Family reactions to rigged game. Silent. B&W. (8)	5	--	Candid Camera
FLOWERS AND BEES—A Spring-time Story. Rhythm of nature in time-lapse and music. (4)	11	1969	Encyc. Brit.
FLY AWAY. Birds, kites, gliders, model and real planes. (5), (9)	11	1967	Doubleday
FOLLOW ME. An easy-to-learn playground game. (9)	5	1969	Encyc. Brit.
FOOD. Productivity of scientific farming. Animated. (3), (13)	4½	--	Nat. Film Board
FOOTBALL FOLLIES. The funny side of professional competition. (8), (9)	25	--	NFL Films
FOREST MURMURS. How careless-ness ruins natural beauty. (4)	8½	--	Perennial Ed.
FOREST PEOPLE. Varied products of Canada, Finland, France. (2)	13	1970	Sterling
THE FOUR SEASONS. Swiss scenes based on Vivaldi's concerto. (1)	14	1968	Thorne Films
FRANCIS BACON: PAINTINGS 1942-1962. Modern man expressed in modern art. (1)	11	1963	Films, Inc.
FREIGHTER. Loading and unloading a foreign ship. Award. (13)	12½	1969	AIMS
FRESCOES IN DANISH CHURCHES. Example of "built-in" Bible history and art. B&W. (1), (13)	10	1954	CCM Films
FROG DEVELOPMENT, Part I. From fertilization to hatching. Silent. (3)	12	--	Mod. Learning
FROG DEVELOPMENT, Part II. From hatching through metamorphosis. Silent. (3)	9½	--	Mod. Learning
FROM THE INSIDE OUT. Teen-age individuality expressed through dance. B&W. (1)	13	1967	Film Images
FROM 3 A.M. TO 10 P.M. A mother's dawn-to-dusk day. Award. B&W. (6)	15	1967	McGraw-Hill
FROM TREE TRUNK TO HEAD. Wood sculpture by Chaim Gross. Silent. B&W. (1)	28	--	Film Images
THE FUGUE. Church music provides treat and retreat. B&W. (1), (6)	19	1966	McGraw-Hill
FULL FATHOM FIVE. Crustaceans, coral, kelp, and sea grasses. (4)	7	1969	Pyramid
GALLERY. 2,000 chronological shots of Western art. (1)	6	1971	Pyramid

Title and Description	Min.	Year	Distributor
GALLERY: A VIEW OF TIME. The Albright-Knox art museum in Buffalo. (1)	14	1969	CCM Films
GAME OF WAR. A half-serious history of war. Animated. (10)	7	--	Film Images
GARBAGE. The world-wide disposal crisis. (13)	10½	1970	King Screen
GATE 73. Simulates the feel of airport and airplane. (9)	13	1970	Holt R&W
GEELONG. City of that name in Victoria, Australia. (6)	22	--	Australia
GEIGER COUNTER. From the Yale Chemistry Films series. Silent. (3)	7	--	CCM Films
THE GENERAL. Civil War adventure and humor. Silent. B&W. (8), (9)	31	1927	Manbeck
GENESIS. Our assembly-line origins. Animated. Award. (11)	6	1966	CCM Films
GENESIS. Old Testament, new approach. Animated. Award. (12), (13)	13	--	CMC/Columbia
GENESIS 1-27: UNDERSEA WORLD. Submarine parallel of a Biblical theme. (4), (13)	8¾	1967	Perennial Ed.
GENIUS MAN. Cave-men reject wheel for weapon. Animated. (10)	1½	1970	ACI Films
GET WET. Activities of swimming, diving, water-skiing. (9)	9	--	Pyramid
GETTING ALONG. Highlights hands in playmates' quarrel. (5)	2	1969	Encyc. Brit.
GETTING EVEN. The reasons for and results of revenge. (7)	3	1969	Encyc. Brit.
GIRL AND THE SPARROW. Fantasy-fable with a Golden Rule moral. (11)	14	1967	Films, Inc.
GLASS. Esthetics and mechanics of glass-blowing. Awards. (1)	11	1958	McGraw-Hill
THE GLOB FAMILY. Human story with ink-blot actors. Animated. (5)	8	--	Learn. Corp.
GO FASTER. Where are we going in such a hurry? Animated. Preview. (6), (7)	9	--	Learn. Corp.
THE GOAL. The ballet-like beauty of basketball. Award. (9)	10	1969	McGraw-Hill
GOIN' HOME. Home, nature, and "the stuff of life." Award. (13)	4	1968	American Ed.
THE GOLDEN FISH. Cat vs. boy's pet fish and canary. Awards. (11)	20	1959	Columbia Pix

Title and Description	Min.	Year	Distributor
GOOD GOODIES. How advertising affects buyer and seller. Animated. (7)	$4\frac{1}{2}$	1971	Bosustow
GRAND CANYON. The American West and Ferde Grofe's suite. (1), (4)	29	--	Walt Disney
GRANTON TRAWLER. Documentary on fishermen off Scotland coast. B&W. (2)	10	1934	McGraw-Hill
GRAY GULL THE HUNTER. Survival of the swiftest among birds of the sea. B&W. (4)	19	1956	Encyc. Brit.
THE GREAT TOY ROBBERY. Santa Claus ambushed! Animated. Awards. (8)	7	1963	McGraw-Hill
THE GREAT TRAIN ROBBERY. The prototype of American westerns. Silent. B&W. (1)	8	1903	Blackhawk
THE GREATER COMMUNITY ANIMAL. Analogy on conformity. Animated. Award. (13)	7	1968	ACI Films
GRINDING WHEAT. From a series on Afghan tribe, the Tajik. B&W. (2)	7	1968	IFF (Bryan)
GROUP HUNTING ON THE SPRING ICE, Part I. From a series on Netsilik Eskimo life. (2)	34	1969	Mod. Media
GROUP HUNTING ON THE SPRING ICE, Part II. From a series on Netsilik Eskimo life. (2)	28	1969	Mod. Media
GROUP HUNTING ON THE SPRING ICE, Part III. From a series on Netsilik Eskimo life. (2)	35	1969	Mod. Media
GROWING (A Computer-Animated Film). Seasonal changes via patterns and music. (1), (3)	7	1970	Encyc. Brit.
GUESSING GAME. Split-screen pantomime matches actions. (5)	7	1969	Encyc. Brit.
GUIDANCE ...DOES COLOR REALLY MAKE A DIFFERENCE? Open-ended problems for group discussion. (7)	11	1969	AIMS
GUIDANCE ... LET'S HAVE RESPECT. Open-ended problems for group discussion. (7)	10	1969	AIMS
GUIDANCE ... WHAT'S RIGHT? Open-ended problems for group discussion. (7)	10	1969	AIMS
GUIDANCE ... WORKING WITH OTHERS. Open-ended problems for group discussion. (7)	10	1969	AIMS

Title and Description	Min.	Year	Distributor
GULL ISLAND. Bird sanctuary near Toronto. Award. (3), (4)	8	1966	A-V Explor.
GYMNASTIC FLASHBACKS. Post-1920 film clips and matching music. (9)	9	1970	Holt R&W
THE HALF-MASTED SCHOONER. Visual accompaniment to song. (5)	$6\frac{1}{2}$	1969	McGraw-Hill
THE HAND. Allegory on mankind vs. force. Animated. Award. (10), (11)	19	1965	McGraw-Hill
HANDS. Preventing accidents, especially on the job. (13)	$3\frac{1}{2}$	1970	Int. Film Bureau
HANDS AND THREADS. Rugs made by a young girl in a village in Mesopotamia. (1)	10	1971	Films, Inc.
HANDS GROW UP. Manual activities of children and adults. (5), (13)	6	1969	Encyc. Brit.
HANG TEN. Likens surfing to ballet. Music. Award. (9)	10	1970	Pyramid
HAPPY ANNIVERSARY. The frustrations of Paris traffic. Awards. B&W. (6), (8)	13	1961	Int. Film Bureau
HAPPY FAMILY PLANNING. Cartoon on contraceptives. Captions in five languages. (13)	8	1969	Plan. Parent.
THE HAPPY PACE OF SWITZERLAND. Musical chase after a dream horse. Award. (11)	11	1963	Thorne Films
HARBOR RHYTHM. Work and recreation at Hamburg's port. Awards. (6)	13	1970	Int. Film Bureau
HARLEM WEDNESDAY. Inner-city activities in paintings and sketches. (1), (6)	10	1959	McGraw-Hill
HARMONIC PHASORS. National Science Foundation-supported lab supplement. Silent. B&W. (3)	7	--	Mod. Media
HARRY BERTOIA'S SCULPTURE. His skill and imagination in metalwork. (1)	23	--	Film Images
HARVEST IN JAPAN. Family work and celebration. Folk music. (2)	10	1964	IFF (Bryan)
HARVESTING. Man and machine in Canadian wheat fields. (2)	10	1968	Pyramid
HAVE I TOLD YOU LATELY THAT I LOVE YOU? Family's dawn-to-dusk communications gap. B&W. (6), (7)	16	1959	U. of So. Cal.
HENRY MOORE AT THE TATE GALLERY. His 1968 sculpture show in England. Silent. (1)	14	1970	Films, Inc.

Title and Description	Min.	Year	Distributor
HERDING CATTLE. From the series African Village Life. (2)	7	1967	IFF (Bryan)
HEY DOC. Black physician and her ghetto clientele. (6)	25	1970	Carousel
THE HIDING PLACE. Joys and fears of a woman's solitude. B&W. (5)	18	1969	Film Images
HIGH SCHOOL. A "good," suburban, middle-class high school. B&W. (6)	75	1969	Zipporah
HIGHLAND INDIANS OF PERU. Man and His World series; minimal narration. (2)	18	1969	Films, Inc.
HIGHLAND PEOPLE. Differentiates hill life in Colombia and Mali. (2)	$12\frac{1}{2}$	1970	Sterling
HIGHWAY. Simulates the sensation of driving. Award. (9)	6	--	Film Images
HIROKO IKOKO. Two Japanese girls get lost in their own city. (2)	20	1970	Xerox Films
THE HOARDER. Bird learns self-defeating results of greed. (7)	$7\frac{1}{2}$	1970	Nat. Film Board
HOBART. About the capital city of Tasmania, Australia. (6)	22	--	Australia
HOLDING ON. Panic of being lost, relief of being found. (5)	4	1969	Encyc. Brit.
HOLLAND: TERRA FERTILIS. Agricultural achievements of the Dutch. (2)	11	1969	ACI Films
HOLY THURSDAY. Based on the William Blake poem. Awards. (4), (12)	18	1969	American Ed.
HOPSCOTCH. The importance of being yourself. Animated. (7)	12	1971	Churchill
HORSES AND HOW THEY LIVE. Environment, behavior, care, and appreciation. (3)	11	1968	AIMS
HOSPITAL. City emergency ward. Awards. Preview. B&W. (6)	85	1970	Zipporah
THE HOUSE. Flashbacks of old house and occupants. Awards. B&W. (11)	32	1961	McGraw-Hill
HOW'S SCHOOL, ENRIQUE? Chicano boy's identity crisis. Awards. (7)	18	1970	AIMS
HUNTER AND THE FOREST. Conscience and the killing of a deer. Open-ended. B&W. (4), (5)	8	1954	Encyc. Brit.

Title and Description	Min.	Year	Distributor
THE HUNTERS. Primitive bushmen of Southwest Africa. Preview. (2), (4)	72	1958	McGraw-Hill
HUNTING WILD DOVES. From the series African Village Life. (2)	8	1967	IFF (Bryan)
HYDROGEN FOUNTAIN. From the Yale Chemistry Films series. Silent. (3)	3	--	CCM Films
HYPOTHESE BETA. Need for reason in a nuclear age. Animated. (10), (11)	7	1966	McGraw-Hill
I AM FIVE. Youngsters' whimsy, logic, and imagination. (11)	10	1967	CCM Films
I KNOW AN OLD LADY WHO SWALLOWED A FLY. Burl Ives' nonsense song. Animated. Awards. (8)	$5\frac{1}{2}$	1963	Int. Film Bureau
IF KANGAROOS JUMP WHY CAN'T YOU? Motivates exercises, written and physical. (9)	8	1971	Atlantis
ILLUSIONS. Eight pantomimes by Marceau student Montanaro. B&W. (1)	15	1969	CMC/Columbia
IMAGE OF A RACE. Tensions of slalom competitor and spectators. (9)	$3\frac{1}{2}$	1971	Thorne Films
IMAGES FROM DEBUSSY. Three of his pieces and their visual equivalents. B&W. (1)	$13\frac{1}{2}$	--	Film Images
IMAGES FROM NATURE. Combines art with "live" seasonal scenes. (4)	7	1962	Thorne Films
IMAGES 67. The forms, man-made and natural, around us. B&W. (1)	9	1967	Assn./Sterl.
IMPRESSIONS OF A GUATEMALA MARKET DAY. Shopping and worshipping on a typical Sunday. (2)	10	1969	Pyramid
IN A BOX. Man's self-imposed havens. Animated. Award. B&W. (13)	4	1968	Learn. Corp.
IN INDIA THE SUN RISES IN THE EAST. Mosaic of contrasting life-styles. Award. (2)	14	1970	McGraw-Hill
IN OUT UP DOWN UNDER OVER UPSIDE DOWN. Captions reinforce song-and-picture story. (5)	8	1970	ACI Films
IN PARIS PARKS. People and activities in the Tuileries Gardens. (6)	14	1955	McGraw-Hill

Title and Description	Min.	Year	Distributor
INDIAN VILLAGERS IN MEXICO. Man and His World series; minimal narration. (2)	12	1970	Films, Inc.
INDUSTRIAL REGION IN SWEDEN. Man and His World series; minimal narration. (2)	18	1969	Films, Inc.
INDUSTRY COMES TO PAKISTAN. Recent changes in manufacturing methods. (2)	17	1972	Films, Inc.
THE INSECTS. Battle of man vs. "things with wings." Animated. (10), (11)	5	1963	McGraw-Hill
INSECTS IN A GARDEN. Aphids, green lacewings, ladybird beetles, ants. (3)	11	--	Encyc. Brit.
INTERNATIONAL SUITCASE. Ethnic differences in gallantry. Silent. B&W. (8)	5	--	Candid Camera
INTERPRETATIONS. Three painters' versions of a single subject. (1)	13	1970	Encyc. Brit.
INTREPID SHADOW. From the Navajo-produced series. Silent. B&W. (2), (13)	18	--	CMC/Columbia
IS THIS OUR FATHER'S WORLD? Man's responsibility for his environment. (7), (13)	10	1971	Family Films
ISLAND PEOPLE. Isolated living in East Africa and off Venezuela. (2)	$13\frac{3}{4}$	1970	Sterling
JAIL KEYS MADE HERE. Advertising signs as an index to society. B&W. (5), (12)	10	1965	McGraw-Hill
JANIE SUE AND TUGALOO. An 8-year-old and her dream horse. (4)	$9\frac{1}{2}$	1970	Centron
JAPANESE FARMERS. Man and His World series; minimal narration. (2)	17	1969	Films, Inc.
JAPAN'S ART—FROM THE LAND. Natural beauty as source of art and serenity. (1)	10	1962	Sterling
JAZZOO. Zoo residents face their visitors. Awards. (Two versions.) (8)	13 & 18	1968	ACI Films
JEFF SETS SAIL. Ten-year-old's trip on a Florida bay. (9)	10	1971	ACI Films
JERUSALEM. A "flash history" of the Holy City. Music. (2)	5	1971	Pyramid
JIGGING FOR LAKE TROUT. From a series on Netsilik Eskimo life. (2)	32	1969	Mod. Media

Title and Description	Min.	Year	Distributor
JOACHIM'S DICTIONARY (Le Dictionnaire de Joachim). A-Z with French words and humor. Animated. Awards. (8)	9	1965	CCM Films
JOIN HANDS, LET GO! Children's game with surprise scenes. (8)	8	1969	Encyc. Brit.
JOSEF HERMAN: 20TH CENTURY ARTIST. Common-man dignity of his subjects. Awards. B&W. (1)	13	--	Time-Life
JOSHUA IN A BOX. Human needs, emotions, and values. Animated. (7)	6	1970	Bosustow
JUGGERNAUT: A FILM OF INDIA. Reactor's impact on Eastern life. Award. (2)	28	1969	Learn. Corp.
THE JUMP and +PLUS - MINUS. Two stories: mechanization; love and war. (7), (10)	11	1966	CCM Films
JUNKYARD. Seasonal beauty in an unlikely spot. (5)	$9\frac{3}{4}$	--	BFA Ed. Media
KANGAROOS. See 'n Tell series; music and natural sound. (4)	10	1970	Films, Inc.
A KEY OF HIS OWN. Loneliness of boy with late-working parents. (6)	$9\frac{1}{4}$	1970	BFA Ed. Media
KEY PEOPLE. Seven individuals, seven ways of life. (6), (8)	5	--	Film Images
KIDS AND BIRDS AND EUROPEAN WINTER. See 'n Tell series; music and natural sound. (4)	10	1971	Films, Inc.
THE KIND-HEARTED ANT. Member upsets colony. Animated. Award. (8), (12)	10	1965	McGraw-Hill
KINDNESS WEEK OR THE SEVEN CAPITAL ELEMENTS. Max Ernst's collages and engravings. Award. B&W. (1)	19	--	Time-Life
A KITE STORY. Fantasy with boy, kites, and a moral. Award. (11)	25	1969	Churchill
KOREAN ALPHABET. Asian ABC's plus music. Animated. Award. (1)	$7\frac{1}{4}$	1968	Universal Ed.
KOSMODROME 1999. Turn-of-the-century traffic jams in space. (8), (11)	12	1969	CCM Films
L.A. 53. Follows train from Chicago to California. (13)	$10\frac{1}{2}$	1970	Journal
L.A. TOO MUCH. Razing a beautiful but "useless" house. (6)	12	1968	Berkeley

Title and Description	Min.	Year	Distributor
LA CATHEDRALE DES MORTS. Sculpture of the Mainz (Germany) cathedral. B&W. (1)	12	1935	Mus./Mod. Art
LA CHAMBRE (The Room). Frustration of confusion and confinement. Animated. (13)	6	1971	Int. Film Bureau
LA POULETTE GRISE. French-Canadian lullaby in single-scene animation. (1), (12)	6	1947	Int. Film Bureau
LADY OF THE LIGHT. Father solves lonely daughter's problem. (12)	19	1967	Walt Disney
LAKE PEOPLE OF SCOTLAND. Man and His World series; minimal narration. (2)	16	1970	Films, Inc.
LAMBING (Parturition in the Ewe). Helping deliver a newborn lamb. Silent. B&W. (13)	20	1966	Encyc. Brit.
LAND FROM THE NORTH SEA. Man and His World series; minimal narration. (2)	18	1969	Films, Inc.
LATE FOR DINNER: Was Dawn Right? Girl's dilemma of honesty vs. obedience. (5)	8	1971	Encyc. Brit.
LAUNCESTON. Life in this city in Tasmania, Australia. (6)	19½	1967	Australia
LAW AND ORDER. Police duty in a black district. Award. B&W. (6), (10)	81	1969	Zipporah
LE CHATELIER'S PRINCIPLE. From the Yale Chemistry Films series. Silent. (3)	3	--	CCM Films
LE FARFALLE. Butterfly's movements, color, and form. (4)	5	--	Xerox Films
LE MERLE. French-Canadian folk song. Animated. Awards. (8)	4	1958	Int. Film Bureau
LEAF. Journey of a leaf in the high Sierras. (4)	7	1962	Holt R&W
LEAVES. Child's paper leaves replace fallen ones. (5)	13	1968	ACI Films
THE LEMONADE STAND: WHAT'S FAIR? A problem situation for viewers to resolve. (7)	14	1970	Encyc. Brit.
LES ESCARGOTS. Man's repeated excesses. Animated. Awards. (11)	11	1966	McGraw-Hill
L'HOMME VITE. Simulates auto-race sensation. French captions. (9)	9	--	Nat. Film Board
LIFE CYCLE. Mankind, from womb to tomb. Animated. (7)	7	1971	ACI Films

Title and Description	Min.	Year	Distributor
LIFE IN NORTH CHINA. Features parade of city and country workers. (2)	18	1971	Films, Inc.
LIFE OF A BUTTERFLY. Life cycle of a black swallowtail. Silent. (3)	18	--	Mod. Learning
LIFE STORY OF A PLANT (About Flowers). How seeds develop, scatter, and "recycle." (3)	7	1964	Encyc. Brit.
THE LINE. First standard gauge railroad across Australia. (2)	13	1969	Australia
LINES AND DOTS. Mediator destroys two combatants. Animated. (10)	7	1970	Sterling
LINES—VERTICAL AND HORIZONTAL. Two films in one. Abstract animation. Awards. (1)	13	--	Int. Film Bureau
LITHO. Lithography: history and technique. Award. (1)	14	1961	McGraw-Hill
THE LITTLE AIRPLANE THAT GREW. Boy's vision: fantasy or reality? Award. (11)	9	1970	Learn. Corp.
THE LITTLE BLUE APRON. The supremacy of good over evil. Animated. (11)	8	1968	BFA Ed. Media
THE LITTLE GIRAFFE. Adventures of a stuffed toy. Animated. (11)	8	--	McGraw-Hill
THE LITTLE MARINER. Boy's toy boat and imaginary voyage. Award. (11)	20	1965	Encyc. Brit.
LIVING (Vivre). Results of war and its impact on witnesses. B&W. (10)	8	1959	McGraw-Hill
LIVING THINGS ARE EVERYWHERE. Variety of plant and animal relationships. (3)	11	--	Encyc. Brit.
LIZARD. See 'n Tell series; music and natural sound. (3)	11	1970	Films, Inc.
L'OISEAU (The Bird). Bird's dream of liberty backfires. Animated. (11)	9	1966	McGraw-Hill
LONG EARS. How rabbits got that way. Animated. (12)	6	--	CCM Films
LOPSIDELAND. Familiar objects from unusual perspectives. (1)	5	1969	Encyc. Brit.
LOREN MacIVER. Contemporary painter's art; two parts. Silent. (1)	46	--	Film Images
THE LOST WORLD. A. C. Doyle's tale of Amazon expedition. Silent. B&W. (11), (12)	48	1925	Cine Concepts
LUCY. Story of an unwed, pregnant teen-ager. (13)	13	1970	Pictura Films

Title and Description	Min.	Year	Distributor
MACHINE. Who's boss: man or inventions? Animated. Award. (11)	10	1966	Pyramid
THE MAGIC BALLOONS. Boy rescues balloon-friend from adults. (11)	17	1969	Learn. Corp.
MAGIC FRAME—ADVENTURES IN SEEING. An exercise in observation; with "song-track." (5)	11	1971	Coronet
MAGIC HANDS. Children's solutions to typical problems. (11)	7	1969	Encyc. Brit.
MAGIC RITES: DIVINATION BY ANIMAL TRACKS. From the series African Village Life. (2)	7	1967	IFF (Bryan)
MAGIC RITES: DIVINATION BY CHICKEN SACRIFICE. From the series African Village Life. (2)	7	1967	IFF (Bryan)
MAGIC SNEAKERS. Boy's adventure with unexpected ending. (11)	8	1969	Encyc. Brit.
THE MAGICIAN. Trickster turns play guns into real ones. B&W. (10)	12	1963	Sterling
THE MAGNETISM OF MAGNETS. Open-ended approach; for primary grades. (3)	10	1966	AIMS
MAGNOLIA. Pantomime of a ghost-town flower spirit. B&W. (11)	7	1963	Thorne Films
MAITRE. Satire on modern artists. Animated. (1), (8)	12	1970	SIM Prod.
MAKING BREAD. From a series on Afghan tribe, the Tajik. B&W. (2)	11	1968	IFF (Bryan)
MAKING FELT. From a series on Afghan tribe, the Pushtu. (1), (2)	9	1968	IFF (Bryan)
MAKING GUN POWDER. From a series on Afghan tribe, the Tajik. B&W. (2), (3)	10	1968	IFF (Bryan)
MAMMALS. On man as exploiter and exploited. Awards. B&W. (7)	10	1959	McGraw-Hill
MAN AND COLOR. Color and motion in nature and in technology. (1)	12	1968	Pyramid
MAN AND HIS WORLD. Metaphor of earth as a soccer ball in our hands. (11)	2	1969	ACI Films
MAN CHANGES THE NILE. Man and His World series; minimal narration. (2)	13	1969	Films, Inc.
MAN OF ARAN. Irish fishermen against the elements. B&W. (2)	77	1934	McGraw-Hill
MAN TO MAN. Alienated 10-year-old boy and his father. (13)	13	--	Perennial Ed.

Title and Description	Min.	Year	Distributor
A MAN'S HANDS. Manual mannerisms and manifestations. (5), (8)	5	1970	Pyramid
MARCH-APRIL: THE COMING OF SPRING. The snow melts as spring returns to a forest (4)	9	1967	Films, Inc.
MARCHING THE COLOURS. Music translated into imagery. Animated. (1)	3	1942	Int. Film Bureau
MARY'S DAY 1965. Modern worship, California-style. Silent. (13)	11	1965	Glascock
MASAI IN TANZANIA. Man and His World series; minimal narration. (2)	13	1970	Films, Inc.
MATCHING UP. Primary test for matching of body parts. (5)	4	1969	Encyc. Brit.
MATRIX. Computer-generated design in motion. Animated. (5)	$5\frac{1}{2}$	1970	Pyramid
ME, TOO? Case study of boy's reaction to rejection. (5)	3	1969	Encyc. Brit.
MELBOURNE. Australian account of one of its major cities. (6)	20	1966	Australia
MEMENTO. Aftermath of three auto accidents. Awards. (13)	9	1967	CMC/Columbia
MEN'S DANCE. From a series on Afghan tribe, the Pushtu. (1), (2)	11	1968	IFF (Bryan)
MERBABIES. Ocean-children's water games. Animated. (11)	9	1970	Walt Disney
THE MERRY-GO-ROUND HORSE. Ragamuffin's steed comes to life. Award. (11)	17	1968	Learn. Corp.
METAMORPHOSIS OF THE CELLO. The technique of cellist Maurice Gendron. B&W. (1)	14	--	Film Images
MICE AND HOW THEY LIVE. Basic concepts of habits and habitat. (3)	11	1969	AIMS
MICROSECOND. 3,000 years in a flash. Animated. Awards. (13)	6	1969	S-L Films
MIKE AND STEVE VISIT THE SHOPPING CENTER. Shopping plaza vs. "mom and pop" stores. (6)	14	1969	Encyc. Brit.
MILLIKAN'S OIL DROP EXPERIMENT. From the Yale Chemistry Films series. Silent. B&W. (3)	6	--	CCM Films
MIME OVER MATTER. Man's relationship to life's "better things." (1), (7)	12	1970	SIM Prod.
MINERS OF BOLIVIA. From Man and His World series. Award. (2)	15	1969	Films, Inc.

Title and Description	Min.	Year	Distributor
MINER'S RIDGE. Park area rescued from industrialization. (4)	22	--	AIM/Assn.
MINT TEA. Parisian's twentieth-century loneliness. Award. B&W. (6)	20	1962	McGraw-Hill
THE MIRACULOUS DREAM OF CIRCLES. Story-song words are seen, heard, and voiced. (5)	15	1971	ACI Films
MR. KOUMAL CARRIES THE TORCH. Cartoon of optimistic, frustrated idea-man. (8)	2	1969	SIM Prod.
MR. KOUMAL CRUSADES FOR LOVE. Cartoon of optimistic, frustrated idea-man. (5)	2	1969	SIM Prod.
MR. KOUMAL DISCOVERS "KOU-MALIA." Cartoon of optimistic, frustrated idea-man. (13)	2	1971	SIM Prod.
MR. KOUMAL FACES DEATH. Cartoon of optimistic, frustrated idea-man. (7)	2	1969	SIM Prod.
MR. KOUMAL FLIES LIKE A BIRD. Cartoon of optimistic, frustrated idea-man. (11)	2	1969	SIM Prod.
MR. KOUMAL GETS INVOLVED. Cartoon of optimistic, frustrated idea-man. (10)	$1\frac{1}{2}$	1971	SIM Prod.
MR. KOUMAL INVENTS A ROBOT. Cartoon of optimistic, frustrated idea-man. (3)	$1\frac{3}{4}$	1969	SIM Prod.
MR. KOUMAL MOVES TO THE COUNTRY. Cartoon of optimistic, frustrated idea-man. (4)	$2\frac{1}{2}$	1969	SIM Prod.
MIXUMMERDAYDREAM. Composer's reveries while at the piano. (11)	10	1971	ACI Films
THE MOCKINGBIRD. Civil War short story by Bierce. Award. B&W. (10), (12)	39	1962	CCM Films
MODEL FOR WEIGHT RELATIONS IN CHEMICAL REACTIONS. From the Yale Chemistry Films series. Silent. B&W. (3)	4	--	CCM Films
MOEBIUS FLIP. Psychedelic "sci-fi" on skis. Awards. (9), (11)	25	1969	Pyramid
MONKEY AND THE ORGAN GRINDER. Life of gradually vanishing entertainers. (5)	11	1971	Encyc. Brit.
MOODS OF SURFING. Pacific Ocean pleasures and perils. Awards. (9)	15	1967	Pyramid
MOON'S MEN. England's shrimp fishermen at ebb tide. B&W. (2)	13	1964	CMC/Columbia

Title and Description	Min.	Year	Distributor
MORNING, NOON, AND EVENING. Compares lives of country and city families. (6)	13½	1970	AIMS
MOSAIC. Cinema "op" art. Animated. Awards. (1)	5½	1965	Int. Film Bureau
MOSLEM FAMILY IN YUGOSLAVIA. The practice of minority customs and religion. (2)	9	1965	IFF (Bryan)
MOTHLIGHT. "Moth's eye view" of life and death. Silent. (1)	4	1963	Pyramid
MOTION PICTURE. "Instant tour" from the Midwest to New York. (1)	4	--	Cinema 16
A MOUNTAIN DAY. Two boys and a girl explore on horseback. (4)	9	1970	Arthur Barr
MOUNTAIN FAMILY IN EUROPE. See 'n Tell series; music and natural sound. (2)	9	1971	Films, Inc.
MOUNTAIN PEOPLE. Compares lives of the Swiss and the Nepalese. (2)	13½	1970	Sterling
MOZART AND BARRIOS ON SIX STRINGS. Guitar recital by pupil of Segovia. B&W. (1)	9	--	Film Images
MROFNOC. World (like title) shown scrambled. Awards. B&W. (7)	7	1965	Film Images
MULTIPLY AND SUBDUE. Man's environmental stewardship. Award. (4)	8	1970	Pyramid
MUSIC. From school bands to Beatles to Bach. (1)	54	1969	NBC-TV
MY FRIEND THE FISH. A five-year-old's love for his new-found pet. (5)	18	1966	CCM Films
MY FRIEND THE ROBIN. Young boy's adoption of a baby bird. (5)	9½	1971	Journal
NAICA AND THE SQUIRRELS. Rumanian boy's love for animals. Awards. (4)	20	1966	McGraw-Hill
NANOOK OF THE NORTH. Flaherty's silent classic on Eskimo life. B&W. (1), (2)	55	1922	McGraw-Hill
NATURE IS FOR PEOPLE. Wilderness peace vs. hectic urban pace. (4)	9	1969	AIMS
THE NAUGHTY DUCKLING. On maturity and responsibility. Animated. (7)	9	1970	Encyc. Brit.
THE NAUGHTY OWLET. Crisis teaches baby owl a lasting lesson. Animated. (7)	8	1970	ACI Films

Title and Description	Min.	Year	Distributor
THE NAVAJO SILVERSMITH. From the Navajo-produced series. Silent. B&W. (1)	20	--	CMC/Columbia
A NAVAJO WEAVER. From the Navajo-produced series. Silent. B&W. (1)	22	--	CMC/Columbia
NAWI. Uganda cattle-drive and temporary camps. (2)	22	1970	Churchill
NEIGHBORS. Trivial dispute's ugly result. Animated. Awards. (10)	8	1952	Int. Film Bureau
NEUF MINUTES. Wrestling match at Quebec Winter Games. (9)	9	--	Nat. Film Board
NEW LIFE FOR A SPANISH FARMER. Man and His World series; minimal narration. (2)	18	1969	Films, Inc.
THE NEWBORN CALF. Delivery, afterbirth, early growth. Preview. (3)	11	1971	Encyc. Brit.
NIGHT ON BALD MOUNTAIN. Animated version of Moussorgsky's piece. B&W. (1)	8	1933	McGraw-Hill
1968 WOMEN'S OLYMPIC COMPULSORY ROUTINES. Japanese and French interpretations. Silent. (9)	10	1968	Athletic
NIOK. Cambodian boy's devotion to pet elephant. (2), (4)	29	1960	Walt Disney
NOBI AND THE SLAVE TRADERS. African boy's defense of his village. Animated. (12)	30	1970	Encyc. Brit.
NOISE. Introduction to sound and "ear pollution." (3)	10	--	BFA Ed. Media
NORTH SEA ISLANDERS. Man and His World series; minimal narration. (2)	19	1970	Films, Inc.
A NORWEGIAN FJORD. Man and His World series; minimal narration. (2)	13	1969	Films, Inc.
THE NOSE (Le Nez). Based on the story by Gogol. Animated. B&W. (12)	11	1963	McGraw-Hill
NOTES ON A TRIANGLE. Geometric "ballet" in waltz rhythm. Awards. (1)	5	1968	Int. Film Bureau
THE NUER. Tribal life in Ethiopia and Sudan. Award. (2)	75	1970	McGraw-Hill
NUMBERS. Digits assume life-like qualities. Animated. (3)	10	1966	McGraw-Hill
NUMERALS EVERYWHERE. Introduces numbers as useful symbols. (3)	9	1969	Encyc. Brit.

Title and Description	Min.	Year	Distributor
N.Y., N.Y. Example of film impressionism. Awards. (1), (6)	16	1959	Pyramid
NZURI: EAST AFRICA. Primitive and civil sides of Nairobi. Awards. (2)	30	1970	Pyramid
O CANADA. "Flash" history: French settlement till present. (2)	4	1970	Pyramid
OASIS IN THE SAHARA. Man and His World series; minimal narration. (2)	16	1970	Films, Inc.
AN OCCURRENCE AT OWL CREEK BRIDGE. Pre-death fantasy of Civil War spy. Awards. B&W. (10), (12)	27	1962	McGraw-Hill
OFFSPRING. Where (and how) all the "flowers" have gone. (10)	5	1968	CCM Films
OIL IN LIBYA. Man and His World series; minimal narration. (2)	16	1969	Films, Inc.
OLD ANTELOPE LAKE. From the Navajo-produced series. Silent. B&W. (4)	11	--	CMC/Columbia
THE OLD MILL. Storm threatens animals' peaceful community. (4)	9	--	Walt Disney
THE OLDER INFANT: FOUR MONTHS TO ONE YEAR. Baboons of Nairobi at four-month intervals. (3)	8	1969	Mod. Media
OMEGA. Symbolic rebirth of mankind. Award. (11)	13	1969	Pyramid
ON THE MOVE. Lockheed planes, past and future. Award. (13)	16	1969	Lockheed
ONCE UPON A TIME THERE WAS A DOT. Exercise in creative configuration. Animated. (1)	8	1964	McGraw-Hill
ONE SPRING DAY. Reversing our self-imposed pollution. (4)	$8\frac{1}{2}$	1970	American Ed.
ONE TURKEY, TWO TURKEYS. Captions reinforce song-and-picture story. (5)	6	1970	ACI Films
ONION FARMING. From the series African Village Life. (2)	7	1967	IFF (Bryan)
ONLY BENJY KNOWS: SHOULD HE TELL? Situation for the pros and cons of tattling. (7)	4	1970	Encyc. Brit.
OPUS: IMPRESSIONS OF BRITISH ART AND CULTURE. Current examples of qualities and trends. Awards. (1)	29	1967	Pyramid
OPUS 3. Geometric forms and matching sound. Award. B&W. (1)	7	1968	Nat. Film Board

Title and Description	Min.	Year	Distributor
ORANGE AND BLUE. Two beach balls playing in a junkyard. (5)	15	1962	McGraw-Hill
THE ORATOR. Dull speeches and empty words. Animated. Awards. (5)	11	1962	McGraw-Hill
ORPHEON. Musical mischief: band vs. baton. Animated. (8)	8	1966	McGraw-Hill
OUR LIVING FORESTS. Balance and interdependence of wildlife. (4)	11	1968	AIMS
OVER THE ANDES IN ECUADOR. Man and His World series; minimal narration. (2)	18	1969	Films, Inc.
OVERTURE/NYITANY. Musical X-ray of chick embryo. Awards. (1), (3)	9	1965	McGraw-Hill
PACIFIC 231. Based on the French symphony of the same name. B&W. (1)	10	1952	Audio/Brandon
PAPUA AND NEW GUINEA. Man and His World series; minimal narration. (2)	17	1970	Films, Inc.
PARABLE. Circus allegory of Christ's passion and death. (13)	20	1963	Nat. Ed. Film
PARADISE LOST. Man's pollution snuffs out wildlife. Animated. (4)	4	1970	Benchmark
PAS DE DEUX. Ballet for two, with special effects. Awards. B&W. (1)	$13\frac{1}{2}$	1969	Learn. Corp.
PATTERNS. Water reflections and musical accompaniment. (5)	6	--	Walt Disney
PAVE IT AND PAINT IT GREEN. Yosemite: example of nature vs. tourism. (4), (7)	27	1970	Berkeley
THE PENNY ARCADE (Capt. Flash vs. The Bat). Vicarious adventures of frustrated cartoonist. B&W. (8)	45	1965	CCM Films
PEOPLE. How we're all alike and still different. Award. (13)	$10\frac{1}{2}$	1969	AIMS
PEOPLE MIGHT LAUGH AT US. Home-made toys of Canadian-Indian children. (1)	9	--	Nat. Film Board
THE PERILS OF PRISCILLA. Lost cat tries to cope with city dangers. (13)	$16\frac{1}{2}$	1969	Churchill
PERMUTATIONS. Recent example of computer graphics. Award. (1)	7	1968	Pyramid
THE PERSISTENT SEED. Nature prevails over steel and concrete. (4)	14	1963	Perennial Ed.
PERTH. About the capital city of Western Australia. (6)	19	1967	Australia

Title and Description	Min.	Year	Distributor
PETS: A BOY AND HIS DOG. Story of pride, affection, and companionship. (6)	11	1969	BFA Ed. Media
A PHANTASY. Early surreal animation by McLaren. Awards. (1)	8	1948	Int. Film Bureau
THE PHANTOM FREIGHTER. Cargo plane that doubles as a passenger flight. (13)	15	--	ACI Films
PHASE DEMONSTRATION. From the Yale Chemistry Films series. Silent. (3)	1	--	CCM Films
PHOSPHINE SMOKE RINGS. From the Yale Chemistry Films series. Silent. (3)	2	--	CCM Films
PHYSICS IN F-MAJOR. Oscilloscope in synch with Scarlatti music. (1), (3)	9	1970	Xerox Films
PICNIC. Captions reinforce song-and-picture story. (5)	7	1970	ACI Films
PIER 73. Simulates the feel of ocean travel. (13)	11	1970	Holt R&W
PIGEONS! PIGEONS! Flight, families, and feeding in the park. (6)	9	1969	Encyc. Brit.
PIGS! Close-up of an unfairly ignored species. (4)	11	1967	Churchill
PITTSBURGH MUSICAL COPS. The motions of directing traffic set to music. B&W. (5), (8)	$2\frac{1}{2}$	--	Candid Camera
A PLACE IN THE SUN. The competition for status. Animated. (7)	7	1960	Films, Inc.
A PLACE TO STAND. A split-screen mosaic of Ontario. Award. (1), (2)	18	1967	McGraw-Hill
PLAINS PEOPLE. Contrasts the Masai of Africa and U.S. Indians. (2)	14	1970	Sterling
PLATEAU FARMERS IN FRANCE. Man and His World series; minimal narration. (2)	15	1969	Films, Inc.
PLAYGROUND. Captions reinforce song-and-picture story. (5)	7	1970	ACI Films
POLICE POWER AND FREEDOM OF ASSEMBLY. Dick Gregory's march on the 1968 Democratic Convention. B&W. (10)	7	1969	Perennial Ed.
POLLUTION. Musical satire with Calypso lyrics. (4), (8)	4	1968	Nat. Med. AV
POOL SHARKS. Romantic rivalry; with W. C. Fields. Silent. B&W. (8)	14	1915	Pyramid

Title and Description	Min.	Year	Distributor
POP SHOW. What was "in" with the jet set of the mid-1960s. (8)	8	1966	Pyramid
POPPYCOCK! Portly hero's amorous competitions. Awards. (8)	16	1966	McGraw-Hill
POPSICLE. The thrills and dangers of motorcycling. Award. (9)	11	1969	American Ed.
PORT MORESBY. City in New Guinea island-territory. (6)	9	1971	Australia
PORTRAIT OF A HORSE. Beast vs. man who would subdue it. Animated. (4)	8	1967	Pyramid
POSADA. Review of this Mexican print-maker's works. B&W. (1)	10	1964	Film Images
POSTERS: MAY-JUNE 1968. Revolutionary art of the French students. (1), (10)	23	1968	Film Images
POTEMKIN. USSR classic about a pre-Bolshevik naval mutiny. B&W. (1), (10)	67	1926	CCM Films
POTTERY MAKING. From a series on Afghan tribe, the Tajik. B&W. (1), (2)	15	1969	IFF (Bryan)
POW WOW. Campus customs and football bands. Awards. B&W. (8), (9)	7	1960	CCM Films
PREPARATION FOR CHILDBIRTH and TWO HOSPITAL DELIVERIES. Prenatal care. Silent, with titles. Color/B&W. (3), (13)	9	1970	Claremont
PRINCIPLES OF MASS SPECTRO-METER. From the Yale Chemistry Films series. Silent. (3)	11	--	CCM Films
THE PRIVATE LIFE OF A CAT. Birth, love, and growth of "common" cats. Silent. B&W. (3)	22	1951	Cinema 16
THE PROBLEM. A burlesque on bureaucratic decisions. Animated. (7), (8)	12	1966	CCM Films
PROPERTIES OF MIXTURES AND COMPOUNDS. From the Yale Chemistry Films series. Silent. (3)	4	--	CCM Films
PSYCHEDELIC WET. Perceptions of, on, and below water. Awards. (9)	8	1967	ACI Films
THE PUFFED-UP DRAGON. Monster and villagers in confrontation. Animated. (5)	10	1966	Sterling
PURSUIT OF HAPPINESS THE MATERIALISTIC WAY. Counterpoints scenes of U.S. plenty and poverty. (6), (7)	4	1965	Thorne Films

Title and Description	Min.	Year	Distributor
THE PUSHER. Self-defeating results of ambition; in mime. B&W. (7)	17	1962	CCM Films
QUEBEC WINTER CARNIVAL. Parade, ice sculpture, and toboggan races. (9)	10	1969	Canada
QUEER BIRDS. Two pelicans team up for self-help. Animated. B&W. (7), (8)	10	1965	McGraw-Hill
THE QUIET RACKET. Man disappointed in search for solitude. (4)	$7\frac{1}{2}$	--	Nat. Film Board
RABBITS. Foods, family life, habits, and hutches. (3)	11	1969	AIMS
RAGAMUFFIN. A small boy's desires, dreams, and disappointments. B&W. (5)	10	1947	Audio/Brandon
RAIL. British trains, past and present. Awards. (13)	13	1968	ACI Films
RAILROADED. Railroad guard's confrontation with intruder. B&W. (11)	10	1968	McGraw-Hill
THE RAILRODDER. Buster Keaton in a right-of-way slapstick. (8)	25	--	McGraw-Hill
RAIN. Captions reinforce song-and-picture story. (5)	8	1970	ACI Films
RAIN (Regen). Filmed during three months in Amsterdam. B&W. (1), (6)	12	1931	Film Images
RAIN IN THE CITY. Reactions and activities, before and after. B&W. (6)	14	1970	Int. Film Bureau
RAINFOREST PEOPLE. The Congo pygmies and Venezuelan Indians. (2)	$13\frac{1}{2}$	1970	Sterling
RAINSHOWER. Rain's effect on plants, animals, and people. (4), (5)	$14\frac{1}{2}$	1965	Churchill
RAINY SEASON IN WEST AFRICA. Man and His World series; minimal narration. (2)	14	1970	Films, Inc.
RANCHERO AND GAUCHOS IN ARGENTINA. Man and His World series; minimal narration. (2)	17	1969	Films, Inc.
RAPIDS OF THE COLORADO. The danger and beauty of river and canyon. (4), (9)	15	1970	Pyramid
RED AND BLACK. Bullfight parody in live action and animation. (8)	7	1965	Sterling
THE RED BALLOON. French boy and friendly toy. Many awards. (11)	33	1956	CCM Films
THE RED KITE. Answers to questions on life, death, and God. (7), (12)	17	1966	Nat. Film Board

Title and Description	Min.	Year	Distributor
RED STONE DANCER. One of Gaudier-Brzeska's sculptures. B&W. (1)	5	--	Film Images
RE-DISCOVERY. New ways of expressing old ideas. (1)	6	1971	AIMS
THE REED. Danube harvesting set to Orff's "Carmina Burana." B&W. (1)	9	1967	CCM Films
THE REFINER'S FIRE. Fate of idealists and pioneers. Animated. (7)	6	1969	Doubleday
REFLECTIONS IN A POND. Includes swans, geese, and great blue heron. (4)	10	1969	Journal
REFLECTIONS OF A COMPANY. A paper producer's "image" film. Awards. (13)	8	1969	Zellerbach
REMBRANDT'S CHRIST. Painter's selection of Biblical models. Awards. B&W. (1), (13)	$40\frac{1}{2}$	--	Time-Life
THE REPORT CARD: HOW DOES RICCARDO FEEL? Reactions to scolding instead of praise. (13)	5	1971	Encyc. Brit.
RESPONSE OF A RESONANT SYSTEM TO A FREQUENCY STEP. National Science Foundation-supported lab demonstration. Silent. B&W. (3)	12	--	Ed. Dev. Ctr.
RESURRECTION. Figurative "end of the line" for steam engine. B&W. (13)	9	1970	American Ed.
THE REVOLUTION. The overthrow of tyrants by dictators. Animated. (10)	8	1970	ACI Films
RHINOCEROS. The Ionesco play on conformity. Animated. (12)	11	1964	McGraw-Hill
RICE FARMERS IN THAILAND. Man and His World series; minimal narration. (2)	19	1969	Films, Inc.
RICKY'S GREAT ADVENTURE. Blind boy uses other senses for discovery. (4), (5)	11	1969	Atlantis
THE RIDE. Oddball is conveyed in variety of vehicles. (8), (9)	7	1965	McGraw-Hill
THE RINK. Ice skaters, young and old, on a Sunday. (9)	10	1963	Films, Inc.
THE RISE AND FALL OF THE GREAT LAKES. The region's past and its probable future. (4)	17	1969	Pyramid
RIVER. From mountain origin, through Yosemite, to valley. B&W. (4)	8	--	Pyramid
THE RIVER. Ecological history from Indian days to now. (3)	9	--	Aim/Assn.

Title and Description	Min.	Year	Distributor
RIVER: AN ALLEGORY. From tiny spring to ocean destination. (4)	11	1968	Int. Film Bureau
RIVER JOURNEY ON THE UPPER NILE. Man and His World series; minimal narration. (2)	18	1969	Films, Inc.
RIVER PEOPLE. Mali's Niger river and Colombia's Magdalena. (2)	12	1970	Sterling
RIVER PEOPLE OF CHAD. Man and His World series; minimal narration. (2)	20	1969	Films, Inc.
RIVER: WHERE DO YOU COME FROM? Water-cycle from origin to ocean. Award. (3)	10	1969	Learn. Corp.
THE ROBBER'S DIRGE. Group attitudes: hostile and passive. Animated. (10)	8	1970	Sterling
THE ROBIN. Telephoto view of life-cycle and enemies. (3), (4)	$5\frac{1}{2}$	1966	A-V Explor.
A ROCK IN THE ROAD. Practical jokes vs. Golden Rule. Animated. (7)	6	1968	BFA Ed. Media
ROMANIA. Man and His World series; minimal narration. (2)	18	1970	Films, Inc.
ROMEO. Boy helps girl pass exam, and fails his own. B&W. (7)	9	1962	CCM Films
ROYAL ROCOCO (1725 - 1750). Examples of eighteenth-century elegance. Award. (1)	12	--	Time-Life
RYTHMETIC. Pictorial pun with animated digits. Awards. (3)	$8\frac{1}{2}$	1956	Nat. Film Board
SAFETY AS WE PLAY. Captions based on song-and-picture story. (13)	7	1971	ACI Films
SAHARA FANTASIA: A DESERT FESTIVAL. Celebration events of the Moroccan nomads. (2), (9)	9	1970	IFF (Bryan)
SAILING. A summer day of sport and storm. Award. (9)	15	1963	McGraw-Hill
SAME SUBJECT, DIFFERENT TREATMENT. Subjective interpretations in varied media. (1)	10	1969	ACI Films
SAN FRANCISCO. Scenes, landmarks, and people. Award. (6)	4	1969	Pyramid
SAND CASTLES. Compares daydreams of parents and children. (11)	6	1970	AIMS
THE SATIRIC EYE. Reversal of customs and pretensions. Animated. (7)	13	1970	Learn. Corp.

Title and Description	Min.	Year	Distributor
SCHOOL DAY IN JAPAN. See 'n Tell series; music and natural sound. (2)	10	1970	Films, Inc.
A SCRAP OF PAPER AND A PIECE OF STRING. Near-human friendship between objects. Animated. (5), (8)	6	1963	McGraw-Hill
THE SCRIBE. Keaton pantomime on construction safety. (8), (13)	30	--	Aim/Assn.
SEA SORCERY. Carribean underwater life and configurations. (4)	15	1970	McGraw-Hill
SEACOAST PEOPLE. Harvest of Maine lobsters and Norway crabs. (2)	$14\frac{1}{4}$	1970	Sterling
SECOND WEAVER. From the Navajo-produced series. Silent. B&W. (1)	9	--	CMC/Columbia
THE SEEING EYE. Lonely boy on a South China Sea island. B&W. (2)	28	1966	McGraw-Hill
SEVEN AUTHORS IN SEARCH OF A READER. The writer-reader relationship. Awards. B&W. (11), (12)	21	1965	McGraw-Hill
SHALLOW WELL PROJECT. From the Navajo-produced series. Silent. B&W. (13)	14	--	CMC/Columbia
THE SHAPE AND COLOR GAME. Study of color, form, texture, and structure. (1)	8	--	Sterling
THE SHAPE OF THINGS. The diversity of 11 sculptors' work. Award. (1)	10	--	Int. Film Bureau
SHEARING YAKS. From a series on Afghan tribe, the Tajik. B&W. (2)	9	1969	IFF (Bryan)
SHEEP AND HOW THEY LIVE. Care and behavior in natural environment. (3)	$13\frac{1}{2}$	1968	AIMS
SHEEP IN WOOD. Ukrainian master making a woodcut. (1)	10	1970	Artscope
SHEEP, SHEEP, SHEEP. Flock behavior in a mountain environment. (4)	11	1970	Churchill
THE SHEPHERD. His flock, dogs, and loneliness. Awards. B&W. (5)	11	1955	Int. Film Bureau
SHEPHERD DOG AND HIS FLOCK. "See 'n Tell" series; music and natural sound. (5)	8	1970	Films, Inc.
SHIBAM. Saudi Arabian city's dependence on water. B&W. (6)	14	1970	McGraw-Hill

Title and Description	Min.	Year	Distributor
A SHIP IS BORN. The relationship of man to his work. B&W. (13)	9	1969	Encyc. Brit.
THE SHOOTING GALLERY. Examines freedom, conformity, and love. (7)	5	1970	SIM Prod.
SHORT AND SUITE. "Visual music" via special effects. Awards. (1)	5	1960	Int. Film Bureau
SIGNS, SIGNALS, AND SYMBOLS. Neons, hands, and other nonverbal communication. (5)	11	1970	AIMS
SILK MOTH. See 'n Tell series; music and natural sounds. (3)	7	1970	Films, Inc.
SING OF THE BORDER. People, history, and landmarks of Scotland. (2)	$19\frac{1}{2}$	--	Int. Film Bureau
THE SINGING STREET. The songs and games of Edinburgh children. B&W. (2), (6)	20	--	British
SIRENE. Modern mermaid vs. bureaucratic machinery. (6), (11)	10	1970	Int. Film Bureau
SISYFOS. Modern version of the Greek myth. Animated. (12)	8	1969	McGraw-Hill
SIU MEI WONG—WHO SHALL I BE? Bicultural conflicts of Chinatown girl. Award. (6), (7)	18	1970	Learn. Corp.
SKATER DATER. Boy gives up skateboard for "love." Awards. (5), (9)	18	1965	Pyramid
SKETCHES. Mime portrays athlete, games, sculptor, and nightmare. B&W. (1)	16	--	CMC/Columbia
SKI FEVER. Asks about skiing, "Why do people do it?" (9)	9	1971	BFA Ed. Media
SKI THE OUTER LIMITS. Esthetic treatment of athletic feats. Awards. (9)	25	1968	Pyramid
SKY. Dawn to dusk in time-lapse. Awards. (1), (4)	10	1958	McGraw-Hill
SKY CAPERS. Gymnastics of free-fall parachuting. Awards. (9)	15	1968	Pyramid
SKYSCRAPER. Impressionist record of a building going up. (6)	20	1960	CCM/Films
SLEEP WELL. Political nightmare of an Everyman. Animated. (13)	9	1969	ACI Films
SLOW REACTION—IRON AND OXYGEN. From the Yale Chemistry Films series. Silent. (3)	2	--	CCM Films

Title and Description	Min.	Year	Distributor
SMOKE SCREEN. Anticigarette message for elementary and high school. (13)	5	1970	Pyramid
SOIR DE FETE. Holiday mood in music and animation. Award. (13)	6	1955	CCM Films
SOLILOQUY OF A RIVER. Prepollution beauty and life. Award. (4)	19	1969	Nature Guide
SOLO. Joy of achievement in mountain climbing. (9)	15	1971	Pyramid
SOLUTION, EVAPORATION, AND CRYSTALLIZATION. From the Yale Chemistry Films series. Silent. (3)	3	--	CCM Films
SOMEDAY. Trip to ball game, market, zoo, and boat ride. (6)	9	1967	Sterling
SOUND ABOUT. Open-ended introduction to concept of sound. (3)	11	1967	AIMS
SOUTH AMERICA: MARKET DAY. Economic and social activity in a village. (2)	$10\frac{1}{2}$	1971	BFA Ed. Media
SPACE PLACE. U.S. Moon program from Mercury to Apollo II. (13)	10	1969	Pyramid
SPANISH GYPSIES. Flamenco songs and dances near Granada. B&W. (1)	11	--	Film Images
A SPECIAL KIND OF MORNING. Young girls' friendship and fun in the zoo. (4), (7)	27	1971	Indiana Univ.
SPHERES. Transfigurations to the music of Bach. (1)	8	1970	Int. Film Bureau
THE SPIRIT OF THE DANCE. Paris Opera Ballet rehearsal and performance. B&W. (1)	21	--	Film Images
THE SPIRIT OF THE NAVAJO. From the Navajo-produced series. Silent. B&W. (13)	21	--	CMC/Columbia
SPRING. A girl's observations on a country stroll. (4)	9	1967	Sterling
SPRING COLOR. The daffodil, hyacinth, tulip, and forsythia. (4)	5	1968	Thorne Films
SPRING IN THE CITY. Easter, kites, buds, birds, and baseball. (6)	11	1969	Encyc. Brit.
SQUARES. Examples of blind obedience. Silent. B&W. (8), (13)	3	--	Candid Camera
STAINED GLASS: A PHOTOGRAPHIC ESSAY. A young craftsman at his labor of love. (1)	$8\frac{1}{2}$	1970	BFA Ed. Media
STALKING SEAL ON THE SPRING ICE, Part I. From a series on Netsilik Eskimo life. (2)	27	1969	Mod. Media

Title and Description	Min.	Year	Distributor
STALKING SEAL ON THE SPRING ICE, Part II. From a series on Netsilik Eskimo life. (2)	35	1969	Mod. Media
STAR OF BETHLEHEM (1700-1750). Nativity scene in Baroque style. (1), (13)	12	--	Time-Life
THE STARFISH'S REALM. The crab, octopus, and other sea animals. Music. (4)	14	--	Rarig's
STARLIGHT. Subjects are interpreted in "personal cinema." (1)	5	1970	Pyramid
STATE OF THE EARTH. Quality and contradictions of life in U.S.A. (6), (7)	18	1969	NBC-TV
STEPPE IN WINTER. Man and beast in the cold of southeastern Europe. B&W. (2)	13	1966	Sterling
STILL WATERS. Scenes include off-beat sounds. Awards. (4)	$14\frac{1}{2}$	1964	Pyramid
STOLEN CHILDHOOD. Young victims of U.S. bombs in North Vietnam. B&W. (10)	10	1967	Amer. Document
THE STORY OF LIGHT. Modern fixtures' development. Animated. (3)	8	--	G. E. Films
THE STRING BEAN (Le Haricot). An old woman's devotion to her plant. B&W. (7)	17	1964	McGraw-Hill
STROMBOLI: A LIVING VOLCANO. Life on an island decimated by disaster. (2)	10	1969	ACI Films
A STUDY IN PAPER. Puppets act out struggle of war vs. peace. B&W. (1), (10)	$4\frac{1}{2}$	--	Int. Film Bureau
STUDY IN WET. Sound and sensation of water forms. Awards. (9)	7	1965	ACI Films
SUGAR IN EGYPT. Man and His World series; minimal narration. (2)	13	1969	Films, Inc.
SUMMER RENDEZVOUS. Track-meet as a mirror of man. Award. (9), (13)	30	1969	Universal Ed.
SUN. Captions based on song-and-picture story. (5)	8	1970	ACI Films
SUNDAY BY THE SEA. British leisure-time activities. Award. B&W. (2)	15	1955	McGraw-Hill
SUNDAY LARK. Six-year-old has Wall Street to herself. Awards. B&W. (8), (11)	12	1963	McGraw-Hill

Title and Description	Min.	Year	Distributor
SUNFLIGHT. Daedalus and Icarus. Animated. Award. (12)	6	1968	IFF (Bryan)
SUR LE PONT D'AVIGNON. Medieval puppets act out old French folk song. (1)	$5\frac{3}{4}$	--	Int. Film Bureau
SURF! Impressions of sun, sea, and sand. Awards. (4), (9)	13	1969	American Ed.
SURFBOARDS, SKATEBOARDS, AND BIG, BIG WAVES. Motion and emotion; Hawaii to California. (9)	10	1970	American Ed.
SURPRISE BOOGIE. Jazz impressions in animation. Awards. (1)	6	1958	CCM Films
SURVIVAL. Traffic and pollution: cope with or cop out? (6), (7)	3	1971	ACI Films
THE SWORD. Antiwar theme. Open-ended; animated. (10)	6	1968	CCM Films
SYDNEY. The capital of New South Wales, Australia. (6)	21	1967	Australia
SYMMETRY. Rhythm and geometric patterns. Animated. (1), (3)	10	1966	McGraw-Hill
SYRINX/CITYSCAPE. Greek fable, plus urban impressions. Award. B&W. (6), (12)	4	1966	Learn. Corp.
TADPOLE TALE. City boy returns his pet to the lake. (3)	14	1967	Universal Ed.
T'AI CHI CH'UAN. Chinese psycho-physical art form and ritual. B&W. (1), (9)	9	1970	Davenport
TAKE OFF. Condensed version of "Ski the Outer Limits." (9)	10	1969	Pyramid
A TALE FOR EVERYBODY. Fable of self-destructive quarrel. Animated. (10)	6	1968	BFA Ed. Media
TEA FOR ELSA. Dramatizes extreme example of indifference. B&W. (7)	10	1971	Counterpoint
TEMPTED (Drugs). Influences of drug-culture on the young. (13)	6	1970	AIMS
THE TENDER GAME. Cartoon couple falls in love musically. (1), (7)	7	1958	McGraw-Hill
TENNESSEE BIRDWALK. What makes a bird a bird? Animated. (5)	6	1970	ABC Media
TERMINUS. The events and people of a London railroad station. B&W. (6)	24	1964	Sterling
TEXTILES. From natural designs to man-made ones. (1)	$15\frac{1}{2}$	--	Mod. Media

Title and Description	Min.	Year	Distributor
TEXTURES. Influence of point of view, distance, and light. (1)	10	1970	ACI Films
TEXTURES OF THE GREAT LAKES. Shore-line waters, beaches, and forests. Award. (4)	6	1965	Thorne Films
THAT ALL MAY BE ONE. A discussion-starter on brotherhood. (7), (13)	32	1970	Syracuse Univ.
THIRD AVENUE EL. The former elevated train in New York City. Awards. (6)	9	1956	ACI Films
THIS IS THE HOME OF MRS. LEVANT GRAHAM. Mother and family in a black D. C. ghetto. Awards. B&W. (6)	15	1970	Pyramid
THIS TRAIN. Night train, railroad station, and pre-Civil War song. (13)	5	1965	Thorne Films
THREE BROTHERS IN HAITI. Overcoming resistance to scientific farming. Minimal narration. (2)	16	1970	Films, Inc.
THRESHING WHEAT. From a series on Afghan tribe, the Tajik. B&W. (2)	9	1969	IFF (Bryan)
THRESHOLD. Amorous dreams of a fugitive outlaw. Award. (11)	25	1970	Pyramid
THROUGH THE LOOKING GLASS. Intentional distortion of familiar forms. (1)	10	1953	Film Images
THE THUNDERSTORM. Boy, dog, and rabbit in a rainstorm. Award. (3)	9	--	Learn. Corp.
TILLIE'S PUNCTURED ROMANCE. Sennett slapstick with Charlie Chaplin. Silent. B&W. (8), (12)	43	1914	CCM Films
TIMBER IN FINLAND. Man and His World series; minimal narration. (2)	15	1969	Films, Inc.
TIME OF THE HORN. A young boy's musical daydream. B&W. (5)	7	--	Journal
TOES TELL. Child senses textures with bare feet. (5)	6	1969	Encyc. Brit.
TOKYO INDUSTRIAL WORKER. Man and His World series; minimal narration. (6)	17	1969	Films, Inc.
TOMATOES—FROM SEED TO TABLE. An example of the food-processing cycle. (13)	11	1970	AIMS
THE TOP. Vanity of material success. Animated. Awards. (7)	8	1965	McGraw-Hill

Title and Description	Min.	Year	Distributor
THE TORCH AND THE TORSO: WORK OF MIGUEL BERROCAL. Welding techniques of contemporary sculptor. B&W. (1)	11	--	Film Images
THE TOWN MUSICIANS. Based on Grimm Bros. Animated. Award. (12)	9	--	CCM Films
TOYS. Store-window war simulates real one. (10)	8	1966	McGraw-Hill
TOYS ON A FIELD OF BLUE. Game revives old man's war memories. B&W. (10)	20	1962	CCM Films
TRACK 73. Simulates the sensation of railroad travel. (13)	10	1970	Holt R&W
TRAINS. Survey of past, present, and future railroads. (13)	15	--	ACI Films
TREES. Joyce Kilmer's poem in song. Animated. (12)	5	--	Walt Disney
THE TRENDSETTER. Ironic results of nonconformity. Animated. (7)	6	--	Pyramid
TRIO FOR THREE ANGLES. Triangles: equilateral, isosceles, and scalene. (3)	8	1968	Int. Film Bureau
THE TRIP. Teen-age drug trip ends in disaster. (7)	$3\frac{1}{2}$	--	Perennial Ed.
TROUT HATCHERY. The change of seasons and the cycle of nature. (3)	15	1970	ACI Films
TUKTU AND HIS ANIMAL FRIENDS. The activities of a Canadian-Eskimo boy. (3)	14	1968	Films, Inc.
TUKTU AND HIS ESKIMO DOGS. The activities of a Canadian-Eskimo boy. (4)	14	1968	Films, Inc.
TUKTU AND HIS NICE NEW CLOTHES. The activities of a Canadian-Eskimo boy. (1)	14	1968	Films, Inc.
TUKTU AND THE BIG KAYAK. The activities of a Canadian-Eskimo boy. (7)	14	1968	Films, Inc.
TUKTU AND THE BIG SEAL. The activities of a Canadian-Eskimo boy. (4)	14	1968	Films, Inc.
TUKTU AND THE CARIBOU HUNT. The activities of a Canadian-Eskimo boy. (9)	14	1968	Films, Inc.
TUKTU AND THE CLEVER HANDS. The activities of a Canadian-Eskimo boy. (1)	14	1968	Films, Inc.

Title and Description	Min.	Year	Distributor
TUKTU AND THE INDOOR GAMES. The activities of a Canadian-Eskimo boy. (2)	14	1968	Films, Inc.
TUKTU AND THE MAGIC BOW. The activities of a Canadian-Eskimo boy. (5), (9)	14	1968	Films, Inc.
TUKTU AND THE MAGIC SPEAR. The activities of a Canadian-Eskimo boy. (5)	14	1968	Films, Inc.
TUKTU AND THE SNOW PALACE. The activities of a Canadian-Eskimo boy. (2)	14	1968	Films, Inc.
TUKTU AND THE TEN THOUSAND FISHES. The activities of a Canadian-Eskimo boy. (4)	14	1968	Films, Inc.
TUKTU AND THE TRIALS OF STRENGTH. The activities of a Canadian-Eskimo boy. (1), (9)	14	1968	Films, Inc.
TURKEY: NATION IN TRANSITION. Animation and live action shows changes. (2)	27	1971	IFF (Bryan)
TURNED ON. Dune buggies, cycles, boats, snowmobiles. (9)	7	1969	Pyramid
TURNER (1775 - 1851). Early liberation of color from subject. Awards. (1)	12	--	Time-Life
TWO. Parody on European film love scenes. Preview. (8)	9	1967	CCM Films
TWO BROTHERS IN GREECE. Man and His World series; minimal narration. (2)	17	1969	Films, Inc.
TWO CASTLES. The nature and futility of war. Animated. B&W. (10)	3	1963	Pyramid
TWO MEN AND A WARDROBE. What is their portable closet? You decide. B&W. (11)	15	1957	McGraw-Hill
THE UGLY DUCKLING. The classic Hans Christian Andersen fable. (12)	8	--	Walt Disney
UIRAPURU. Brazilian primitive legend. Awards. Preview. (2)	17	--	Audio/Brandon
UMBRELLA. Couple's pursuit of happiness. Awards. B&W. (11)	20	1967	McGraw-Hill
UN CHIEN ANDALOU (An Andalusian Dog). Avant-garde surrealism. Silent. Preview. B&W. (1), (11)	16	1929	Pyramid
UNDALA. Village life and leisure in India. Awards. (2)	28	1967	CMC/Columbia

Title and Description	Min.	Year	Distributor
UNE BOMBE PAR HASARD. Re-action of town in crisis. Animated. Awards. (5)	8	1970	Sterling
UNTITLED 2. Modern art: fashionable or fraudulent? (1)	9	--	Xerox Films
UP TO THE SEQUOIAS. Wild life in the Sierra Nevada foothills. (4)	$7\frac{1}{2}$	--	A-V Explor.
URBANIA. Need for civic planning vs. urban decay. (6)	$7\frac{1}{4}$	1971	Thorne Films
VARIATIONS ON A THEME. An anti-war treatise from three points of view. Award. B&W. (10)	11	1961	CCM Films
VENEZUELA. Man and His World series; minimal narration. (2)	12	1970	Films, Inc.
VENICE, ETUDE NO. 1. Subjective vision of Venetian canals and palaces. (6)	8	1961	Film Images
VERGETTE MAKING A POT. A master at work on creative ceramics. Award. (1)	9	1966	ACI Films
VERY FAST REACTION—AM-MONIUM DICTROMATE. From the Yale Chemistry Films series. Silent. (3)	1	--	CCM Films
VERY NICE, VERY NICE. Chaos of life expressed in chaos of images. B&W. (13)	7	1961	McGraw-Hill
VILLAGE LIFE IN TONGA. The people of a peaceful Polynesian island. (2)	20	1971	ACI Films
THE VIOLIN LESSON. Maestro and pupil in classic confrontation. (1)	10	1970	McGraw-Hill
VIVALDI'S VENICE. Concerto parallels four-season scenes. Award. (1), (6)	27	1968	Time-Life
VOLLEYBALL. Interprets match be-tween U.S. and Russian teams. B&W. (9)	10	1967	Universal Ed.
WALKING. Correlates posture and mood. Animated. Awards. Preview. (5), (8)	5	1968	Learn. Corp.
THE WALL. Example of "people users." Animated. Award. (13)	4	1965	McGraw-Hill
WARGAMES. Goat becomes victim of senseless "sport." B&W. (10)	19	1963	CCM Films
WATER BIRDS. Loon, tern, heron, and ring-billed gull. (4)	$5\frac{1}{2}$	1966	A-V Explor.
THE WATER SAYS. Raindrop's journey from cloud to sea. (4)	11	1971	Churchill

Title and Description	Min.	Year	Distributor
WATER'S EDGE. Variety of water-forms set to music. Award. (4)	12	--	Films, Inc.
WATERS OF YOSEMITE. Stream's origin and path. Minimal narration. (4)	10	1967	Holt R&W
WATERS RETURNING. Water cycle, from clouds to rain or snow. (3)	$5\frac{1}{2}$	--	Aim/Assn.
THE WAYS OF WATER. The wilderness of Washington's Olympic Peninsula. (4)	13	1971	Encyc. Brit.
WEAVES. A textile designer's work and exhibit. (1)	12	--	Int. Film Bureau
WEAVING CLOTH (Pushtu). From a series on Afghan tribe, the Pushtu. (1), (2)	9	1968	IFF (Bryan)
WE'RE GONNA HAVE RECESS. Spontaneous display of playground emotions. (5)	$9\frac{1}{2}$	--	Nat. Film Board
WHAT CAN YOU FIND? Basis for observing natural relationships. (3)	$11\frac{1}{2}$	1967	Thorne Films
WHAT IF? Four problems for children to resolve. (5), (7)	3	1969	Encyc. Brit.
WHAT IS A COMMUNITY? Common needs and group cooperation. (6)	14	1969	Encyc. Brit.
WHAT WOULD YOU DO? Problem-situation with three alternatives. (5)	8	1971	Atlantis
WHATEVER THE WEATHER. Introduction to wind, rain, snow, and sun. (3)	10	--	Encyc. Brit.
WHAT'S HAPPENING? Five story-starts for viewers to complete. (5)	5	1969	Encyc. Brit.
A WHEEL IS ROUND. Captions reinforce song-and-picture story. (5)	8	1970	ACI Films
WHERE TIME IS A RIVER. The art of Gauguin, Rousseau, Chagall, and Leger. (1)	18	1965	CMC/Columbia
WHITE MANE (Crin Blanc). Love of a French boy for a wild horse. Awards. B&W. (1), (5)	39	1953	Mus./Mod. Art
WHITE THROAT. Sparrow's forest-home in Canada. Awards. (4)	10	1965	A-V Explor.
WHOSE SHOES? Five incidents to be completed by viewers. (5)	3	1969	Encyc. Brit.
WILLOW. Tree-study forms example of cinema principles. (1), (4)	7	1971	Syracuse Univ.

Title and Description	Min.	Year	Distributor
WIND. Captions reinforce song-and-picture story. (3)	8	1970	ACI Films
WINDOWS. Stained glass, from design to installation. Awards. (1)	11	1969	ACI Films
WINEMAKERS IN FRANCE. Man and His World series; minimal narration. (2)	15	1969	Films, Inc.
WINTER. Boy's fun with snow, ice, and frosty windows. (4), (5)	11	1967	Sterling
WINTER COLOR. Seasonal compositions in picture and music. (4)	5	1963	Thorne Films
WINTER COMES TO THE CITY. Southern boy's first Christmas in Chicago. (6)	11	1969	Coronet
WINTER GEYSER. Split-screen scenes of Yellowstone. Award. (4)	7	1967	Holt R&W
WOMEN OF RUSSIA. Diversity of roles among young and old. (2)	12	1968	IFF (Bryan)
WOOL IN AUSTRALIA. Man and His World series; minimal narration. (2)	19	1969	Films, Inc.
WORKOUT. Boy and horse in training for the Olympics. B&W. (9)	9	1967	Australia
WORLD. Novel version of earth's origin. Animated. (3)	6	1970	Pyramid
THE WORLD OF THREE. Sibling rivalry and how to prevent it. B&W. (13)	28	1967	McGraw-Hill
YOUNG INFANT: BIRTH TO FOUR MONTHS. Baby baboon behavior on an East African reserve. (3)	10	1969	Mod. Media
YOUR BODY AND ITS PARTS. Interrelation of five major body systems. (3)	12	1966	Encyc. Brit.
YUGOSLAV FARM FAMILY. Struggles and successes of individualism. (2)	14	1965	IFF (Bryan)
YUGOSLAVIAN COASTLINE. Man and His World series; minimal narration. (2)	14	1970	Films, Inc.
Z IS FOR ZOO. Captions reinforce song-and-picture story. (5)	9	1970	ACI Films

FILMS
INDEXED BY SUBJECT

190

ANIMALS (Cont.)

Horses and How They Live (3)
Kangaroos (4)
Mice and How They Live (3)
Pigs! (4)
Rabbits (3)
Sheep, Sheep, Sheep (4)

ARCHITECTURE

Architecture, USA (1), (6)
Brand New Day (6)
Bridges-Go-Round (6)
The Builders (3)
Frescoes in Danish Churches (1),
    (13)
Gallery: A View of Time (1)
La Cathedrale des Morts (1)
Royal Rococo (1725-1750) (1)
Skyscraper (6)

ARTS, CONTEMPORARY

Art Expert (1), (8)
Art Scene, USA (1)
Creation: The Artist at Work (1)
Day of the Painter (1), (8)
Ernst Barlach: The Fighter (1)
Ernst Barlach: The Victor (1)
Francis Bacon: Paintings (1)
From Tree Trunk to Head (1)
Gallery: A View of Time (1)
Harry Bertoia's Sculpture (1)
Henry Moore at the Tate Gallery (1)
Images 67 (1)
Josef Herman: Twentieth-Century
    Artist (1)
Kindness Week or The Seven Capital
    Elements (1)
Litho (1)
Loren MacIver (1)
Maitre (1), (8)
Man and Color (1)
Opus: Impressions of British Art
    and Culture (1)
Posada (1)
Posters: May-June 1968 (1), (10)
Red Stone Dancer (1)
The Shape of Things (1)
The Torch and the Torso: Work of
    Miguel Berrocal (1)
Untitled 2 (1)

ASIA

Baking Bread (2)
Bangkok (6)

Boys' Games (2), (9)
Building a Bridge (2), (3)
Buzkashi (2), (9)
Casting Iron Plow-Shares (2)
Fishing on the Coast of Japan (2)
Grinding Wheat (2)
Harvest in Japan (2)
Hiroko Ikoko (2)
In India the Sun Rises in the East
    (2)
Industry Comes to Pakistan (2)
Japanese Farmers (2)
Japan's Art—From the Land (1)
Juggernaut: A Film of India (2)
Life in North China (2)
Making Bread (2)
Making Felt (1), (2)
Making Gunpowder (2), (3)
Men's Dance (1), (2)
Mountain People (2)
Niok (2), (4)
Pottery Making (1), (2)
Rice Farmers in Thailand (2)
School Day in Japan (2)
The Seeing Eye (2)
Shearing Yaks (2)
Threshing Wheat (2)
Tokyo Industrial Worker (6)
Undala (2)
Weaving Cloth (1), (2)

AUSTRALIA

Adelaide (6)
Australian Animals (4)
Geelong (6)
Hobart (6)
Kangaroos (4)
Launceston (6)
The Line (2)
Melbourne (6)
Perth (6)
Port Moresby (6)
Sydney (6)
Wool in Australia (2)
Workout (9)

BIRDS

The Bird (7)
Birds of the Forest (3), (4)
Birds on a Sea Shore (3), (4)
Blackbird Family (3), (4)
The Canada Goose (3), (4)
Carp in a Marsh (3), (4)
Chickens (3)
Chicks and Chickens (3)
Ducks, Geese, and Swans (3)
Gray Gull the Hunter (4)

BIRDS (Cont.)

Gull Island (3), (4)
Hunting Wild Doves (2)
Kids and Birds and European
    Winter (4)
Pigeons! Pigeons! (6)
Reflections in a Pond (4)
The Robin (3), (4)
Tennessee Birdwalk (5)
Uirapuru (2)
Waterbirds (4)
White Throat (4)

BLACK STUDIES

The Blue Dashiki (6)
Harlem Wednesday (1), (6)
Hey Doc (6)
Nobi and the Slave Traders (12)
Time of the Horn (5)

BRITISH ISLES

Granton Trawler (2)
Lake People of Scotland (2)
Moon's Men (2)
Sing of the Border (2)
Sunday by the Sea (2)

CANADA

Deep Sea Trawler (2)
Gull Island (3), (4)
La Poulette Grise (1), (12)
Le Merle (8)
L'Homme Vite (9)
O Canada (2)
A Place to Stand (1), (2)
Quebec Winter Carnival (9)
The Railrodder (8)
The Rink (9)
The Rise and Fall of the Great
    Lakes (4)
The Shepherd (5)
Sky (1), (4)

CHEMISTRY

Acid Base Reaction in Electrolysis
    of Water (3)
Ammonia Fountain (3)
Building Atom Models—Isomerism
    (3)
Crooke's Tubes (3)
Diffusion along a Bar (3)
Fast Reaction—Mercury and Silver
    Nitrate (3)
Geiger Counter (3)

Harmonic Phasors (3)
Hydrogen Fountain (3)
Le Chatelier's Principle (3)
Millikan's Oil Drop Experiment (3)
Model for Weight Relations in
    Chemical Reactions (3)
Phase Demonstration (3)
Phosphine Smoke Rings (3)
Principles of Mass Spectrometer
    (3)
Properties of Mixtures and Com-
    pounds (3)
Slow Reaction—Iron and Oxygen (3)
Solution, Evaporation, and Crystal-
    lization (3)
Very Fast Reaction—Ammonium
    Dictromate (3)

CHILDREN'S STORIES

Alexander and the Car with a Miss-
    ing Headlight (12)
A Bell for Ursli (5)
The Carnival (5)
Caterpillar (3)
Changing of the Guard (13)
Circus (1)
Clown (5), (7)
The Clown (8)
Coat from Heaven (11)
County Fair (5)
The Curious Mouse (8)
Faroun, the Little Clown (11)
Fine Feathers (7)
Girl and the Sparrow (11)
The Golden Fish (11)
Hiroko Ikoko (2)
The Hoarder (7)
Janie Sue and Tugaloo (4)
Jeff Sets Sail (9)
The Kind-Hearted Ant (8), (12)
A Kite Story (11)
Lady of the Light (12)
Leaves (5)
The Little Airplane That Grew (11)
The Little Blue Apron (11)
The Little Giraffe (11)
The Little Mariner (11)
Long Ears (12)
The Magic Balloons (11)
Merbabies (11)
The Merry-Go-Round Horse (11)
Mr. Koumal Discovers "Koumalia"
    (13)
Mr. Koumal Moves to the Country
    (4)
Monkey and the Organ Grinder (5)
My Friend the Fish (5)
My Friend the Robin (5)

CHILDREN'S STORIES (Cont.)

Naica and the Squirrels (4)
The Naughty Duckling (7)
The Naughty Owlet (7)
Niok (2), (4)
Nobi and the Slave Traders (12)
The Old Mill (4)
The Perils of Priscilla (13)
Pets: A Boy and His Dog (6)
Queer Birds (7), (8)
Ragamuffin (5)
Red and Black (8)
The Red Balloon (11)
The Red Kite (7), (12)
A Rock in the Road (7)
The Shepherd (5)
A Special Kind of Morning (4), (7)
The String Bean (Le Haricot) (7)
Sunday Lark (8), (11)
Sunflight (12)
Tadpole Tale (3)
The Thunderstorm (3)
Time of the Horn (5)
The Town Musicians (12)
The Ugly Duckling (12)
White Mane (1), (5)

COMMUNICATION

Chickens (3)
Electrocution of the Word (11)
Enter Hamlet (8), (12)
From the Inside Out (1)
Getting Along (5)
Have I Told You Lately That I
    Love You? (6), (7)
Numerals Everywhere (3)
The Orator (5)
Orpheon (8)
Pittsburgh Musical Cops (5), (8)
Posters: May-June 1968 (1), (10)
Seven Authors in Search of a
    Reader (11), (12)
Signs, Signals, and Symbols (5)
A Study in Paper (1), (10)
Untitled 2 (1)

CRAFTS

At Your Fingertips—Boxes (1)
At Your Fingertips—Cylinders (1)
At Your Fingertips—Floats (1), (3)
At Your Fingertips—Grasses (1),
    (3)
At Your Fingertips—Play Clay (1)
At Your Fingertips—Sugar and Spice
    (1)

Bakery Beat (13)
Baking Bread (2)
The Builders (3)
Building a Boat (2)
Building a House (2)
Building a Kayak, Part I (2)
Building a Kayak, Part II (2)
Casting Iron Plow-Shares (2)
Cotton Growing and Spinning (2)
Cut-ups (1)
Encre (1)
Glass (1)
Hands and Threads (1)
Images 67 (1)
Litho (1)
Making Bread (2)
Making Felt (1), (2)
Metamorphosis of the Cello (1)
The Navajo Silversmith (1)
A Navajo Weaver (1)
People Might Laugh at Us (1)
Pottery Making (Tajik) (1), (2)
Re-discovery (1)
Second Weaver (1)
A Ship Is Born (13)
Skyscraper (6)
Stained Glass: A Photographic Essay
    (1)
Star of Bethlehem (1700-1750) (1),
    (13)
Textiles (1)
Tuktu and the Big Kayak (7)
Tuktu and the Clever Hands (1)
Tuktu and His Nice New Clothes (1)
Vergette Making a Pot (1)
Weaves (1)
Weaving Cloth (Pushtu) (1), (2)
Windows (1)

CREATIVITY

The Art of Seeing (1)
Bronze (1)
Creation: The Artist at Work (1)
Cut-ups (1)
Day of the Painter (1), (8)
Delacroix (1798-1863) (1)
The Desert (10), (11)
The Dreamer (11)
Encre (1)
From the Inside Out (1)
Genius Man (10)
Get Wet (9)
Glass (1)
The Glob Family (5)
Good Goodies (7)
Le Farfalle (4)
Lopsideland (1)

CREATIVITY (Cont.)

Magic Frame—Adventures in
    Seeing (5)
Magic Hands (11)
Notes on a Triangle (1)
Numbers (3)
Once upon a Time There Was a
    Dot (1)
Patterns (5)
Re-discovery (1)
Rythmetic (3)
The Satiric Eye (7)
The Shape and Color Game (1)
Sheep in Wood (1)
Study in Wet (9)
Tennessee Birdwalk (5)
Tuktu and the Clever Hands (1)
Un Chien Andalou (An Andalusian
    Dog) (1), (11)
Windows (1)

DANCE

Ballet by Degas (1)
Child of Dance (1)
Crystals (1), (3)
Dance Squared (1)
Danze Cromatiche (1)
Degas Dancers (1)
From the Inside Out (1)
Hang Ten (9)
Men's Dance (1), (2)
Mixummerdaydream (11)
Pas de Deux (1)
Spanish Gypsies (1)
The Spirit of the Dance (1)
T'ai Chi Ch'uan (1), (9)

DREAMS

Children's Dreams (1), (11)
Day Dreams (8), (12)
Dream of the Wild Horses (11)
The Dreamer (11)
Mixummerdaydream (11)
The Penny Arcade (Captain Flash
    vs. The Bat) (8)
Sand Castles (11)
Sleep Well (13)

DRUGS

Choice (7)
Hey Doc (6)
Hospital (6)
Tempted (13)
The Trip (7)

ECOLOGY

Animals in Amboseli (3)
Animals in Autumn (3), (4)
Animals in Summer (3), (4)
Birds of the Forest (3), (4)
A Boy's Journey through a Day (4)
Buttercup (4)
Carp in a Marsh (3), (4)
Discovering the Forest (1)
Holy Thursday (4), (12)
The Hunters (2), (4)
Insects in a Garden (3)
Living Things Are Everywhere (3)
Miner's Ridge (4)
Multiply and Subdue (4)
Nature Is for People (4)
Old Antelope Lake (4)
Our Living Forests (4)
The River (3)
Textures of the Great Lakes (4)
The Thunderstorm (3)
Trout Hatchery (3)
Up to the Sequoias (4)

ECONOMICS

Bakery Beat (13)
Co-operative Farming in East
    Germany (2)
Dairy—Farm to Door (13)
Dairy Farming in the Alps (2)
Day of the Painter (1), (8)
Deep Sea Trawler (2)
Economics: Newspaper Boy (13)
Economics: The Credit Card (13)
Economics: Workers Who Build
    Houses (13)
Forest People (2)
Genius Man (10)
Granton Trawler (2)
Island People (2)
Mike and Steve Visit the Shopping
    Center (6)
Oil in Libya (2)
On the Move (13)
Pursuit of Happiness the Materi-
    alistic Way (6), (7)
Reflections of a Company (13)
A Scrap of Paper and a Piece of
    String (5), (8)
Seacoast People (2)
Sunday Lark (8), (11)
Tokyo Industrial Worker (6)
Tomatoes—From Seed to Table (13)
The Top (7)
Winemakers in France (2)
What Is a Community? (6)

EDUCATION

The Card Catalog (13)
Dialectics of a Dropout (13)
High School (6)
How's School, Enrique? (7)
I Am Five (11)
The Report Card: How Does
  Riccardo Feel? (13)
Romeo (7)
School Day in Japan (2)
Seven Authors in Search of a
  Reader (11), (12)
Siu Mei Wong—Who Shall I Be?
  (6), (7)
We're Gonna Have Recess (5)
The World of Three (13)

ESKIMO LIFE

Arctic People (2)
At the Caribou Crossing Place,
  Part I (2)
At the Caribou Crossing Place,
  Part II (2)
Building a Kayak, Part I (2)
Building a Kayak, Part II (2)
The Eskimo: Fight For Life (2)
Fishing at the Stone Weir, Part I
  (2)
Fishing at the Stone Weir, Part II
  (2)
Group Hunting on the Spring Ice,
  Part I (2)
Group Hunting on the Spring Ice,
  Part II (2)
Group Hunting on the Spring Ice,
  Part III (2)
Jigging for Lake Trout (2)
Nanook of the North (1), (2)
Stalking Seal on the Spring Ice,
  Part I (2)
Stalking Seal on the Spring Ice,
  Part II (2)
Tuktu (series of 13 films) (1), (2),
  (3), (4), (5), (7), (9)

EUROPE

Bargemen on the Rhine (2)
Berlin, Berlin, Berlin (6)
Children Adrift (6)
Children of Paris (2), (6)
Circus in Europe (5)
Co-operative Farming in East Ger-
  many (2)
Cork from Portugal (2)
Czechoslovakia 1918-1968 (10)

Dairy Farming in the Alps (2)
The Family Farm (2)
Fishing in Romania (2)
Fishing on the Danube Delta (2)
The Happy Pace of Switzerland (11)
Harbor Rhythm (6)
Holland: Terra Fertilis (2)
In Paris Parks (6)
Industrial Region in Sweden (2)
Kids and Birds and European
  Winter (4)
La Cathedrale des Morts (1)
Moslem Family in Yugoslavia (2)
Mountain Family in Europe (2)
Mountain People (2)
New Life for a Spanish Farmer (2)
A Norwegian Fjord (2)
Plateau Farmers in France (2)
Rain (Regen) (1), (6)
Rain in the City (6)
Romania (2)
Seacoast People (2)
Spanish Gypsies (1)
Steppe in Winter (2)
Stromboli: A Living Volcano (2)
Timber in Finland (2)
Two Brothers in Greece (2)
Venice, Etude No. 1 (6)
Winemakers in France (2)
Women of Russia (2)
Yugoslav Farm Family (2)
Yugoslavian Coastline (2)

EVOLUTION

Ai-Ye (2)
Clay (Origin of the Species) (3)
The Endless Cycle (4)
Genesis (11)
Genesis 1-27: Undersea World
  (4), (13)
Life Cycle (7)
Omega (11)
Tadpole Tale (3)
World (3)

FAMILY

The Adventures of * (5)
Amazon Family (2)
The Endless Cycle (4)
The Family Farm (2)
Family of the Mountains: A Peruvian
  Village (2)
The House (11)
Is This Our Father's World?
  (7), (13)
A Key of His Own (6)
Late for Dinner: Was Dawn Right?
  (5)

FAMILY (Cont.)

Life Cycle (7)
Lucy (13)
Man to Man (13)
Morning, Noon, and Evening (6)
Moslem Family in Yugoslavia (2)
Mountain Family in Europe (2)
Siu Mei Wong ... Who Shall I Be?
    (6), (7)
This Is the Home of Mrs. Levant
    Graham (6)
Yugoslav Farm Family (2)

FILM STUDY: CINEMA VERITE

Basic Training (10)
Cicero March (6), (10)
The Faces of Patriots (5)
Hey Doc (6)
High School (6)
Hospital (6)
Law and Order (6), (10)
Police Power and Freedom of
    Assembly (6)
This Is the Home of Mrs. Levant
    Graham (6)

FILM STUDY: DOCUMENTARIES

Changing Greenland (2)
Children Adrift (6)
Day after Day (7)
The Eskimo: Fight for Life (2)
Evening Activity (3)
Exposition (1)
From 3 AM to 10 PM (6)
Man of Aran (2)
Nanook of the North (1), (2)
The Nuer (2)
Pow Wow (8), (9)
The Private Life of a Cat (3)

FILM STUDY: EXPERIMENTAL

The Admiral (10), (11)
Airborn (9)
Blinkity Blank (1)
Boiled Egg (11)
Candleflame (1)
Dance Squared (1)
Dom (The House) (11)
Energies (3)
Exercises #4 (1)
Highway (9)
Marching the Colours (1)
Matrix (5)
Microsecond (13)
Mosaic (1)

Mothlight (1)
Opus 3 (1)
Orange and Blue (5)
Permutations (1)
A Phantasy (1)
The Robber's Dirge (1)
Starlight (1)
Surprise Boogie (1)
Through the Looking Glass (1)
Un Chien Andalou (An Andalusian
    Dog) (1), (11)
Une Bombe Par Hasard (5)

FILM STUDY: TECHNIQUES

Autumn Fire (1)
Begone Dull Care (1)
Bouquet (1), (4)
A Bowl of Cherries (8)
Catch the Joy (9)
Chronology (10)
Corral (9)
Corrida Interdite (Forbidden
    Bullfight) (9)
Day Dreams (8), (12)
Death and Sunrise (12)
Devil's Work (11)
The Director (1)
Dream of the Wild Horses (11)
Ersatz (8), (11)
Ethiopian Mosaic (2)
Fiddle-de-Dee (1), (8)
Film Impressions (1)
Gallery (1)
The General (8), (9)
Get Wet (9)
Glass (1)
The Goal (9)
The Great Train Robbery (1)
Growing (A Computer-Animated
    Film) (1), (3)
Hang Ten (9)
Image of a Race (9)
Korean Alphabet (1)
L'Homme Vite (9)
Lines—Vertical and Horizontal
    (1)
The Lost World (11), (12)
Mammals (7)
Man and Color (1)
Mary's Day 1965 (13)
Memento (13)
Moebius Flip (9) (11)
Moods of Surfing (9)
Motion Picture (1)
Neighbors (10)
The Nose (Le Nez) (12)
N.Y., N.Y. (1), (6)

FILM STUDY: TECHNIQUES (Cont.)

An Occurrence at Owl Creek
  Bridge (10), (12)
Omega (11)
Pas de Deux (1)
A Place to Stand (1), (2)
Pool Sharks (8)
Potemkin (1), (10)
The Railrodder (8)
Rain (Regen) (1), (6)
Rain in the City (6)
Rainshower (4), (5)
The Red Balloon (11)
Short and Suite (1)
Skater Dater (5), (9)
Ski the Outer Limits (9)
Sky (1), (4)
Skyscraper (6)
Space Place (13)
Spheres (1)
Take Off (9)
Third Avenue El (6)
Tillie's Punctured Romance (8),
  (12)
Two (8)
Water's Edge (4)
Willow (1), (4)
Where Time Is a River (1)
White Mane (1), (5)

FISHING

Deep Sea Trawler (2)
Fishing at the Stone Weir, Part I
  (2)
Fishing at the Stone Weir, Part II
  (2)
Fishing in Romania (2)
Fishing on the Coast of Japan (2)
Fishing on the Danube Delta (2)
Fishing on the Niger River (2)
Granton Trawler (2)
Jigging for Lake Trout (2)
Man of Aran (2)
Moon's Men (2)

GAMES

Boys' Games (2), (9)
Choosing Up (9)
Clap! (5), (9)
Fantasy of Feet (9)
Fixed Bowling (8)
Follow Me (9)
Football Follies (8), (9)
Get Wet (9)
The Glob Family (5)
Guessing Game (5)

Gymnastic Flashbacks (9)
Hands Grow Up (5), (13)
If Kangaroos Jump, Why Can't
  You? (9)
Join Hands, Let Go! (8)
Matching Up (5)
Neuf Minutes (9)
1968 Women's Olympic Compul-
  sory Routines (9)
Quebec Winter Carnival (9)
The Rink (9)
The Shape and Color Game (1)
The Singing Street (2), (6)
Tuktu and the Indoor Games (2)
Volleyball (9)
We're Gonna Have Recess (5)
What Can You Find? (3)

GEOMETRY

Dance Squared (1)
Notes on a Triangle (1)
Opus 3 (1)
Symmetry (1), (3)
Trio for Three Angles (3)

HISTORY

An American Time Capsule (13)
Chronology (10)
Currier and Ives (1)
Czechoslovakia 1918-1968 (10)
Durer: The Great Passion (1), (13)
Game of War (10)
Genius Man (10)
Jerusalem (2)
Microsecond (13)
An Occurrence at Owl Creek
  Bridge (10), (12)
Posada (1)
Resurrection (13)
Sing of the Border (2)
Space Place (13)
Sur le Pont D'Avignon (1)

HOBBIES

Catch the Joy (9)
Deep Sea Trawler (2)
The Empty Hand (9)
Fishing at the Stone Weir,
  Part I (2)
Fishing at the Stone Weir,
  Part II (2)
Hang Ten (9)
Highway (9)
Hunter and the Forest (4), (5)
Interpretations (1)
Jigging for Lake Trout (2)

MUSIC (Cont.)

Rythmetic (3)
San Francisco (6)
A Scrap of Paper and a Piece of
    String (5), (8)
The Seeing Eye (2)
Sheep in Wood (1)
Short and Suite (1)
Sing of the Border (2)
The Singing Street (2), (6)
Spanish Gypsies (1)
Spheres (1)
Summer Rendezvous (9), (13)
Sunday by the Sea (2)
Sur Le Pont D'Avignon (1)
Surprise Boogie (1)
Symmetry (1), (3)
Syrinx/Cityscape (6), (12)
The Tender Game (1), (7)
This Train (13)
Time of the Horn (5)
The Town Musicians (12)
Trees (12)
Undala (2)
The Violin Lesson (1)
Vivaldi's Venice (1), (6)

OPEN-ENDED

The Beginning (7)
The Big Shave (11)
The Bird (7)
Boiled Egg (11)
The Box (5)
Boynng! (8)
A Boy's Journey through a Day (4)
The Deer and the Forest (4)
The Faces of Patriots (5)
Fly Away (5), (9)
The Hiding Place (5)
Holding On (5)
Hunter and the Forest (4), (5)
Le Farfalle (4)
Leaf (4)
Les Escargots (11)
Magic Sneakers (11)
Man and His World (11)
A Man's Hands (5), (8)
Mr. Koumal Carries the Torch (8)
Mr. Koumal Faces Death (7)
Mr. Koumal Flies Like a Bird (11)
Moebius Flip (9), (11)
A Mountain Day (4)
An Occurrence at Owl Creek
    Bridge (10), (12)
The Old Mill (4)
Only Benjy Knows: Should He Tell?
    (7)

The Perils of Priscilla (13)
Police Power and Freedom of As-
    sembly (10)
The Problem (7), (8)
Psychedelic Wet (9)
The Puffed-Up Dragon (5)
Railroaded (11)
Reflections in a Pond (4)
Sky (1), (4)
Soir de Fete (13)
Solo (9)
Someday (6)
Terminus (6)
Textures of the Great Lakes (4)
Threshold (11)
Toes Tell (5)
Turned On (9)
Two Men and a Wardrobe (11)
Une Bombe par Hasard (5)
The Water Says (4)
Water's Edge (4)
What Is a Community? (6)
What Would You Do? (5)
What's Happening? (5)
Whose Shoes? (5)
Workout (9)

OPPRESSION AND PROTEST

"A" (5)
The Chess Game (10)
Chromophobia (10)
Cicero March (6), (10)
Czechoslovakia 1918-1968 (10)
The Hand (10, (11)
Law and Order (6), (10)
L'Oiseau (The Bird) (11)
Police Power and Freedom of
    Assembly (10)
Portrait of a Horse (4)
Posters: May-June 1968 (1), (10)
Potemkin (1), (10)
The Refiner's Fire (7)
The Revolution (10)
The Robber's Dirge (10)
The Shooting Gallery (7)
Sisyfos (12)
Sleep Well (13)

PANTOMIME

Act without Words (12)
Baggage (11), (13)
Illusions (1)
Magnolia (11)
Mime over Matter (1), (7)
The Pusher (7)
The Scribe (8), (13)
Sketches (1)

POLLUTION

The Abandoned (7), (13)
America the Ugly (4)
Boomsville (6)
Buttercup (4)
The End of One (4)
Forest Murmurs (4)
Garbage (13)
Is This Our Father's World? (7), (13)
One Spring Day (4)
Paradise Lost (4)
Pave It and Paint It Green (4), (7)
Pollution (4), (8)
The Quiet Racket (4)
The Rise and Fall of the Great Lakes (4)
Soliloquy of a River (4)
Survival (6), (7)
Urbania (6)

PSYCHOLOGY

Acceptance (13)
Art Expert (1), (8)
Baggage (11), (13)
The Bird (7)
Blessings of Love (7)
Conformity (10), (13)
The Crowd (6), (13)
Curiosity (8), (13)
The Curious Habits of Man (8), (13)
Dialectics of a Dropout (13)
The Dreamer (11)
East Lynne (8), (13)
Elegy (7)
Evening Activity (3)
Face the Rear (8), (13)
The Family—The Boy Who Lived Alone (7)
The Fireman Is Sad and Cries (1)
Fixed Bowling (8)
From the Inside Out (1)
Genius Man (10)
Getting Even (7)
The Greater Community Animal (13)
I Am Five (11)
In a Box (13)
The Insects (10), (11)
International Suitcase (8)
Joshua in a Box (7)
La Chambre (The Room) (13)
Late For Dinner: Was Dawn Right? (5)
Me, Too? (5)
Mrofnoc (7)
The Older Infant: Four Months to One Year (3)

People (13)
The Problem (7), (8)
The Pusher (7)
The Refiner's Fire (7)
The Report Card: How Does Riccardo Feel? (13)
Rhinoceros (12)
The Robber's Dirge (10)
Squares, (8), (13)
Summer Rendezvous (9), (13)
Tea for Elsa (7)
The Trendsetter (7)
Umbrella (11)
Walking (5), (8)
The World of Three (13)
Young Infant: Birth to Four Months (3)

QUALITY OF LIFE

America the Ugly (4)
Cities in Crisis: What's Happening? (6)
City . . . One Day (6)
Day after Day (7)
Evasion (4), (6)
Go Faster (6), (7)
The Greater Community Animal (13)
Hey Doc (6)
Jail Keys Made Here (5), (12)
The Jump and + Plus - Minus (7), (10)
Key People (6), (8)
L. A. Too Much (6)
Pursuit of Happiness the Materialistic Way (6), (7)
State of the Earth (6), (7)
Survival (6), (7)
This Is the Home of Mrs. Levant Graham (6)
Very Nice, Very Nice (13)

RACISM

The Ballad of Crowfoot (10)
Exchanges (7), (11)
Guidance: Does Color Really Make a Difference? (7)
High School (6)
How's School, Enrique? (7)
Law and Order (6) (10)
This Is the Home of Mrs. Levant Graham (6)

RELATIONSHIPS

Alf, Bill, and Fred (7)
The Brand-New Basketball (7)
Douglas, James, and Joe (7)

RELATIONSHIPS (Cont.)

Duet (7)
The Family—The Boy Who Lived
  Alone (7)
Family Teamwork and You (7)
The Fence (7)
Getting Along (5)
Getting Even (7)
Guidance: Let's Have Respect (7)
Guidance: Working with Others (7)
Hopscotch (7)
The Lemonade Stand: What's Fair?
  (7)
Mammals (7)
Me, Too? (5)
Mint Tea (6)
Mr. Koumal Gets Involved (10)
Neighbors (10)
A Place in the Sun (7)
Romeo (7)
A Scrap of Paper and a Piece of
  String (5), (8)
A Tale for Everybody (10)
That All May Be One (7), (13)
The Wall (13)
What If? (5), (7)
What Would You Do? (5)

RELIGION

Christmas Eve Service in the Black
  Forest (13)
Durer: The Great Passion (1), (13)
Ecce Homo (Czech Art 1400-1600)
  (1), (13)
Ernst Barlach: The Victor (1)
Frescoes in Danish Churches (1),
  (13)
The Fugue (1), (6)
Genesis (12), (13)
Guidance: What's Right? (7)
Intrepid Shadow (2), (13)
Is This Our Father's World? (7), (13)
Jerusalem (2)
La Cathedrale des Morts (1)
Magic Rites: Divination by Animal
  Tracks (2)
Magic Rites: Divination by Chicken
  Sacrifice (2)
Mary's Day 1965 (13)
Moslem Family in Yugoslavia (2)
Multiply and Subdue (4)
Omega (11)
Parable (13)
The Red Kite (7), (12)
Rembrandt's Christ (1), (13)
The Spirit of the Navajo (13)
Star of Bethlehem (1700-1750) (1),
  (13)

T'ai Chi Ch'uan (1), (9)
That All May Be One (7), (13)
Threshold (11)
The Top (7)
Umbrella (Kobakhidze) (11)

RIVERS

Amazon Family (2)
Man Changes the Nile (2)
Rapids of the Colorado (4), (9)
The River (3)
River: An Allegory (4)
River Journey on the Upper Nile (2)
River People (2)
River People of Chad (2)
River: Where Do You Come From?
  (3)
Soliloquy of a River (4)
Waters of Yosemite (4)

SAFETY

Eyes (1), (13)
Feet (13)
Fire Safety in the Laboratory
  (3), (13)
Hands (13)
Memento (13)
Moods of Surfing (9)
Safety as We Play (13)
The Scribe (8), (13)
Smoke Screen (13)

SCIENCE, EARTH

Aetna (3), (4)
A Day at the Beach (3)
Dunes (4)
Earth: Man's Home (3)
The Endless Cycle (4)
Fire Mountain (4)
If You Could See the Earth (3)
The Persistent Seed (4)
Rapids of the Colorado (4), (9)
River (4)
The River (3)
River: An Allegory (4)
River: Where Do You Come From? (3)
Stromboli: A Living Volcano (2)
Waters of Yosemite (4)
Waters Returning (3)
The Ways of Water (4)
Wind (3)
Winter Geyser (4)

SCIENCE, GENERAL

Bang! (3), (5)

SCIENCE, GENERAL (Cont.)

Cosmic Zoom (3)
Dimensions (3)
Electricity (3)
Energy (3)
Physics in F-Major (1), (3)
River: Where Do You Come From?
 (3)
The Story of Light (3)
Tadpole Tale (3)
Your Body and Its Parts (3)

SEASONS

Autumn (4)
Autumn Color (4)
Autumn Comes to the City (6)
Autumn Pastorale (4)
An Autumn Story—Mrs. Penny-
 packer's Package (6)
City in Winter (5), (6)
Flowers and Bees—A Springtime
 Story (4)
The Four Seasons (1)
Growing (A Computer-Animated
 Film) (1), (3)
Images from Nature (4)
Junkyard (5)
Leaf (4)
Loren MacIver (1)
March-April: The Coming of
 Spring (4)
Quebec Winter Carnival (9)
The Rink (9)
Spring (4)
Spring Color (4)
Spring in the City (6)
Steppe in Winter (2)
What Can You Find? (3)
Winter (4), (5)
Winter Color (4)
Winter Comes to the City (6)
Winter Geyser (4)

SEX EDUCATION

Blessings of Love (7)
Brine Shrimp (3)
Butterfly (two films) (3)
Embryo (3)
Flowers and Bees—A Springtime
 Story (4)
Frog Development: Fertilization
 to Hatching (3)
Frog Development: Hatching
 through Metamorphosis (3)
Happy Family Planning (13)

Lambing (Parturition in the Ewe)
 (13)
Life Cycle (7)
Lizard (3)
The Newborn Calf (3)
Overture/Nyitany (1), (3)
Preparation for Childbirth and Two
 Hospital Deliveries (3), (13)
The Private Life of a Cat (3)
Skater Dater (5), (9)

SMOKING

Smoke Screen (13)

SOUND

Auditory Responses of Newborn
 Infants (3)
Noise (3)
Sound About (3)

SOUTH AMERICA

Amazon Family (2)
Family of the Mountains: A Peruvian
 Village (2)
Highland Indians of Peru (2)
Highland People (2)
Impressions of a Guatemala Mar-
 ket Day (2)
Island People (2)
Miners of Bolivia (2)
Over the Andes in Ecuador (2)
Rainforest People (2)
Ranchero and Gauchos in Argentina
 (2)
River People (2)
South America: Market Day (2)
Uirapuru (2)
Venezuela (2)

TECHNOLOGY AND AUTOMATION

Bakery Beat (13)
Food (3), (13)
Genius Man (10)
Glass (1)
Go Faster (6), (7)
Growing (A Computer-Animated
 Film) (1), (13)
Harvesting (2)
Hypothese Beta (10), (11)
Juggernaut: A Film of India (2)
The Jump and + Plus - Minus
 (7), (10)
Kosmodrome 1999 (8), (11)
L. A. Too Much (6)
Machine (11)

TECHNOLOGY
AND AUTOMATION (Cont.)

Mr. Koumal Invents a Robot (3)
Sirene (6), (11)
Skyscraper (6)
Sunday Lark (8), (11)

TRANSPORTATION

Barges (13)
Big, Big Harbor (6)
Boat Families (2)
Freighter (13)
Gate 73 (9)
L. A. 53 (13)
The Line (2)
On the Move (13)
Pacific 231 (1)
The Phantom Freighter (13)
Pier 73 (13)
Popsicle (9)
Rail (13)
Resurrection (13)
The Ride (8), (9)
River Journey on the Upper Nile
    (2)
A Ship is Born (13)
Sunflight (12)
Terminus (6)
Third Avenue El (6)
This Train (13)
Track 73 (13)
Train (13)
Tuktu and His Eskimo Dogs (4)

VIOLENCE

The Big Shave (11)
Neighbors (10)
A Tale for Everybody (10)

Tea for Elsa (7)
Toys (10)
Wargames (10)

VISUAL LITERACY

Art of Seeing (1)
Esther (12)
Eyes Are for Seeing (1)
Film (8), (12)
Interpretations (1)
The Little Blue Apron (11)
Living Things Are Everywhere (3)
Lopsideland (1)
Magic Frame—Adventures in
    Seeing (5)
Portrait of a Horse (4)
Ricky's Great Adventure (4), (5)
Same Subject, Different Treatment
    (1)
Textures (1)
Turner (1775-1851) (1)
What Can You Find? (3)

WEATHER

Concert for Clouds (1), (3)
Rain (5)
Rain in the City (6)
Rainshower (4), (5)
Rainy Season in West Africa (2)
Sun (5)
The Thunderstorm (3)
Waters Returning (3)
Whatever the Weather (3)
Wind (3)

ZOO

Jazzoo (two versions) (8)
Z Is for Zoo (5)

PRODUCER/ DISTRIBUTOR DIRECTORY

With only a few exceptions, all films noted here are available for purchase from the producers or distributors identified in the descriptions. As for rental, the producer/distributor will either rent directly or refer you to the nearest source. Of course, a good place to start looking is your school district's A-V office, your public library, the university film library in your area, or your state department of education. You may be pleasantly surprised to find a good selection of titles relatively close at hand, and at little—if any—expense or inconvenience.

Consult the producer/distributors themselves for detailed information such as research findings, preview-for-purchase arrangements, catalogs, study guides, or TV rights. Check with them, too, about availability of their material on videotape, super 8mm sound, or other formats that are "coming soon." Some of them are on the way now. Meanwhile, 16mm is already here.

ABC MEDIA
ABC Media Concepts
1001 North Poinsettia Place
Hollywood, Calif. 90046

ACI FILMS
ACI Films
35 West 45th Street
New York, N.Y. 10036

AIM/ASSN.
Association Instructional Materials
866 Third Avenue
New York, N.Y. 10022

AIMS
AIMS Instructional Media
P.O. Box 1010
Hollywood, Calif. 90028

AMERICAN DOCUMENT
American Documentary Films
336 West 84th Street
New York, N.Y. 10024

AMERICAN ED.
American Educational Films
331 North Maple Drive
Beverly Hills, Calif. 90210

ARTHUR BARR
(Arthur) Barr Productions
1029 North Allen Avenue
Pasadena, Calif. 91104

ARTSCOPE
Artscope, Ltd.
310 West 53rd Street
New York, N.Y. 10019

ASSN./STERL.
Association/Sterling Movies
600 Madison Avenue
New York, N.Y. 10022

ATHLETIC
The Athletic Institute
705 Merchandise Mart
Chicago, Ill. 60654

ATLANTIS
Atlantis Productions
1252 LaGranada Drive
Thousand Oaks, Calif. 91360

AUDIO/BRANDON
Audio/Brandon/Ideal Films
34 MacQuesten Parkway South
Mt. Vernon, N.Y. 10550

205

AUSTRALIA
Australian News and Information
    Bureau
636 Fifth Avenue
New York, N.Y. 10020

A-V EXPLOR.
A-V Explorations
505 Delaware Avenue
Buffalo, N.Y. 14202

BENCHMARK
Benchmark Films
145 Scarborough Road
Briarcliff Manor, N.Y. 10510

BERKELEY
University of California
Extension Media Center
2223 Fulton Street
Berkeley, Calif. 94720

BFA ED. MEDIA
BFA Educational Media
2211 Michigan Avenue
Santa Monica, Calif. 90404

BLACKHAWK
Blackhawk Films
Eastin-Phelan Building
Davenport, Iowa 52808

BLUMENTHAL
(Roy) Blumenthal International
    Associates
1 East 57th Street
New York, N.Y. 10022

BOSUSTOW
(Stephen) Bosustow Productions
1610 Butler Avenue
West Los Angeles, Calif. 90425

BRITISH
British Information Service
45 Rockefeller Plaza
New York, N.Y. 10020

CANADA
Canadian Travel Film Library
680 Fifth Avenue, Suite 819
New York, N.Y. 10019

CANDID CAMERA
Candid Camera Collection
Du Art Film Labs.
245 West 55th Street
New York, N.Y. 10019

CAROUSEL
Carousel Films
1501 Broadway
New York, N.Y. 10036

CATHEDRAL
Cathedral Films
P.O. Box 1608
Burbank, Calif. 91505

CCM FILMS
CCM Films
866 Third Avenue
New York, N.Y. 10022

CENTRON
Centron Educational Films
1621 West Ninth Street
Lawrence, Kansas 66044

CHURCHILL
Churchill Films
622 North Robertson
Los Angeles, Calif. 90069

CINE CONCEPTS
Cinema Concepts
245 East 80th Street
New York, N.Y. 10022

CINEMA 16
Cinema 16/Grove Press
214 Mercer Street
New York, N.Y. 10012

CLAREMONT
The Claremont Foundation
Claremont, Calif. 91711

CLARK BELL
Clark Bell Films
P.O. Box 1686
Studio City, Calif. 91604

CMC/COLUMBIA
Center for Mass Communication
Columbia University Press
562 West 113th Street
New York, N.Y. 10025

COLUMBIA PIX
Columbia Pictures
711 Fifth Avenue
New York, N.Y. 10022

CORONET
Coronet Films
65 East South Water Street
Chicago, Ill. 60601

COUNTERPOINT
Counterpoint Films
5823 Santa Monica Blvd.
Hollywood, Calif. 90038

DA SILVA
da Silva Motion Pictures
1400 East Avenue
Rochester, N.Y. 14610

DAVENPORT
(Tom) Davenport Films
Pearlstone
Delaplane, Va. 22025

DOUBLEDAY
Doubleday Multimedia
1371 Reynolds Avenue
Santa Ana, Calif. 92705

ED. DEV. CTR.
Education Development Center
39 Chapel Street
Newton, Mass. 02160

ENCYC. BRIT.
Encyclopaedia Britannica
425 North Michigan Avenue
Chicago, Ill. 60611

FAMILY FILMS
Family Films
5823 Santa Monica Blvd.
Hollywood, Calif. 90038

FILM IMAGES
Film Images/Radim
17 West 60th Street
New York, N.Y. 10023

FILMS, INC.
Films, Incorporated
1144 Wilmette Avenue
Wilmette, Ill. 60091

G.E. FILMS
General Electric
    Educational Films
60 Washington Avenue
Schenectady, N.Y. 12305

GLASCOCK
(Baylis) Glascock Films
1901 Avenue of the Stars, Suite 700
Los Angeles, Calif. 90067

HOLT R&W
Holt, Rinehart, and Winston
383 Madison Avenue
New York, N.Y. 10017

IFF (BRYAN)
International Film Foundation
475 Fifth Avenue, Suite 916
New York, N.Y. 10017

INDIANA UNIV.
Indiana University
Audio-Visual Center
Bloomington, Ind. 47401

INT. FILM BUR.
International Film Bureau
332 South Michigan Avenue
Chicago, Ill. 60604

JOURNAL
Journal Films
909 Diversey Parkway
Chicago, Ill. 60614

KING SCREEN
King Screen Productions
320 Aurora Avenue North
Seattle, Wash. 98101

KODAK
Eastman Kodak Company
A-V Services Department
Rochester, N.Y. 14650

LEARN. CORP.
Learning Corporation of America
711 Fifth Avenue
New York, N.Y. 10022

LOCKHEED
Lockheed-Georgia Co.
Motion Picture Library
Marietta, Ga. 30060

McGRAW-HILL
McGraw-Hill/Contemporary Films
1221 Avenue of the Americas
New York, N.Y. 10020

MANBECK
Manbeck Pictures
3621 Wakonda Drive
Des Moines, Iowa 50321

MINI FILMS
Mini-Films Productions
229 South East 1st Avenue
Ft. Lauderdale, Fla. 33301

MOD. LEARNING
Modern Learning Aids
Ward's Natural Science
P.O. Box 302
Rochester, N.Y. 14603

MOD. MEDIA
Modern Media Services
1212 Avenue of the Americas
New York, N.Y. 10036

MUS./MOD. ART
Museum of Modern Art
11 West 53rd Street
New York, N.Y. 10019

NAT. ED. FILM
National Educational Film Center
P.O. Box 010
Westminster, Md. 21157

NAT. FILM BOARD
National Film Board of Canada
680 Fifth Avenue, Suite 819
New York, N.Y. 10019

NAT. MED. AV
National Medical AV Center
(Annex) Station K
Atlanta, Ga. 30324

NAT'L. AV CTR.
National Audio-Visual Center
National Archives (GSA)
Washington, D.C. 20409

NATURE GUIDE
Nature Guide Films
Shadow Canyon
Springdale, Utah 84767

NBC-TV
NBC Educational Enterprises
30 Rockefeller Plaza
New York, N.Y. 10020

NFL FILMS
NFL Football Films
410 Park Avenue
New York, N.Y. 10022

PERENNIAL ED.
Perennial Education
1825 Willow Road
Northfield, Ill. 60093

PICTURA FILMS
Pictura Films
43 West 16th Street
New York, N.Y. 10011

PLAN. PARENT.
Planned Parenthood Federation
515 Madison Avenue
New York, N.Y. 10022

PYRAMID
Pyramid Films
P.O. Box 1048
Santa Monica, Calif. 90406

RARIG'S
Rarig's Inc.
P.O. Box 548
Edmonds, Wash. 98020

SIM PROD.
SIM Productions
Weston Woods Studio
Weston, Conn. 06880

S-L FILMS
S-L Film Productions
5126 Hartwick Street
Los Angeles, Calif. 90041

STERLING
Sterling Educational Films
241 East 34th Street
New York, N.Y. 10016

SYRACUSE UNIV.
Syracuse University
1455 East Colvin Street
Syracuse, N.Y. 13210

THORNE FILMS
Thorne Films
1229 University Avenue
Boulder, Colo. 80302

TIME-LIFE
Time-Life Films
43 West 16th Street
New York, N.Y. 10011

U. OF SO. CAL.
Univ. of Southern California
Film Library, University Park
Los Angeles, Calif. 90007

UNITED PROD.
United Productions of America
600 Madison Avenue
New York, N.Y. 10022

UNIVERSAL ED.
Universal Education and Visual Arts
221 Park Avenue South
New York, N.Y. 10003

USIA
U.S. Information Agency
Department of State
Washington, D.C. 20547

WALT DISNEY
Walt Disney (Education)
800 Sonora Avenue
Glendale, Calif. 91201

WESTON WOODS
Weston Woods Studio
Weston, Conn. 06880

WOMBAT PROD.
Wombat Productions
87 Main Street
Hastings-on-Hudson, N.Y. 10706

XEROX FILMS
Xerox Films
245 Long Hill Road
Middletown, Conn. 06457

ZELLERBACH
Crown-Zellerbach Corp.
1 Bush Street
San Francisco, Calif. 94119

ZIPPORAH
Zipporah Films
54 Lewis Wharf
Boston, Mass. 02110